CONTENTS

December U.S. Light-Vehicle Sales Give Strong Finish to 2011

U.S. light-vehicle sales finished better than expected in December, further cementing the industry's long-term growth pattern as deliveries climbed 10.2% for the year compared with 2010.

The U.S. ended 2011 with 12.7 million LV sales, compared with prior-year's 11.6 million, the highest since 2008's 13.2 million.

Though it marks two straight years of increases since hitting bottom in 2009 with 10.4 million, the total still is comparatively low. Prior to 2009, the last time LV sales were lower was 1991, when volume was 12.3 million.

On the positive side, as long as the U.S. economy does not return to recessionary levels, steady long-term growth is inevitable.

Several auto makers posted hefty year-over-year gains in 2011. Sales leader General Motors delivered 2.504 million light vehicles for a 13.2% gain on 2010, while its share climbed to 19.7% compared with prior-year's 19.1%.

Ford's volume increased 10.8% compared with year-ago. Sales totaled 2.11 million for the year, vs. 1.91 million in 2010. Ford's annual share inched up to 16.6% from year-ago's 16.5%.

Toyota, still hampered by low inventory of some models due to the disruption caused by Japan's natural disasters earlier in the year, saw deliveries fall 6.7% to 1.645 million units. As a result, its share dropped to 12.9% vs. 15.3% in 2010 and 17.0% in 2009. It was Toyota's lowest U.S. share since 12.2% in 2004.

Chrysler returned to the No.4 sales position last year for the first time in three years by overtaking Honda, due to a combination of refreshed products and the depleted inventory suffered by the Asian auto maker.

Chrysler delivered 1.362 million units in 2011, up 26.1% compared with year-ago, with its share climbing to 10.7% from 2010's 9.3%. The auto maker ended the year with a whopping 37.4% sales increase in December and 11.1% market penetration.

Honda's sales nosedived in 2011, tumbling 6.8% to 1.147 million. The auto maker's share dropped to 9.0% from 10.6% in 2010 and 11.1% in 2009.

Nissan ended 2011 with its highest annual share ever, more impressive because it also incurred some inventory shortages due to Japan's natural disasters. Market penetration of 8.2% edged out 2010's 7.9%.

The auto maker sold 1.043 million units for a 14.7% year-over-year increase, marking its third-best year on record. December deliveries totaled 100,927, up 7.7% from like-2010.

Hyundai and Kia both posted major increases for the month

and for the year. Hyundai's December sales grew 13.3%, compared with year-ago, while Kia's deliveries soared 42.5%. Hyundai posted a 20.0% gain for the year, and Kia was up 36.3%.

Hyundai-Kia combined earned their highest U.S. annual share ever of 8.9% in 2011, compared with 7.8% in 2010, and beat Nissan for the first time.

In Canada, dealers closed the books on 2011 with sales of 1,581,733 cars and light trucks, a 1.7% gain over the 1,554,700 in 2010, despite weakened demand in December.

The gain was led by a 4.6% rise in light-truck deliveries, to 899,777 units from year-ago's 860,351, that more than compensated for a 1.8% decline in new-car sales, to 681,956 from 694,349, largely due to Japanese-make inventory shortages.

Ford again led the industry with 2011 LV sales up 2.5%, and deliveries including medium-duty trucks up 3.0%. It also was tops in total sales, though its volume gain was the lowest among the Detroit Three.

The F-150 fullsize truck remained the country's top-selling vehicle for a second consecutive year and the best-selling pickup for the 46th year.

GM nailed down second place for the year in spite of a 1.6% overall decline, while Chrysler ranked third on the strength of its 12.5% year-over-year gain.

In Europe, signs of sluggish growth and high public debt had auto makers concerned. EU new-vehicle registrations in 2011 were relatively flat at 15,094,222 compared with 15,140,977 in 2010, according to the ACEA, the European auto makers' group.

Several car companies were cutting back production or overtime at their plants because of the weakening market, including General Motors, Ford, Renault and PSA Peugeot Citroen. GM was planning about 60 non-working days at its Opel/Vauxhall plant in Zaragoza, Spain, through the end of 2012 and another 20 in Eisenach, Germany. A GM spokesman said demand was soft for vehicles built at those plants and the European market itself was expected to be softer in 2012.

Globally, even emerging markets, on which so many hopes rode, were showing signs of fatigue from Brazil to South Africa to China. Analysts particularly were watching to see whether China could rein in its fast-paced economy without seriously curtailing growth. Beijing put increasing focus on fighting inflation, leading to concerns that the economy could cool significantly. Reflecting the sales slowdown, China vehicle production for the year reached 18.4 million units, just 0.8% ahead of prior year's 18.3 million, but a sharp contrast with 2010's 33.8% gain over 2009. ❏

U.S. Production of Cars and Trucks

U.S. VEHICLE PRODUCTION

Year	Cars	Trucks	Total	Year	Cars	Trucks	Total
2011	2,976,397	5,678,606	8,655,003	1957	6,115,458	1,090,200	7,205,658
2010	2,731,105	5,011,988	7,743,093	1956	5,801,864	1,104,325	6,906,189
2009	2,195,588	3,513,843	5,709,431	1955	7,942,132	1,246,442	9,188,574
2008	3,731,241	4,940,900	8,672,141	1954	5,509,550	1,022,609	6,532,159
2007	3,867,268	6,885,042	10,752,310	1953	6,134,534	1,203,835	7,338,369
2006	4,311,696	6,948,581	11,260,277	1952	4,337,481	1,218,045	5,555,526
2005	4,265,872	7,680,781	11,946,653	1951	5,338,820	1,412,149	6,750,969
2004	4,165,925	7,794,429	11,960,354	1950	6,672,132	1,344,227	8,016,359
2003	4,453,369	7,633,659	12,087,028	1949	5,126,060	1,132,138	6,258,198
2002	4,957,377	7,322,205	12,279,582	1948	3,910,213	1,369,472	5,279,685
2001	4,808,019	6,616,670	11,424,689	1947	3,555,924	1,236,703	4,792,627
2000	5,470,917	7,302,797	12,773,714	1946	2,155,924	942,317	3,098,241
1999	5,577,749	7,447,229	13,024,978	1945	83,786	701,090	784,876
1998	5,492,473	6,510,190	12,002,663	1944	NA	791,357	791,357
1997	5,878,221	6,252,354	12,130,575	1943	NA	751,698	751,698
1996	6,035,235	5,794,922	11,830,157	1942	206,274	876,812	1,083,086
1995	6,325,967	5,669,281	11,995,248	1941	3,760,501	1,093,868	4,854,369
1994	6,601,220	5,638,068	12,239,288	1940	3,728,491	784,404	4,512,895
1993	5,982,120	4,873,342	10,855,462	1939	2,866,796	710,496	3,577,292
1992	5,666,891	4,024,552	9,691,443	1938	2,000,985	488,100	2,489,085
1991	5,439,864	3,349,976	8,789,840	1937	3,915,889	893,085	4,808,974
1990	6,077,903	3,689,536	9,767,439	1936	3,669,528	784,587	4,454,115
1989	6,821,291	4,035,501	10,856,792	1935	3,252,244	694,690	3,946,934
1988	7,137,433	4,084,575	11,222,008	1934	2,177,919	575,192	2,753,111
1987	7,099,854	3,812,074	10,911,928	1933	1,573,512	346,545	1,920,057
1986	7,829,271	3,490,853	11,320,124	1932	1,135,491	235,187	1,370,678
1985	8,186,043	3,452,094	11,638,137	1931	1,973,090	416,648	2,389,738
1984	7,773,342	3,165,716	10,939,058	1930	2,784,745	571,241	3,355,986
1983	6,782,061	2,443,637	9,225,698	1929	4,587,400	771,020	5,358,420
1982	5,073,214	1,912,099	6,985,313	1928	3,815,417	543,342	4,358,759
1981	6,251,003	1,689,778	7,940,781	1927	2,936,533	464,793	3,401,326
1980	6,372,304	1,638,259	8,010,563	1926	3,783,987	516,947	4,300,934
1979	8,422,074	3,053,033	11,475,107	1925	3,735,171	530,659	4,265,830
1978	9,173,606	3,721,680	12,895,286	1924	3,185,881	416,659	3,602,540
1977	9,211,411	3,487,675	12,699,086	1923	3,624,717	409,295	4,034,012
1976	8,492,473	2,993,063	11,485,536	1922	2,274,185	269,991	2,544,176
1975	6,705,837	2,259,576	8,965,413	1921	1,468,067	148,052	1,616,119
1974	7,290,258	2,693,676	9,983,934	1920	1,905,560	321,789	2,227,349
1973	9,660,821	3,002,098	12,662,919	1919	1,651,625	224,731	1,876,356
1972	8,821,737	2,475,786	11,297,523	1918	943,436	227,250	1,170,686
1971	8,578,349	2,071,407	10,649,756	1917	1,745,792	128,157	1,873,949
1970	6,545,908	1,716,749	8,262,657	1916	1,525,578	92,130	1,617,708
1969	8,219,463	1,963,099	10,182,562	1915	895,930	74,000	969,930
1968	8,843,031	1,950,713	10,793,744	1914	548,139	24,900	573,039
1967	7,406,788	1,585,481	8,992,269	1913	461,500	23,500	485,000
1966	8,598,917	1,764,337	10,363,254	1912	356,000	22,000	378,000
1965	9,329,104	1,785,109	11,114,213	1911	199,319	10,681	210,000
1964	7,739,034	1,560,644	9,299,678	1910	181,000	6,000	187,000
1963	7,637,173	1,463,412	9,100,585	1909	123,990	3,297	127,287
1962	6,935,182	1,254,220	8,189,402	1908	63,500	1,500	65,000
1961	5,516,317	1,127,505	6,643,822	1907	43,000	1,000	44,000
1960	6,696,108	1,198,112	7,894,220	1906	33,200	800	34,000
1959	5,593,707	1,139,958	6,733,665	1905	24,250	750	25,000
1958	4,244,045	871,330	5,115,375	1900	4,192	NA	4,192

NA - Not available.
SOURCE: *WardsAuto Group.*

N. America Vehicle Production by Model

NORTH AMERICA VEHICLE PRODUCTION BY MODEL

	Canada		Mexico		United States		North America	
	2011	2010	2011	2010	2011	2010	2011	2010
Ford Mustang	—	—	—	—	78,286	77,586	78,286	77,586
Mazda6	—	—	—	—	39,550	45,168	39,550	45,168
AUTOALLIANCE TOTAL	—	—	—	—	117,836	122,754	117,836	122,754
Chrysler 200 Series	—	—	—	—	122,625	2,197	122,625	2,197
Chrysler 300 Series	55,072	39,688	—	—	—	—	55,072	39,688
Chrysler Sebring Convertible	—	—	—	—	—	7,829	—	7,829
Chrysler Sebring Sedan	—	—	—	—	—	32,157	—	32,157
Dodge Avenger	—	—	—	—	75,951	59,170	75,951	59,170
Dodge Caliber	—	—	—	—	51,841	67,586	51,841	67,586
Dodge Challenger	44,068	40,042	—	—	—	—	44,068	40,042
Dodge Charger	91,523	83,527	—	—	—	—	91,523	83,527
Dodge Viper	—	—	—	—	—	459	—	459
Fiat 500 Convertible	—	—	6,729	—	—	—	6,729	—
Fiat 500 Sedan	—	—	50,243	724	—	—	50,243	724
Lancia Thema	3,968	—	—	—	—	—	3,968	—
CHRYSLER TOTAL	194,631	163,257	56,972	724	250,417	169,398	502,020	333,379
Ford Crown Victoria	66,096	52,148	—	—	—	—	66,096	52,148
Ford Fiesta	—	—	125,971	77,358	—	—	125,971	77,358
Ford Focus	—	—	—	—	221,514	199,502	221,514	199,502
Ford Fusion	—	—	294,110	267,533	—	—	294,110	267,533
Ford Taurus	—	—	—	—	77,664	83,052	77,664	83,052
Lincoln MKS	—	—	—	—	12,636	16,085	12,636	16,085
Lincoln MKZ	—	—	35,399	24,342	—	—	35,399	24,342
Lincoln Town Car	10,192	12,088	—	—	—	—	10,192	12,088
Mercury Grand Marquis	165	31,765	—	—	—	—	165	31,765
Mercury Milan	—	—	—	21,155	—	—	—	21,155
FORD TOTAL	76,453	96,001	455,480	390,388	311,814	298,639	843,747	785,028
Buick LaCrosse	—	—	—	—	64,729	73,480	64,729	73,480
Buick Lucerne	—	—	—	—	15,882	29,654	15,882	29,654
Buick Regal	23,715	—	—	—	—	—	23,715	—
Buick Verano	—	—	—	—	4,471	—	4,471	—
Cadillac CTS	—	—	—	—	64,935	60,688	64,935	60,688
Cadillac DTS	—	—	—	—	6,515	21,023	6,515	21,023
Cadillac STS	—	—	—	—	1,907	4,792	1,907	4,792
Chevrolet Aveo	—	—	68,428	55,141	—	—	68,428	55,141
Chevrolet Camaro	105,387	94,433	—	—	—	—	105,387	94,433
Chevrolet Chevy	—	—	37,183	48,971	—	—	37,183	48,971
Chevrolet Cobalt	—	—	—	—	—	91,796	—	91,796
Chevrolet Corvette	—	—	—	—	13,222	15,791	13,222	15,791
Chevrolet Cruze	—	—	—	—	281,810	66,303	281,810	66,303
Chevrolet Impala	188,838	177,772	—	—	—	—	188,838	177,772
Chevrolet Malibu	—	—	—	—	214,388	235,956	214,388	235,956
Chevrolet Sonic	—	—	—	—	36,527	—	36,527	—
Chevrolet Volt	—	—	—	—	14,510	1,219	14,510	1,219
Opel Ampera	—	—	—	—	2,605	—	2,605	—
Pontiac G6	—	—	—	—	—	1	—	1
GM TOTAL	317,940	272,205	105,611	104,112	721,501	600,703	1,145,052	977,020
Acura CSX	1,170	1,979	—	—	—	—	1,170	1,979
Acura TL	—	—	—	—	35,763	35,294	35,763	35,294
Honda Accord	—	—	—	—	229,439	295,709	229,439	295,709
Honda Civic	178,732	207,555	—	—	84,767	95,116	263,499	302,671
HONDA TOTAL	179,902	209,534	—	—	349,969	426,119	529,871	635,653
Hyundai Elantra	—	—	—	—	112,665	19,780	112,665	19,780
Hyundai Sonata	—	—	—	—	225,462	218,607	225,462	218,607
HYUNDAI TOTAL	—	—	—	—	338,127	238,387	338,127	238,387
Kia Optima	—	—	—	—	35,132	—	35,132	—
KIA TOTAL	—	—	—	—	35,132	—	35,132	—

N. America Vehicle Production by Model

NORTH AMERICA VEHICLE PRODUCTION BY MODEL – continued

	Canada		Mexico		United States		North America	
	2011	2010	2011	2010	2011	2010	2011	2010
Mitsubishi Eclipse	—	—	—	—	7,142	6,424	7,142	6,424
Mitsubishi Galant	—	—	—	—	19,441	16,545	19,441	16,545
MITSUBISHI TOTAL	**—**	**—**	**—**	**—**	**26,583**	**22,969**	**26,583**	**22,969**
Nissan Altima	—	—	—	—	319,203	275,115	319,203	275,115
Nissan Maxima	—	—	—	—	65,906	71,776	65,906	71,776
Nissan March	—	—	44,688	115	—	—	44,688	115
Nissan Sentra	—	—	156,704	146,753	—	—	156,704	146,753
Nissan Tiida	—	—	133,369	—	—	—	133,369	—
Nissan Tiida/Versa	—	—	61,814	234,868	—	—	61,814	234,868
Nissan Tsuru	—	—	57,844	74,503	—	—	57,844	74,503
Nissan Versa	—	—	74,557	—	—	—	74,557	—
NISSAN TOTAL	**—**	**—**	**528,976**	**456,239**	**385,109**	**346,891**	**914,085**	**803,130**
Toyota Corolla	—	—	—	—	—	63,319	—	63,319
NUMMI TOTAL	**—**	**—**	**—**	**—**	**—**	**63,319**	**—**	**63,319**
Subaru Legacy	—	—	—	—	46,568	43,791	46,568	43,791
Toyota Camry	—	—	—	—	79,170	87,731	79,170	87,731
SUBARU TOTAL	**—**	**—**	**—**	**—**	**125,738**	**131,522**	**125,738**	**131,522**
Toyota Avalon	—	—	—	—	38,684	40,155	38,684	40,155
Toyota Camry	—	—	—	—	227,663	270,249	227,663	270,249
Toyota Corolla	204,276	192,271	—	—	1,967	—	206,243	192,271
Toyota Matrix	17,280	33,809	—	—	—	—	17,280	33,809
TOYOTA TOTAL	**221,556**	**226,080**	**—**	**—**	**268,314**	**310,404**	**489,870**	**536,484**
Volkswagen Beetle	—	—	21,299	31,447	—	—	21,299	31,447
Volkswagen Beetle Cabrio	—	—	197	8,640	—	—	197	8,640
Volkswagen Bora	—	—	551	12,249	—	—	551	12,249
Volkswagen Jetta	—	—	487,994	382,349	—	—	487,994	382,349
Volkswagen Passat*	—	—	—	—	45,857	—	45,857	—
VOLKSWAGEN TOTAL	**—**	**—**	**510,041**	**434,685**	**45,857**	**—**	**555,898**	**434,685**
TOTAL CARS	**990,482**	**967,077**	**1,657,080**	**1,386,148**	**2,976,397**	**2,731,105**	**5,623,959**	**5,084,330**
BMW X3	—	—	—	—	121,561	16,078	121,561	16,078
BMW X5	—	—	—	—	110,605	98,245	110,605	98,245
BMW X6	—	—	—	—	43,899	43,380	43,899	43,380
BMW TOTAL	**—**	**—**	**—**	**—**	**276,065**	**157,703**	**276,065**	**157,703**
Chrysler PT Cruiser	—	—	—	11,083	—	—	—	11,083
Chrysler Town & Country	110,483	130,845	—	—	—	—	110,483	130,845
Dodge Caravan	169,234	165,594	—	—	—	—	169,234	165,594
Dodge Durango	—	—	—	—	71,796	3,429	71,796	3,429
Dodge Journey	—	—	108,601	128,203	—	—	108,601	128,203
Dodge Nitro	—	—	—	—	26,042	27,562	26,042	27,562
Fiat Freemont	—	—	33,192	—	—	—	33,192	—
Jeep Commander	—	—	—	—	—	5,582	—	5,582
Jeep Compass	—	—	—	—	103,671	34,412	103,671	34,412
Jeep Grand Cherokee	—	—	—	—	174,664	125,142	174,664	125,142
Jeep Liberty	—	—	—	—	77,923	64,411	77,923	64,411
Jeep Patriot	—	—	—	—	81,732	66,427	81,732	66,427
Jeep Wrangler	—	—	—	—	62,798	59,181	62,798	59,181
Jeep Wrangler Unlimited	—	—	—	—	102,368	85,504	102,368	85,504
Lancia Voyager	4,555	—	—	—	—	—	4,555	—
Mitsubishi Raider	—	—	—	—	193,752	178,406	193,752	178,406
Ram Cargo Van	2,827	—	—	—	—	—	2,827	—
Ram Pickup	—	—	132,818	110,673	17,390	19,043	150,208	129,716
Volkswagen Routan	14,351	15,686	—	—	—	—	14,351	15,686
CHRYSLER TOTAL	**301,450**	**312,125**	**274,611**	**249,959**	**912,136**	**669,099**	**1,488,197**	**1,231,183**
Ford Econoline	—	—	—	—	133,850	121,471	133,850	121,471
Ford Edge	171,285	150,157	—	—	—	—	171,285	150,157

N. America Vehicle Production by Model

NORTH AMERICA VEHICLE PRODUCTION BY MODEL – continued

	Canada		Mexico		United States		North America	
	2011	2010	2011	2010	2011	2010	2011	2010
Ford Escape	—	—	—	—	320,859	275,646	320,859	275,646
Ford Expedition	—	—	—	—	59,073	51,295	59,073	51,295
Ford Explorer	—	—	—	—	170,676	97,312	170,676	97,312
Ford F-Series	—	—	—	—	686,598	616,541	686,598	616,541
Ford Flex	31,163	41,081	—	—	—	—	31,163	41,081
Ford Ranger	—	—	—	—	97,222	70,666	97,222	70,666
Lincoln Mark LT	—	—	—	—	408	847	408	847
Lincoln MKT	5,873	5,961	—	—	—	—	5,873	5,961
Lincoln MKX	35,622	27,408	—	—	—	—	35,622	27,408
Lincoln Navigator	—	—	—	—	9,785	9,636	9,785	9,636
Mercury Mariner	—	—	—	—	—	25,050	—	25,050
Mercury Mountaineer	—	—	—	—	—	4,564	—	4,564
Mazda Pickup	—	—	—	—	—	2,395	—	2,395
Mazda Tribute	—	—	—	—	3,977	9,273	3,977	9,273
FORD TOTAL	**243,943**	**224,607**	**—**	**—**	**1,482,448**	**1,284,696**	**1,726,391**	**1,509,303**
Buick Enclave	—	—	—	—	70,244	74,414	70,244	74,414
Cadillac Escalade	—	—	—	—	17,085	22,753	17,085	22,753
Cadillac Escalade ESV	—	—	—	—	7,769	12,693	7,769	12,693
Cadillac Escalade EXT	—	—	2,404	2,649	—	—	2,404	2,649
Cadillac SRX	—	—	85,465	76,589	—	—	85,465	76,589
Chevrolet Avalanche	—	—	25,407	26,956	—	—	25,407	26,956
Chevrolet Captiva Sport	—	—	42,798	30,618	—	—	42,798	30,618
Chevrolet Colorado	—	—	—	—	41,012	34,509	41,012	34,509
Chevrolet Equinox	233,244	180,522	—	—	—	—	233,244	180,522
Chevrolet Express	—	—	—	—	79,162	69,328	79,162	69,328
Chevrolet HHR	—	—	29,460	72,892	—	—	29,460	72,892
Chevrolet Silverado	—	—	165,783	162,141	326,950	294,802	492,733	456,943
Chevrolet Suburban	—	—	—	—	58,185	58,889	58,185	58,889
Chevrolet Tahoe	—	—	—	—	100,134	101,499	100,134	101,499
Chevrolet Traverse	—	—	—	—	118,846	118,220	118,846	118,220
GMC Acadia	—	—	—	—	92,747	82,555	92,747	82,555
GMC Canyon	—	—	—	—	13,208	12,436	13,208	12,436
GMC Savana	—	—	—	—	26,214	21,688	26,214	21,688
GMC Sierra	—	—	86,518	80,594	124,741	124,846	211,259	205,440
GMC Terrain	110,700	76,841	—	—	—	—	110,700	76,841
GMC Yukon	—	—	—	—	50,091	50,402	50,091	50,402
GMC Yukon XL	—	—	—	—	34,965	35,793	34,965	35,793
Hummer H3	—	—	—	—	—	1,183	—	1,183
Hummer H3T	—	—	—	—	—	321	—	321
Saab 9-4X	—	—	700	—	—	—	700	—
Saturn Outlook	—	—	—	—	—	2,507	—	2,507
Saturn Vue	—	—	—	2,886	—	—	—	2,886
GM TOTAL	**343,944**	**257,363**	**438,535**	**455,325**	**1,161,353**	**1,118,838**	**1,943,832**	**1,831,526**
Acura MDX	52,069	63,859	—	—	—	—	52,069	63,859
Acura RDX	—	—	—	—	19,377	20,550	19,377	20,550
Acura ZDX	1,940	4,879	—	—	—	—	1,940	4,879
Honda CR-V	140	—	45,426	55,001	165,840	196,743	211,406	251,744
Honda Crosstour	—	—	—	—	18,839	33,200	18,839	33,200
Honda Element	—	—	—	—	7,500	16,800	7,500	16,800
Honda Odyssey	—	—	—	—	130,443	119,580	130,443	119,580
Honda Pilot	—	—	—	—	118,326	121,330	118,326	121,330
Honda Ridgeline	—	—	—	—	13,356	20,180	13,356	20,180
HONDA TOTAL	**54,149**	**68,738**	**45,426**	**55,001**	**473,681**	**528,383**	**573,256**	**652,122**
Hyundai Santa Fe	—	—	—	—	—	62,113	—	62,113
HYUNDAI TOTAL	**—**	**—**	**—**	**—**	**—**	**62,113**	**—**	**62,113**

N. America Vehicle Production by Model

NORTH AMERICA VEHICLE PRODUCTION BY MODEL – continued

	Canada		Mexico		United States		North America	
	2011	2010	2011	2010	2011	2010	2011	2010
Hyundai Santa Fe	—	—	—	—	91,155	30,093	91,155	30,093
Kia Sorento	—	—	—	—	146,017	122,268	146,017	122,268
KIA TOTAL	**—**	**—**	**—**	**—**	**237,172**	**152,361**	**237,172**	**152,361**
Mercedes GL*	—	—	—	—	39,067	31,995	39,067	31,995
Mercedes M-Class*	—	—	—	—	87,699	76,472	87,699	76,472
Mercedes R-Class*	—	—	—	—	19,075	16,870	19,075	16,870
MERCEDES TOTAL	**—**	**—**	**—**	**—**	**145,841**	**125,337**	**145,841**	**125,337**
Mitsubishi Endeavor	—	—	—	—	10,567	6,406	10,567	6,406
MITSUBISHI TOTAL	**—**	**—**	**—**	**—**	**10,567**	**6,406**	**10,567**	**6,406**
Infiniti QX56	—	—	—	—	—	3,466	—	3,466
Nissan Armada	—	—	—	—	20,794	26,260	20,794	26,260
Nissan Chassis	—	—	27,447	20,907	—	—	27,447	20,907
Nissan Frontier	—	—	3,486	589	55,653	48,658	59,139	49,247
Nissan NV	—	—	—	—	13,830	—	13,830	—
Nissan Pathfinder	—	—	—	—	35,454	29,786	35,454	29,786
Nissan Pickup	—	—	47,178	28,755	—	—	47,178	28,755
Nissan Titan	—	—	—	—	26,254	28,022	26,254	28,022
Nissan Xterra	—	—	—	—	23,931	26,180	23,931	26,180
Suzuki Equator	—	—	—	—	2,190	1,630	2,190	1,630
NISSAN TOTAL	**—**	**—**	**78,111**	**50,251**	**178,106**	**164,002**	**256,217**	**214,253**
Toyota Tacoma	—	—	—	—	—	27,495	—	27,495
NUMMI TOTAL	**—**	**—**	**—**	**—**	**—**	**27,495**	**—**	**27,495**
Subaru Outback	—	—	—	—	108,752	108,686	108,752	108,686
Subaru Tribeca	—	—	—	—	6,396	5,543	6,396	5,543
SUBARU TOTAL	**—**	**—**	**—**	**—**	**115,148**	**114,229**	**115,148**	**114,229**
Lexus RX350	65,242	81,618	—	—	—	—	65,242	81,618
Toyota Highlander	—	—	—	—	101,502	86,527	101,502	86,527
Toyota RAV4	126,030	151,031	—	—	—	—	126,030	151,031
Toyota Sequoia	—	—	—	—	19,841	24,685	19,841	24,685
Toyota Sienna	—	—	—	—	126,475	132,780	126,475	132,780
Toyota Tacoma	—	—	49,596	53,829	65,122	42,139	114,718	95,968
Toyota Tundra	—	—	—	—	83,895	107,959	83,895	107,959
Toyota Venza	—	—	—	—	48,892	61,290	48,892	61,290
TOYOTA TOTAL	**191,272**	**232,649**	**49,596**	**53,829**	**445,727**	**455,380**	**686,595**	**741,858**
TOTAL LIGHT TRUCKS	**1,134,758**	**1,095,482**	**886,279**	**864,365**	**5,438,244**	**4,866,042**	**7,459,281**	**6,825,889**
TOTAL LIGHT VEHICLES	**2,125,240**	**2,062,559**	**2,543,359**	**2,250,513**	**8,414,641**	**7,597,147**	**13,083,240**	**11,910,219**
Blue Diamond	—	—	12,328	5,589	—	—	12,328	5,589
Chrysler	—	—	8,800	7,100	—	—	8,800	7,100
Dina Camiones**	—	—	701	143	—	—	701	143
Ford	—	—	—	—	42,765	30,052	42,765	30,052
Freightliner	—	—	62,601	46,643	45,532	24,756	108,133	71,399
Hino**	—	—	319	354	4,777	3,484	5,096	3,838
International	1	8	36,363	23,701	42,998	32,479	79,362	56,188
Kenworth	9,880	5,622	15,870	10,325	30,625	14,916	56,375	30,863
Mack	—	—	—	—	20,299	13,546	20,299	13,546
MAN**	—	—	903	651	—	—	903	651
Peterbilt	—	—	—	—	28,124	13,853	28,124	13,853
Volvo Truck**	—	—	142	85	25,209	12,836	25,351	12,921
Other	—	—	—	—	33	24	33	24
TOTAL MED.HVY. TRUCKS	**9,881**	**5,630**	**138,027**	**94,591**	**240,362**	**145,946**	**388,270**	**246,167**
TOTAL TRUCKS	**1,144,639**	**1,101,112**	**1,024,306**	**958,956**	**5,678,606**	**5,011,988**	**7,847,551**	**7,072,056**
TOTAL VEHICLES	**2,135,121**	**2,068,189**	**2,681,386**	**2,345,104**	**8,655,003**	**7,743,093**	**13,471,510**	**12,156,386**

* *WardsAuto* estimates for U.S. units for 2011.
** *WardsAuto* estimates for Mexico units for 2011.
SOURCE: *WardsAuto* InfoBank.

U.S. Factory Sales of Trucks and Buses by Gross Vehicle Weight Rating

U.S. FACTORY SALES OF TRUCKS AND BUSES BY GROSS VEHICLE WEIGHT RATING

	Gross Vehicle Weight Rating (Pounds)								
	6,000 & Less	6,001- 10,000	10,001- 14,000	14,001- 16,000	16,001- 19,500	19,501- 26,000	26,001- 33,000	33,001 & Over	Total
U.S. TOTAL									
2011	2,288,126	1,975,924	119,924	3,123	32,867	29,489	29,748	162,395	4,641,596
2010	2,051,050	1,820,898	94,777	3,979	16,342	26,466	28,063	90,618	4,132,193
2009	1,624,363	1,248,435	80,176	15,301	15,215	16,443	31,100	76,393	3,107,426
2008	2,317,625	1,655,766	99,692	21,420	27,558	27,977	44,943	127,880	4,322,861
2007	3,232,324	2,504,072	156,610	35,293	34,478	46,158	54,761	137,016	6,200,712
2006	3,459,190	2,381,970	115,140	31,471	33,757	68,069	78,754	274,480	6,442,831
2005	4,059,286	2,585,660	146,809	36,812	37,359	55,666	71,305	253,840	7,246,737
2004	4,176,947	2,767,305	136,229	36,203	26,058	67,252	61,918	194,827	7,466,739
2003	4,238,125	2,503,395	116,416	26,888	20,086	46,211	56,225	136,083	7,143,429
2002	4,279,792	2,274,661	121,867	29,277	15,913	40,507	62,070	139,633	6,963,720
2001	3,915,731	1,968,010	66,787	29,876	22,616	35,815	69,749	115,002	6,223,586
2000	4,533,600	1,973,801	100,293	48,572	25,137	36,874	106,750	197,451	7,022,478
1999	4,876,534	1,891,397	116,868	44,250	19,699	25,528	122,411	248,332	7,345,019
1998	4,458,970	1,431,110	147,839	33,513	17,441	19,850	116,412	210,050	6,435,185
1997	4,377,340	1,366,899	47,022	32,286	4,056	16,687	128,245	180,282	6,152,817
1996	4,073,778	1,344,826	38,525	32,912	4,127	12,379	106,657	162,526	5,775,730
1995	3,742,739	1,583,878	901	37,073	1,549	16,369	125,703	205,257	5,713,469
1994	3,811,837	1,478,854	848	29,585	550	13,559	115,334	189,708	5,640,275
1993	3,488,278	1,124,106	—	8,149	—	21,943	93,939	158,809	4,895,224
1992	2,978,214	850,876	—	7,193	2	21,993	81,601	122,123	4,062,002
1991	2,533,904	658,425	—	3,820	56	19,498	77,850	93,950	3,387,503
U.S. DOMESTIC									
2011	2,008,291	1,697,134	110,928	2,893	29,138	28,642	26,595	129,167	4,032,788
2010	1,823,848	1,568,311	87,855	3,561	14,674	25,763	25,651	68,461	3,618,124
2009	1,485,453	1,069,687	74,899	13,994	13,428	15,772	29,317	61,769	2,764,319
2008	1,975,203	1,392,987	92,105	19,680	25,311	26,929	39,315	97,015	3,668,545
2007	2,745,028	2,185,881	146,794	32,162	31,123	45,195	50,747	102,614	5,339,544
2006	3,005,776	2,125,307	111,461	29,255	30,804	66,753	73,039	231,418	5,673,813
2005	3,569,546	2,333,147	142,116	33,926	33,446	54,557	65,524	213,873	6,446,135
2004	3,795,422	2,530,711	131,889	33,870	23,702	65,869	56,579	164,711	6,802,753
2003	3,818,750	2,300,058	112,745	24,960	18,304	45,515	50,927	114,990	6,486,249
2002	3,827,782	2,073,553	117,927	26,986	14,279	39,607	56,691	120,409	6,277,234
2001	3,511,326	1,794,251	61,168	27,038	20,216	34,905	64,454	99,422	5,612,780
2000	4,070,026	1,757,683	97,697	35,407	22,602	35,752	100,175	171,565	6,290,907
1999	4,453,332	1,723,012	112,349	37,328	17,542	24,362	113,147	218,041	6,699,113
1998	4,053,521	1,303,786	141,781	29,629	15,779	18,989	105,874	177,852	5,847,211
1997	3,894,222	1,236,119	44,893	28,428	3,931	15,609	116,922	149,183	5,489,307
1996	3,699,385	1,225,792	37,559	30,309	4,056	11,717	97,720	141,941	5,248,479
1995	3,405,062	1,458,713	780	35,427	1,471	15,046	114,194	180,652	5,211,345
1994	3,475,044	1,353,576	848	28,437	533	12,123	102,745	165,375	5,138,681
1993	3,187,731	1,031,829	—	7,630	—	19,277	84,779	140,247	4,471,493
1992	2,711,172	785,198	—	6,612	2	19,160	71,899	108,003	3,702,046
1991	2,281,761	594,435	—	3,547	28	16,536	69,703	83,875	3,049,885

* Reporting firms do not represent the entire industry.
SOURCE: *WardsAuto Group*.

U.S. FACTORY SALES OF TRUCKS AND BUSES BY GROSS VEHICLE WEIGHT RATING, 1991-2011

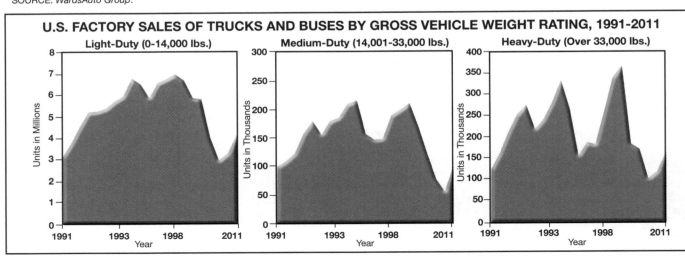

Light-Duty (0-14,000 lbs.) — Medium-Duty (14,001-33,000 lbs.) — Heavy-Duty (Over 33,000 lbs.)

U.S. Factory Sales of Diesel Trucks and Vehicle Factory Sales from U.S. and Canadian Plants

U.S. FACTORY SALES OF DIESEL TRUCKS BY GROSS VEHICLE WEIGHT RATING

	Gross Vehicle Weight Rating (Pounds)								
	6,000 & Less	6,001- 10,000	10,001- 14,000	14,001- 16,000	16,001- 19,500	19,501- 26,000	26,001- 33,000	33,001 & Over	Total
U.S. TOTAL									
2011	529	349,966	50,602	2,566	26,410	27,889	14,463	162,262	634,687
2010	635	282,134	45,476	3,739	15,140	24,346	10,893	90,547	472,910
2009	492	201,621	37,277	13,350	13,894	9,148	11,090	76,335	363,207
2008	1,126	213,647	44,000	17,320	25,441	16,238	22,588	127,549	467,909
2007	1,292	260,435	66,575	27,631	31,665	24,170	27,592	136,839	576,199
2006	1,598	240,289	78,943	23,817	30,935	51,224	46,103	274,459	747,368
2005	2,258	246,744	100,773	27,158	34,457	40,869	39,820	253,828	745,907
2000	2,580	279,224	50,571	30,223	23,422	19,807	72,509	197,451	675,787
1995	5,995	225,968	150	25,241	1,346	11,403	93,237	205,254	568,594
1990	449	102,051	—	81	51	12,567	61,010	116,931	293,140
1985	15,447	132,871	5,870	—	—	16,537	57,238	132,429	360,392
U.S. DOMESTIC									
2011	59	280,332	48,922	2,388	23,192	26,138	12,183	129,159	522,373
2010	54	222,846	43,966	3,333	13,498	22,633	9,508	68,447	384,285
2009	38	159,701	36,039	12,084	12,434	8,827	10,015	61,761	300,899
2008	81	164,700	42,539	15,674	23,267	15,626	18,689	96,899	377,475
2007	105	207,668	64,365	24,632	28,425	23,645	24,836	102,570	476,246
2006	135	194,968	76,322	21,707	28,109	50,372	41,881	231,397	644,891
2005	192	204,413	97,427	24,431	30,692	39,939	36,183	213,861	647,138
2000	271	221,830	48,911	26,997	20,921	18,812	68,678	171,565	577,985
1995	4,579	191,758	92	23,913	1,272	10,597	84,213	180,652	497,076
1990	337	94,030	—	55	51	11,458	53,957	107,002	266,890
1985	9,663	123,882	5,870	—	—	14,253	50,492	120,311	324,471

* Reporting firms do not represent the entire industry.
SOURCE: *WardsAuto Group.*

U.S. AND CANADA TRUCK AND BUS FACTORY SALES

	U.S. Plants				Canadian Plants			
	U.S Total	Exports to Canada	Other Exports	U.S. Domestic	Canada Total	Exports to U.S.	Other Exports	Canada Domestic
2011	4,641,596	271,555	337,253	4,032,788	865,773	737,749	16,028	111,996
2010	4,132,193	255,408	258,661	3,618,124	785,087	648,199	16,704	120,184
2009	3,107,426	190,641	152,466	2,764,319	493,856	407,087	11,534	75,235
2008	4,322,861	296,702	357,614	3,668,545	684,183	555,449	24,896	103,838
2007	6,200,712	374,739	486,429	5,339,544	861,711	746,417	13,004	102,290
2006	6,442,831	388,689	380,329	5,673,813	713,960	626,986	9,841	77,133
2005	7,246,737	424,819	375,783	6,446,135	830,683	747,926	7,558	75,199
2004	7,466,739	419,384	244,602	6,802,753	923,873	837,521	8,542	77,810
2003	7,143,429	411,539	245,641	6,486,249	917,240	806,830	8,648	101,762
2002	6,963,720	446,775	239,711	6,277,234	1,003,861	845,602	8,187	150,072
2001	6,223,586	384,775	226,031	5,612,780	982,983	851,884	5,868	125,231
2000	7,022,478	410,698	320,873	6,290,907	1,161,654	954,641	8,899	198,114
1999	7,345,059	416,010	229,936	6,699,113	1,241,442	1,017,982	11,814	211,646
1998	6,435,185	364,865	223,109	5,847,211	1,041,626	814,961	10,223	216,442
1997	6,152,817	402,138	261,372	5,489,307	1,153,540	924,837	11,329	217,374
1996	5,775,730	327,701	199,550	5,248,479	1,058,106	891,117	11,772	155,217
1995	5,713,469	318,470	183,654	5,211,345	1,004,717	871,134	5,180	128,403
1994	5,640,275	340,606	160,988	5,138,681	1,031,795	896,608	5,408	129,779
1993	4,895,224	286,348	137,383	4,471,493	842,468	732,189	5,297	104,982
1992	4,062,002	242,944	117,012	3,702,046	907,346	779,824	24,725	102,797
1991	3,387,503	235,432	102,186	3,049,885	790,485	648,973	33,621	107,891

* Reporting firms do not represent the entire industry.
SOURCE: *WardsAuto Group.*

Vehicle Production by State and Plant

U.S. VEHICLE PRODUCTION BY STATE AND PLANT, 2011

ALABAMA					**KANSAS**			
Lincoln	Light Truck	Honda Odyssey	130,443		Fairfax	Car	Buick LaCrosse	64,729
Lincoln	Light Truck	Honda Pilot	118,326		Fairfax	Car	Chevrolet Malibu	214,388
Lincoln	Light Truck	Honda Ridgeline	13,356		**GM Total**			**279,117**
Honda Total			**262,125**		**Total Kansas**			**279,117**
Montgomery	Car	Hyundai Elantra	112,665		**KENTUCKY**			
Montgomery	Car	Hyundai Sonata	225,462		Kentucky Truck	Light Truck	Ford Expedition	59,073
Hyundai Total			**338,127**		Kentucky Truck	Light Truck	Ford F-Series	207,290
Vance	Light Truck	Mercedes GL	39,067		Kentucky Truck	Light Truck	Lincoln Navigator	9,785
Vance	Light Truck	Mercedes M-Class	87,699		Kentucky Truck	Med./Hvy. Truck	Ford F-Series	34,849
Vance	Light Truck	Mercedes R-Class	19,075		**Ford Total**			**310,997**
Mercedes Total*			**145,841**		Bowling Green	Car	Chevrolet Corvette	13,222
Total Alabama			**746,093**		**GM Total**			**13,222**
GEORGIA					Georgetown	Car	Toyota Avalon	38,684
West Point	Car	Kia Optima	35,132		Georgetown	Car	Toyota Camry	227,663
West Point	Light Truck	Hyundai Santa Fe	91,155		Georgetown	Light Truck	Toyota Venza	48,892
West Point	Light Truck	Kia Sorento	146,017		**Toyota Total**			**315,239**
Kia Total			**272,304**		**Total Kentucky**			**639,458**
Total Georgia			**272,304**		**LOUISIANA**			
ILLINOIS					Shreveport	Light Truck	Chevrolet Colorado	41,012
Belvidere	Car	Dodge Caliber	51,841		Shreveport	Light Truck	GMC Canyon	13,208
Belvidere	Light Truck	Jeep Compass	103,671		**GM Total**			**54,220**
Belvidere	Light Truck	Jeep Patriot	81,732		**Total Louisiana**			**54,220**
Chrysler Total			**237,244**		**MICHIGAN**			
Chicago	Car	Ford Taurus	77,664		Flat Rock	Car	Ford Mustang	78,286
Chicago	Car	Lincoln MKS	12,636		Flat Rock	Car	Mazda6	39,550
Chicago	Light Truck	Ford Explorer	170,676		**AutoAlliance Total**			**117,836**
Ford Total			**260,976**		Detroit (Jefferson N.)	Light Truck	Dodge Durango	71,796
Normal	Car	Mitsubishi Eclipse	7,142		Detroit (Jefferson N.)	Light Truck	Jeep Grand Cherokee	174,664
Normal	Car	Mitsubishi Galant	19,441		Sterling Heights	Car	Chrysler 200 Series	122,625
Normal	Light Truck	Mitsubishi Endeavor	10,567		Sterling Heights	Car	Dodge Avenger	75,951
Mitsubishi Total			**37,150**		Warren	Light Truck	Ram Dakota	17,390
Total Illinois			**535,370**		Warren	Light Truck	Ram Pickup	193,752
INDIANA					**Chrysler Total**			**656,178**
Fort Wayne	Light Truck	Chevrolet Silverado	222,585		Dearborn Truck	Light Truck	Ford F-Series	344,038
Fort Wayne	Light Truck	GMC Sierra	84,775		Dearborn Truck	Light Truck	Lincoln Mark LT	408
GM Total			**307,360**		Detroit	Med./Hvy. Truck	Ford Chassis	7,916
Greensburg	Car	Honda Civic	84,767		Wayne (MI Assem.)	Car	Ford Focus	221,514
Honda Total			**84,767**		**Ford Total**			**573,876**
Lafayette	Car	Subaru Legacy	46,568		Flint 1	Light Truck	Chevrolet Silverado	104,365
Lafayette	Car	Toyota Camry	79,170		Flint 1	Light Truck	GMC Sierra	39,966
Lafayette	Light Truck	Subaru Outback	108,752		Hamtramck	Car	Buick Lucerne	15,882
Lafayette	Light Truck	Subaru Tribeca	6,396		Hamtramck	Car	Cadillac DTS	6,515
Subaru Total			**240,886**		Hamtramck	Car	Chevrolet Volt	14,510
Princeton	Light Truck	Toyota Highlander	101,502		Hamtramck	Car	Opel Ampera	2,605
Princeton	Light Truck	Toyota Sequoia	19,841		Lansing Delta	Light Truck	Buick Enclave	70,244
Princeton	Light Truck	Toyota Sienna	126,475		Lansing Delta	Light Truck	Chevrolet Traverse	118,846
Toyota Total			**247,818**		Lansing Delta	Light Truck	GMC Acadia	92,747
Total Indiana			**880,831**		Lansing Grand River	Car	Cadillac CTS	64,935

Vehicle Production by State and Plant

U.S. VEHICLE PRODUCTION BY STATE AND PLANT, 2011 — continued

Lansing Grand River	Car	Cadillac STS	1,907
Orion	Car	Buick Verano	4,471
Orion	Car	Chevrolet Sonic	36,527
GM Total			**573,520**
Total Michigan			**1,921,410**
MINNESOTA			
Twin Cities	Light Truck	Ford Ranger	97,222
Ford Total			**97,222**
Total Minnesota			**97,222**
MISSISSIPPI			
Canton	Car	Nissan Altima	168,453
Canton	Light Truck	Nissan Armada	20,794
Canton	Light Truck	Nissan NV	13,830
Canton	Light Truck	Nissan Titan	26,254
Nissan Total			**229,331**
Blue Springs	Car	Toyota Corolla	1,967
Toyota Total			**1,967**
Total Mississippi			**231,298**
MISSOURI			
Kansas City 1	Light Truck	Ford Escape	320,859
Kansas City 1	Light Truck	Mazda Tribute	3,977
Kansas City 2	Light Truck	Ford F-Series	135,270
Ford Total			**460,106**
Wentzville	Light Truck	Chevrolet Express	79,162
Wentzville	Light Truck	GMC Savana	26,214
GM Total			**105,376**
Total Missouri			**565,482**
OHIO			
Toledo North	Light Truck	Dodge Nitro	26,042
Toledo North	Light Truck	Jeep Liberty	77,923
Toledo South	Light Truck	Jeep Wrangler	62,798
Toledo South	Light Truck	Jeep Wrangler Unlimited	102,368
Chrysler Total			**269,131**
Avon Lake	Light Truck	Ford Econoline	133,850
Ford Total			**133,850**
Lordstown	Car	Chevrolet Cruze	281,810
GM Total			**281,810**
East Liberty	Light Truck	Honda CR-V	165,840
East Liberty	Light Truck	Honda Crosstour	18,839
East Liberty	Light Truck	Honda Element	7,500
Marysville	Car	Acura TL	35,763
Marysville	Car	Honda Accord	229,439
Marysville	Light Truck	Acura RDX	19,377
Honda Total			**476,758**
Total Ohio			**1,161,549**
SOUTH CAROLINA			
Spartanburg	Light Truck	BMW X3	121,561
Spartanburg	Light Truck	BMW X5	110,605
Spartanburg	Light Truck	BMW X6	43,899
BMW Total			**276,065**
Total South Carolina			**276,065**
TENNESSEE			
Smyrna	Car	Nissan Altima	150,750
Smyrna	Car	Nissan Maxima	65,906
Smyrna	Light Truck	Nissan Frontier	55,653
Smyrna	Light Truck	Nissan Pathfinder	35,454
Smyrna	Light Truck	Nissan Xterra	23,931
Smyrna	Light Truck	Suzuki Equator	2,190
Nissan Total			**333,884**
Chattanooga	Car	Volkswagen Passat	45,857
Volkswagen Total*			**45,857**
Total Tennessee			**379,741**
TEXAS			
Arlington	Light Truck	Cadillac Escalade	17,085
Arlington	Light Truck	Cadillac Escalade ESV	7,769
Arlington	Light Truck	Chevrolet Suburban	58,185
Arlington	Light Truck	Chevrolet Tahoe	100,134
Arlington	Light Truck	GMC Yukon	50,091
Arlington	Light Truck	GMC Yukon XL	34,965
GM Total			**268,229**
San Antonio	Light Truck	Toyota Tacoma	65,122
San Antonio	Light Truck	Toyota Tundra	83,895
Toyota Total			**149,017**
Total Texas			**417,246**
OTHER			
Freightliner	Med./Hvy. Truck		45,532
Hino	Med./Hvy. Truck		4,777
International	Med./Hvy. Truck		42,998
Kenworth	Med./Hvy. Truck		30,625
Mack	Med./Hvy. Truck		20,299
Peterbilt	Med./Hvy. Truck		28,124
Volvo Truck	Med./Hvy. Truck		25,209
Other	Med./Hvy. Truck		33
TOTAL U.S. CARS			**2,976,397**
TOTAL U.S. LIGHT TRUCKS			**5,438,244**
TOTAL U.S. MED./HVY. TRUCKS			**240,362**
TOTAL U.S. VEHICLES			**8,655,003**

TOP STATES IN CALENDAR 2011 U.S. PRODUCTION

Rank	Cars	Rank	Trucks
1. Michigan	685,278	1. Michigan	1,236,132
2. Ohio	547,012	2. Indiana	670,326
3. Alabama	338,127	3. Ohio	657,535
4. Kentucky	279,569	4. Missouri	565,482
5. Kansas	279,117	5. Texas	417,246

* *WardsAuto* estimates. SOURCE: *WardsAuto InfoBank.*

Factory Installations of Selected Equipment

FACTORY INSTALLATIONS OF SELECTED EQUIPMENT BY MODEL YEAR

	2011 Units (000)	2011 % of Total	2010 Units (000)	2010 % of Total	2009 Units (000)	2009 % of Total	2008 Units (000)	2008 % of Total
CARS								
Automatic Transmission	4,183	91.2	4,171	91.1	3,556	91.4	5,281	91.5
5-Speed Transmission	126	2.8	174	3.8	241	6.2	373	6.5
6-Speed Transmission	276	6.0	236	5.1	93	2.4	115	2.0
All-Wheel Drive	173	3.8	141	3.1	150	3.9	158	2.7
4-Cylinder Engine	2,933	64.0	2,953	64.5	2,539	65.3	3,186	55.2
5-Cylinder Engine	316	6.9	221	4.8	221	5.7	438	7.6
6-Cylinder Engine	1,084	23.6	1,147	25.0	938	24.1	1,804	31.3
8-Cylinder Engine	253	5.5	260	5.7	191	4.9	341	5.9
Stability Control	4,331	94.4	3,563	77.8	1,690	43.5	953	16.5
Antilock Brakes	4,585	100.0	4,484	97.9	3,494	89.8	4,524	78.4
Power Door Locks	4,472	97.5	4,474	97.7	3,756	96.6	5,571	96.6
Power Seats, 4 or 6 way	2,125	46.4	2,057	44.9	2,038	52.4	2,761	47.9
Memory Seats	263	5.7	188	4.1	220	5.5	384	6.7
Power Windows	4,491	97.9	4,474	97.7	3,750	96.4	5,561	96.4
Sun Roof	1,230	26.8	1,246	27.2	1,006	25.9	1,531	26.5
Side Airbags	4,550	99.2	4,436	96.8	3,455	88.8	4,190	72.6
Side Curtain Airbags	4,474	97.6	4,332	94.6	3,561	91.5	4,603	79.8
Navigation System	349	7.6	292	6.4	191	4.9	262	4.5
Keyless Remote	4,375	95.4	4,384	95.7	3,663	94.2	5,341	92.6
Air Conditioning,Automatic Temp. Control	1,236	26.9	1,011	22.1	843	21.7	1,196	20.7
Air Conditioning, Manual Temp. Control	3,340	72.8	3,550	77.5	3,020	77.6	4,532	78.6
Limited-Slip Differential	240	5.2	234	5.1	157	4.0	256	4.4
Styled Wheels	2,838	61.9	2,765	60.3	2,499	64.3	3,603	62.5
Automatic Headlamp	2,999	65.4	2,829	61.7	2,050	52.7	3,365	58.3
Cruise Control	4,345	94.8	4,392	95.9	3,653	93.9	5,369	93.1
LIGHT TRUCKS (0-10,000 lbs. G.V.W.R.)								
AutomaticTransmission	6,862	98.7	5,192	98.1	3,983	98.2	6,860	97.8
Four Wheel Antilock Brakes	6,950	100.0	5,284	99.8	4,024	99.3	6,690	95.3
Rear Antilock Brakes	—	—	9	0.2	5	0.1	203	2.9
Keyless Entry	6,179	88.9	4,740	89.6	3,549	87.5	6,135	87.4
Side Airbag	4,956	71.3	3,207	60.6	2,068	51.0	3,471	49.5
Four-Wheel Drive	3,694	53.2	2,561	48.4	1,913	47.2	3,411	48.6
Diesel Engine	437	6.3	177	3.3	236	5.8	459	6.5
4-Cylinder Gasoline Engine	1,159	16.7	940	17.8	600	14.8	706	10.1
5-Cylinder Gasoline Engine	27	0.4	41	0.8	36	0.9	88	1.3
6-Cylinder Gasoline Engine	3,281	47.1	2,457	46.4	1,742	43.0	3,248	46.3
8-Cylinder Gasoline Engine	2,039	29.4	1,666	31.5	1,429	35.3	2,487	35.5
10-Cylinder Gasoline Engine	7	0.1	12	0.2	11	0.3	29	0.4
Air Conditioning	6,893	99.2	5,224	98.7	4,032	99.5	7,006	99.8
Cruise Control	6,578	94.7	4,982	94.1	3,751	92.5	6,422	91.5
Limited-Slip Differential	1,709	24.6	1,165	22.0	1,149	28.4	2,049	29.2

* Based on production in the United States, Canada and Mexico for the United States market.
SOURCE: WardsAuto Group.

Recreation Vehicle Shipments

U.S. RECREATION VEHICLE SHIPMENTS BY TYPE

Year	Total All Types	Travel Trailers		Folding Camping Trailers	Truck Campers	Motor Homes			Multi-use Van Conversions
		Conventional	Fifth Wheel[1]			Type A Conventional	Type B Van Campers[2]	Type C Chopped Vans[3]	
2011	252,300	153,300	59,600	11,800	2,800	12,700	1,900	10,200	NA
2010	242,300	144,500	54,700	15,000	2,900	13,100	1,600	10,500	NA
2009	165,700	101,500	36,800	12,300	1,900	5,900	1,200	6,100	NA
2008	237,000	128,100	57,000	18,900	4,700	14,900	1,900	11,500	NA
2007	353,500	180,200	81,500	28,800	7,500	32,900	3,100	19,500	NA
2006	416,800	203,600	88,800	34,000	8,200	32,700	3,000	20,200	26,300
2005	419,500	196,600	84,800	32,800	8,800	37,900	2,600	20,900	35,100
2004	412,100	163,600	91,000	34,100	9,600	46,300	2,500	23,000	42,000
2003	377,800	139,800	74,600	35,700	8,800	41,500	2,100	18,300	57,000
2002	378,700	129,700	66,100	44,800	10,000	39,600	2,800	18,000	67,700
2001	321,000	102,200	54,700	40,800	9,900	33,400	2,600	13,200	64,200
2000	418,300	114,500	62,300	51,300	11,100	41,000	3,400	16,500	118,200
1999	473,800	117,500	60,500	60,100	11,500	49,400	3,600	18,600	152,600
1998	441,300	98,600	56,500	63,300	10,800	42,900	3,600	17,000	148,600
1997	438,800	78,800	52,800	57,600	10,300	37,600	3,800	13,600	184,300
1996	466,800	75,400	48,500	57,300	11,000	36,500	4,100	14,700	219,300
1995	475,200	75,300	45,900	61,100	11,900	33,000	4,100	15,700	228,200
1994	518,800	79,100	48,900	61,700	11,400	37,300	3,500	17,300	259,600
1993	420,200	69,700	43,900	51,900	10,900	31,900	3,000	16,500	192,400
1992	382,700	63,600	38,900	43,300	10,600	27,300	2,900	16,800	179,300
1991	293,700	49,300	28,300	33,900	9,600	23,500	3,500	15,200	130,400
1990	347,300	52,500	27,900	30,700	9,700	29,000	5,900	17,400	174,200
1989	388,300	53,500	29,400	33,900	9,900	35,400	5,000	20,800	200,400
1988	420,000	58,300	31,300	42,300	11,000	41,500	5,200	26,200	204,200
1987	393,600	59,100	27,100	41,600	10,100	40,800	6,600	26,400	181,900

(1) To be towed by pickup truck with fifth-wheel hitch mounted on the truck bed.
(2) Panel-type trucks with interior converted to living area.
(3) Chopped Vans: Mini - unit over 8' high attaches to van chassis of 6,500 lbs. GVWR or more; Low Profile - unit less than 8' high attaches to van chassis of 6,500 lbs. GVWR or more: Compact - unit attaches to van chassis less than 6,500 lbs. GVWR.
SOURCE: Recreation Vehicle Industry Assn.

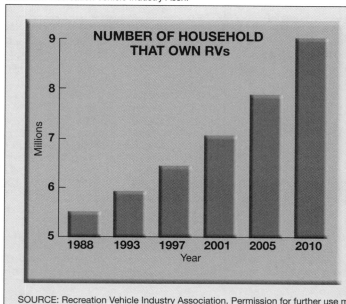

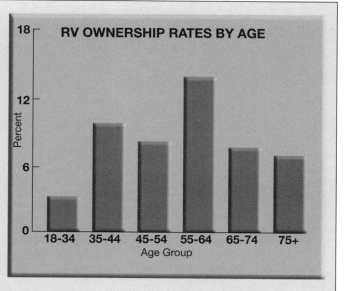

SOURCE: Recreation Vehicle Industry Association. Permission for further use must be obtained from the Recreation Vehicle Industry Association.

World Vehicle Production by Country

WORLD VEHICLE PRODUCTION IN MAJOR COUNTRIES, 2011

Region/Country	Cars	Commercial Vehicles	Total
North America			
Canada	990,482	1,144,639	2,135,121
Mexico	1,657,080	1,024,306	2,681,386
United States	2,976,397	5,678,606	8,655,003
Total	**5,623,959**	**7,847,551**	**13,471,510**
Western Europe			
Austria	130,343	22,162	152,505
Belgium	566,128	34,470	600,598
France	1,914,399	363,376	2,277,775
Germany	5,871,918	439,400	6,311,318
Italy	485,606	304,742	790,348
Netherlands	40,772	69,611	110,383
Portugal	141,779	50,463	192,242
Spain	1,867,657	486,025	2,353,682
Sweden	188,969	42,960	231,929
United Kingdom	1,343,794	120,189	1,463,983
Total	**12,551,365**	**1,933,398**	**14,484,763**
Eastern/Central Europe			
Czech Republic	1,191,968	7,866	1,199,834
Poland	722,285	113,030	835,315
Russia	1,738,162	250,757	1,988,919
Slovakia	585,518	0	585,518
Turkey	639,734	549,397	1,189,131
Other	978,264	85,135	1,063,399
Total	**5,855,931**	**1,006,185**	**6,862,116**
Asia/Pacific			
Australia	189,503	29,873	219,376
China	10,052,854	8,366,022	18,418,876
India	2,479,131	1,461,229	3,940,360
Japan	7,158,525	1,240,129	8,398,654
South Korea	2,901,707	1,755,387	4,657,094
Other	1,897,867	1,437,723	3,335,590
Total	**24,679,587**	**14,290,363**	**38,969,950**
South America			
Argentina	577,233	251,538	828,771
Brazil	2,339,741	804,425	3,144,166
Venezuela	58,032	44,377	102,409
Total	**2,975,006**	**1,100,340**	**4,075,346**
South Africa	**312,265**	**220,280**	**532,545**
Total Vehicles	**51,998,113**	**26,398,117**	**78,396,230**

NOTE: North America excludes buses. Table excludes smaller non-reporting countries.
SOURCE: Compiled by *Ward's* from various industry sources.

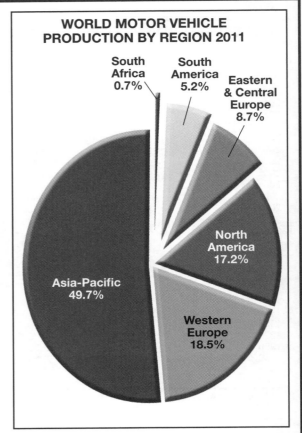

WORLD MOTOR VEHICLE PRODUCTION BY REGION 2011

- South Africa 0.7%
- South America 5.2%
- Eastern & Central Europe 8.7%
- North America 17.2%
- Asia-Pacific 49.7%
- Western Europe 18.5%

WORLD VEHICLE PRODUCTION

Year	United States	Canada	U.S. & Canada Total	Western Europe	China	Japan	Other	World Total	Percent of World Total United States	Percent of World Total U.S. & Canada
2011	8,655	2,135	10,790	14,485	18,419	8,399	26,303	78,396	11.0	13.8
2010	7,743	2,068	9,811	13,863	18,265	9,626	24,808	76,373	10.1	12.8
2009	5,709	1,490	7,199	12,315	13,649	7,935	19,156	60,254	9.5	11.9
2008	8,673	2,082	10,755	15,310	9,233	11,564	22,722	69,584	12.5	15.5
2007	10,752	2,579	13,331	16,892	8,885	11,596	21,936	72,640	14.8	18.4
2005	11,947	2,688	14,635	16,806	5,668	10,780	18,196	66,085	18.1	22.1
2000	12,771	2,962	15,732	16,749	2,069	10,145	14,251	58,946	21.7	26.7
1995	11,985	2,408	14,393	17,045	1,435	10,196	6,914	49,983	24.0	28.8
1990	9,783	1,928	11,711	18,866	509	13,487	3,981	48,554	20.1	24.1
1985	11,653	1,933	13,586	16,113	443	12,271	2,496	44,909	25.9	30.3
1980	8,010	1,324	9,334	15,496	141	11,043	2,551	38,565	20.8	24.2
1975	8,987	1,385	10,372	13,581	NA	6,942	2,211	33,106	27.1	31.3
1970	8,284	1,160	9,444	13,049	NA	5,289	1,637	29,419	28.2	32.1
1965	11,138	847	11,985	9,576	NA	1,876	834	24,271	45.9	49.4
1960	7,905	398	8,303	6,837	NA	482	866	16,488	47.9	50.4
1955	9,204	452	9,656	3,741	NA	68	163	13,628	67.5	70.9
1950	8,006	388	8,394	1,991	NA	32	160	10,577	75.7	79.4

NA - Not available.
NOTE: Units in thousands.
SOURCE: *Ward's Automotive Group.*

World Vehicle Production by Manufacturer

WORLD VEHICLE PRODUCTION FOR SELECT MANUFACTURERS BY REGION

Manufacturer/Region	2010 Cars	2010 Commercial Vehicles	2010 Total	2009 Cars	2009 Commercial Vehicles	2009 Total
BMW						
Africa	50,203	—	50,203	47,749	—	47,749
Asia/Pacific	10,902	—	10,902	7,602	—	7,602
Europe	1,215,345	—	1,215,345	1,087,017	—	1,087,017
North America	—	157,703	157,703	—	121,666	121,666
Total BMW	**1,276,450**	**157,703**	**1,434,153**	**1,142,368**	**121,666**	**1,264,034**
Chrysler						
Africa	657	—	657	655	—	655
Europe	5,497	—	5,497	5,376	—	5,376
North America	333,379	1,238,283	1,571,662	205,784	747,910	953,694
South America	1,881	8,254	10,135	2,734	10,311	13,045
Total Chrysler	**341,414**	**1,246,537**	**1,587,951**	**214,549**	**758,221**	**972,770**
Daimler						
Africa	53,353	3,570	56,923	42,585	3,355	45,940
Asia/Pacific	17,169	201,976	219,145	11,249	129,092	140,341
Europe	1,086,775	288,670	1,375,445	888,579	198,041	1,086,620
North America	—	196,736	196,736	—	140,996	140,996
South America	12,260	90,863	103,123	15,211	66,962	82,173
Total Daimler	**1,169,557**	**781,815**	**1,951,372**	**957,624**	**538,446**	**1,496,070**
Fiat						
Africa	—	1,795	1,795	—	1,550	1,550
Asia/Pacific	23,113	—	23,113	23,677	—	23,677
Europe	1,222,985	440,033	1,663,018	1,365,167	345,864	1,711,031
South America	672,366	206,611	878,977	681,681	148,546	830,227
Total Fiat	**1,918,464**	**648,439**	**2,566,903**	**2,070,525**	**495,960**	**2,566,485**
Ford						
Africa	18,001	14,579	32,580	13,622	24,822	38,444
Asia/Pacific	230,308	160,140	390,448	85,783	120,972	206,755
Europe	1,252,600	282,275	1,534,875	1,269,297	201,146	1,470,443
North America	907,782	1,539,355	2,447,137	650,492	1,241,737	1,892,229
South America	299,241	172,674	471,915	290,806	157,100	447,906
Total Ford	**2,707,932**	**2,169,023**	**4,876,955**	**2,310,000**	**1,745,777**	**4,055,777**
General Motors						
Africa	42,812	46,848	89,660	42,526	38,915	81,441
Asia/Pacific	794,509	195,512	990,021	583,985	119,290	703,275
Europe	1,277,030	114,262	1,391,292	1,176,702	86,836	1,263,538
North America	977,020	1,831,526	2,808,546	698,729	1,185,242	1,883,971
South America	698,339	133,459	831,798	601,924	124,587	726,511
Total General Motors	**3,789,710**	**2,321,607**	**6,111,317**	**3,103,866**	**1,554,870**	**4,658,736**
Honda						
Asia/Pacific	1,331,135	58,521	1,389,656	1,130,221	33,186	1,163,407
Europe	159,583	—	159,583	93,847	—	93,847
North America	635,653	652,122	1,287,775	617,967	412,991	1,030,958
South America	131,455	—	131,455	132,122	—	132,122
Total Honda	**2,257,826**	**710,643**	**2,968,469**	**1,974,157**	**446,177**	**2,420,334**
Hyundai-Kia						
Africa	11,317	53	11,370	15,354	86	15,440
Asia/Pacific	2,543,576	1,245,673	3,789,249	2,311,240	1,017,167	3,328,407
Europe	506,604	—	506,604	316,667	—	316,667
North America	238,387	214,474	452,861	103,876	107,185	211,061
South America	3,972	24,777	28,749	3,061	6,814	9,875
Total Hyundai-Kia	**3,303,856**	**1,484,977**	**4,788,833**	**2,750,198**	**1,131,252**	**3,881,450**

World Vehicle Production by Manufacturer

WORLD VEHICLE PRODUCTION FOR SELECT MANUFACTURERS BY REGION — continued

Manufacturer/Region	2010 Cars	2010 Commercial Vehicles	2010 Total	2009 Cars	2009 Commercial Vehicles	2009 Total
Mitsubishi						
Africa	—	2,582	2,582	—	2,500	2,500
Asia/Pacific	614,989	257,843	872,832	382,537	158,339	540,876
Europe	48,025	—	48,025	50,620	—	50,620
North America	22,969	6,406	29,375	14,798	3,703	18,501
South America	3,438	37,981	41,419	2,005	32,560	34,565
Total Mitsubishi	**689,421**	**304,812**	**994,233**	**449,960**	**197,102**	**647,062**
Nissan						
Africa	13,502	31,861	45,363	9,063	27,974	37,037
Asia/Pacific	1,210,580	244,352	1,454,932	852,702	186,294	1,038,996
Europe	486,784	67,418	554,202	361,054	33,207	394,261
North America	803,130	214,253	1,017,383	582,311	147,401	729,712
South America	10,578	7,577	18,155	11,966	6,942	18,908
Total Nissan	**2,524,574**	**565,461**	**3,090,035**	**1,817,096**	**401,818**	**2,218,914**
PSA						
Africa	387	—	387	688	—	688
Asia/Pacific	2,863	—	2,863	1,673	—	1,673
Europe	1,713,174	469,835	2,183,009	1,581,851	343,493	1,925,344
South America	248,702	26,485	275,187	191,486	13,648	205,134
Total PSA	**1,965,126**	**496,320**	**2,461,446**	**1,775,698**	**357,141**	**2,132,839**
Renault						
Asia/Pacific	226,520	48,749	275,269	161,098	28,733	189,831
Europe	1,651,886	205,747	1,857,633	1,537,879	145,383	1,683,262
South America	240,034	27,967	268,001	168,978	18,021	186,999
Total Renault	**2,118,440**	**282,463**	**2,400,903**	**1,867,955**	**192,137**	**2,060,092**
Suzuki						
Africa	337	2,072	2,409	569	2,584	3,153
Asia/Pacific	2,084,817	375,121	2,459,938	1,701,184	277,769	1,978,953
Europe	170,031	—	170,031	180,170	—	180,170
Total Suzuki	**2,255,185**	**377,193**	**2,632,378**	**1,881,923**	**280,353**	**2,162,276**
Toyota						
Africa	47,069	76,415	123,484	40,018	62,804	102,822
Asia/Pacific	4,363,759	1,175,203	5,538,962	3,741,050	889,257	4,630,307
Europe	695,153	2,553	697,706	744,548	1,967	746,515
North America	599,803	773,191	1,372,994	650,966	525,269	1,176,235
South America	71,502	77,283	148,785	71,977	68,528	140,505
Total Toyota	**5,777,286**	**2,104,645**	**7,881,931**	**5,248,559**	**1,547,825**	**6,796,384**
Volkswagen						
Africa	93,953	706	94,659	59,529	309	59,838
Asia/Pacific	55,020	431	55,451	8,920	—	8,920
Europe	4,076,511	167,594	4,244,105	3,543,089	129,388	3,672,477
North America	434,685	—	434,685	319,743	—	319,743
South America	1,011,199	142,979	1,154,178	842,434	67,070	909,504
Total Volkswagen	**5,671,368**	**311,710**	**5,983,078**	**4,773,715**	**196,767**	**4,970,482**
Other Manufacturers	**13,273,618**	**11,272,497**	**24,546,115**	**10,034,829**	**8,024,210**	**18,059,039**
Total World	**51,040,227**	**25,235,845**	**76,276,072**	**42,373,022**	**17,989,722**	**60,362,744**

Compiled by *Ward's* from various industry sources.

U.S. Sales of Cars and Trucks

U.S. VEHICLE SALES

Year	Cars Domestic	Cars Import	Cars Total	Trucks Domestic	Trucks Import	Trucks Total	Total Vehicles Domestic	Total Vehicles Import	Total Vehicles Total
2011	4,239,526	1,849,896	6,089,422	5,958,483	992,727	6,951,210	10,198,009	2,842,623	13,040,632
2010	3,791,877	1,843,556	5,635,433	5,228,589	908,198	6,136,787	9,020,466	2,751,754	11,772,220
2009	3,557,608	1,843,282	5,400,890	4,309,483	890,995	5,200,478	7,867,091	2,734,277	10,601,368
2008	4,490,836	2,278,271	6,769,107	5,616,890	1,107,168	6,724,058	10,107,726	3,385,439	13,493,165
2007	5,197,271	2,365,063	7,562,334	7,489,745	1,408,236	8,897,981	12,687,016	3,773,299	16,460,315
2006	5,416,828	2,344,764	7,761,592	7,918,015	1,369,374	9,287,389	13,334,843	3,714,138	17,048,981
2005	5,473,450	2,186,533	7,659,983	8,547,078	1,237,268	9,784,346	14,020,528	3,423,801	17,444,329
2004	5,333,496	2,149,059	7,482,555	8,546,755	1,269,263	9,816,018	13,880,251	3,418,322	17,298,573
2003	5,472,500	2,083,051	7,555,551	8,165,851	1,246,040	9,411,891	13,638,351	3,329,091	16,967,442
2002	5,816,671	2,225,584	8,042,255	8,012,897	1,083,500	9,096,397	13,829,568	3,309,084	17,138,652
2001	6,254,371	2,097,629	8,352,000	8,118,253	1,002,125	9,120,378	14,372,624	3,099,754	17,472,378
2000	6,761,603	2,016,120	8,777,723	8,161,045	872,905	9,033,950	14,922,648	2,889,025	17,811,673
1999	6,918,781	1,718,927	8,637,708	7,982,485	794,535	8,777,020	14,901,266	2,513,462	17,414,728
1998	6,705,208	1,379,781	8,084,989	7,207,820	674,478	7,882,298	13,913,028	2,054,259	15,967,287
1997	6,862,175	1,355,305	8,217,480	6,687,076	593,304	7,280,380	13,549,251	1,948,609	15,497,860
1996	7,206,349	1,272,196	8,478,545	6,526,030	451,537	6,977,567	13,732,379	1,723,733	15,456,112
1995	7,113,902	1,506,257	8,620,159	6,078,959	417,207	6,496,166	13,192,861	1,923,464	15,116,325
1994	7,255,303	1,735,214	8,990,517	5,995,895	424,962	6,420,857	13,251,198	2,160,176	15,411,374
1993	6,741,667	1,776,192	8,517,859	5,287,384	393,611	5,680,995	12,029,051	2,169,803	14,198,854
1992	6,285,916	1,927,197	8,213,113	4,481,769	422,562	4,904,331	10,767,685	2,349,759	13,117,444
1991	6,161,573	2,023,406	8,184,979	3,814,225	550,319	4,364,544	9,975,798	2,573,725	12,549,523
1990	6,918,869	2,384,346	9,303,215	4,216,644	629,519	4,846,163	11,135,513	3,013,865	14,149,378
1989	7,098,098	2,680,419	9,778,517	4,405,286	661,458	5,066,744	11,503,384	3,341,877	14,845,261
1988	7,543,116	3,003,692	10,546,808	4,511,065	733,671	5,244,736	12,054,181	3,737,363	15,791,544
1987	7,085,279	3,106,598	10,191,877	4,058,996	942,073	5,001,069	11,144,275	4,048,671	15,192,946
1986	8,215,017	3,189,222	11,404,239	3,930,067	988,715	4,918,782	12,145,084	4,177,937	16,323,021
1985	8,204,670	2,774,517	10,979,187	3,905,329	840,775	4,746,104	12,109,999	3,615,292	15,725,291
1984	7,951,523	2,372,172	10,323,695	3,480,209	679,237	4,159,446	11,431,732	3,051,409	14,483,141
1983	6,795,299	2,352,739	9,148,038	2,663,022	500,456	3,163,478	9,458,321	2,853,195	12,311,516
1982	5,756,658	2,199,802	7,956,460	2,145,793	436,109	2,581,902	7,902,451	2,635,911	10,538,362
1981	6,180,784	2,308,418	8,489,202	1,820,693	468,085	2,288,778	8,001,477	2,776,503	10,777,980
1980	6,579,778	2,369,457	8,949,235	2,014,709	479,669	2,494,378	8,594,487	2,849,126	11,443,613
1979	8,341,000	2,332,000	10,673,000	3,010,000	470,000	3,480,000	11,351,000	2,802,000	14,153,000
1978	9,312,000	2,002,000	11,314,000	3,773,000	336,000	4,109,000	13,085,000	2,338,000	15,423,000
1977	9,109,000	2,074,000	11,183,000	3,352,000	323,000	3,675,000	12,461,000	2,397,000	14,859,000
1976	8,611,000	1,499,000	10,110,000	2,944,000	237,000	3,181,000	11,555,000	1,736,000	13,291,000
1975	7,053,000	1,571,000	8,624,000	2,249,000	229,000	2,478,000	9,302,000	1,800,000	11,103,000
1974	7,454,000	1,399,000	8,853,000	2,512,000	176,000	2,688,000	9,966,000	1,575,000	11,541,000
1973	9,676,000	1,748,000	11,424,000	2,916,000	233,000	3,148,000	12,592,000	1,981,000	14,572,000
1972	9,327,000	1,614,000	10,940,000	2,486,000	143,000	2,629,000	11,813,000	1,757,000	13,569,000
1971	8,681,000	1,561,000	10,242,000	2,011,000	85,000	2,096,000	10,692,000	1,646,000	12,338,000
1970	7,119,000	1,280,000	8,400,000	1,746,000	65,000	1,811,000	8,865,000	1,345,000	10,211,000
1969	8,464,000	1,118,000	9,582,000	1,936,000	34,000	1,970,000	10,400,000	1,152,000	11,552,000
1968	8,625,000	1,031,000	9,656,000	1,807,000	24,000	1,831,000	10,432,000	1,055,000	11,487,000
1967	7,568,000	769,000	8,337,000	1,524,000	21,000	1,545,000	9,092,000	790,000	9,882,000
1966	8,377,000	651,000	9,028,000	1,619,000	17,000	1,636,000	9,996,000	668,000	10,664,000
1965	8,763,000	569,000	9,332,000	1,539,000	14,000	1,553,000	10,302,000	583,000	10,885,000
1964	7,617,000	484,000	8,101,000	1,351,000	42,000	1,393,000	8,968,000	526,000	9,494,000
1963	7,334,000	386,000	7,720,000	1,230,000	40,000	1,270,000	8,564,000	426,000	8,990,000
1961	5,556,000	379,000	5,935,000	908,000	29,000	937,000	6,464,000	408,000	6,872,000
1959	5,486,000	614,000	6,100,000	928,000	37,000	965,000	6,414,000	651,000	7,065,000
1957	5,826,000	207,000	6,033,000	878,000	16,000	894,000	6,704,000	223,000	6,927,000
1955	7,408,000	58,000	7,466,000	1,012,000	3,000	1,015,000	8,420,000	61,000	8,481,000
1953	5,775,000	33,000	5,808,000	965,000	NA	965,000	6,740,000	33,000	6,773,000
1951	5,143,000	21,000	5,164,000	1,111,000	NA	1,111,000	6,254,000	21,000	6,275,000

Note: NA is not available.

U.S. Vehicle Sales by Model

U.S. VEHICLE SALES BY MODEL

Model	2011	2010	2009	2008	2007
A3*	6,561	6,558	3,874	4,759	6,354
A4*	31,022	30,816	31,461	36,930	35,606
A4 Cabrio*	—	107	4,501	4,709	6,975
A5*	11,389	12,206	6,845	4,120	—
A6*	11,065	8,465	6,606	11,406	11,239
A7*	6,270	—	—	—	—
A8*	5,700	1,515	1,334	2,433	3,059
R8*	1,145	799	699	900	241
S4*	4,212	3,749	1,108	1,705	2,830
S5*	3,996	4,173	2,955	2,162	625
S6*	59	210	180	550	762
S8*	—	6	129	392	767
TT*	2,236	1,531	1,935	4,486	4,355
AUDI TOTAL	**83,655**	**70,135**	**61,627**	**74,552**	**72,813**
1-Series*	8,832	13,132	11,182	12,018	—
3-Series*	94,371	100,910	90,960	112,464	142,490
5-Series*	51,491	39,488	40,109	45,915	54,142
6-Series*	3,903	2,418	3,549	6,533	9,033
7-Series*	11,299	12,253	9,254	12,276	14,773
Z4	—	—	125	5,879	10,097
Z4*	3,479	3,804	3,398	—	—
BMW Total	**173,375**	**172,005**	**158,577**	**195,085**	**230,535**
Mini Cooper*	40,828	45,644	45,225	54,077	42,045
BMW TOTAL	**214,203**	**217,649**	**203,802**	**249,162**	**272,580**
200 Series	87,033	—	—	—	—
300 Series	36,285	37,116	38,606	62,352	120,636
Crossfire*	—	—	499	2,021	8,774
PT Cruiser Convertible	—	—	2	1,094	10,978
Sebring Convertible	—	7,027	5,139	27,437	21,599
Sebring Sedan	2,380	31,558	22,321	44,226	71,531
Chrysler Total	**125,698**	**75,701**	**66,567**	**137,130**	**233,518**
Avenger	64,023	50,923	38,922	61,963	83,804
Caliber	35,049	45,082	36,098	84,158	101,079
Challenger	39,534	36,791	25,852	17,423	—
Charger	70,089	75,397	60,651	97,367	119,289
Magnum	—	—	113	6,912	30,256
Stratus Sedan	—	—	—	—	1,478
Viper	197	392	482	1,172	435
Dodge Total	**208,892**	**208,585**	**162,118**	**268,995**	**336,341**
Fiat 500	19,769	—	—	—	—
CHRYSLER TOTAL	**354,359**	**284,286**	**228,685**	**406,125**	**569,859**
B-Class*	19	1	—	—	—
C-Class*	69,314	58,785	52,427	72,471	63,701
CL*	943	1,035	1,220	2,733	3,672
CLK*	6	585	7,150	10,844	15,009
CLS*	5,665	2,135	2,527	5,775	7,906
E-Class*	62,736	60,922	43,072	38,576	48,950
S-Class*	12,258	13,608	11,199	17,787	26,081
SL*	1,449	2,385	4,025	5,464	6,126
SLK*	3,220	1,980	2,566	4,941	7,270
SLS*	722	499	—	—	—
Mercedes Total	**156,332**	**141,935**	**124,186**	**158,591**	**178,715**
Smart Fortwo*	5,208	5,927	14,595	24,622	—
DAIMLER TOTAL	**161,540**	**147,862**	**138,781**	**183,213**	**178,715**
Crown Victoria	46,725	33,722	33,255	48,557	60,901
Fiesta	68,574	23,273	—	—	—
Five Hundred	—	—	—	—	35,146
Focus	175,717	172,421	160,433	195,823	173,213
Ford GT	—	—	—	—	231
Fusion	248,067	219,219	180,671	147,569	149,552
Mustang	70,438	73,716	66,623	91,251	134,626
Taurus	63,526	68,859	45,617	52,667	33,032
Ford Total	**673,047**	**591,210**	**486,599**	**535,867**	**586,701**
MKS	12,217	14,417	17,174	12,982	—
MKZ	27,529	22,535	22,081	30,117	34,363
Town Car	9,460	11,264	11,375	15,653	26,739
Lincoln Total	**49,206**	**48,216**	**50,630**	**58,752**	**61,102**
Grand Marquis	248	28,543	24,783	29,766	50,664
Milan	—	28,912	27,403	31,393	37,244
Montego	—	—	—	—	10,755
Sable	—	37	6,256	16,187	10,366
Mercury Total	**248**	**57,492**	**58,442**	**77,346**	**109,029**

U.S. Vehicle Sales by Model

U.S. VEHICLE SALES BY MODEL — continued

Model	2011	2010	2009	2008	2007
FORD TOTAL	**722,501**	**696,918**	**595,671**	**671,965**	**756,832**
Century	—	—	—	—	5
LaCrosse	58,474	61,178	27,818	36,873	47,747
LeSabre	—	—	—	—	121
Lucerne	20,358	26,459	31,292	54,930	82,923
Park Ave	—	—	—	—	26
Regal	11,883	—	—	—	—
Regal*	28,261	12,326	—	—	—
Verano	265	—	—	—	—
Buick Total	**119,241**	**99,963**	**59,110**	**91,803**	**130,822**
CTS	55,042	45,656	38,817	58,774	57,029
Deville	—	—	—	—	71
DTS	11,589	18,640	17,330	30,479	51,469
STS	3,338	4,473	6,037	14,790	20,873
XLR	12	188	787	1,250	1,750
Cadillac Total	**69,981**	**68,957**	**62,971**	**105,293**	**131,192**
Aveo*	28,601	48,623	38,516	55,360	67,028
Camaro	88,249	81,299	61,648	—	—
Caprice*	880	—	—	—	—
Cavalier	—	—	—	—	57
Classic	—	—	—	—	17
Cobalt	856	97,376	104,724	188,045	200,620
Corvette	13,164	12,624	13,934	26,971	33,685
Cruze	231,732	24,495	—	—	—
Impala	171,434	172,078	165,565	265,840	311,128
Malibu	204,808	198,770	161,568	178,253	128,312
Monte Carlo	—	—	6	711	15,784
Sonic	15,778	—	—	—	—
Volt	7,671	326	—	—	—
Chevrolet Total	**763,173**	**635,591**	**545,961**	**715,180**	**756,631**
Bonneville	—	—	—	—	130
G3*	—	14	6,223	—	—
G5	—	86	12,362	25,439	27,928
G6	—	479	87,171	140,240	150,001
G8*	—	274	23,157	15,002	—
Grand Am	—	—	—	—	99
Grand Prix	—	7	265	8,636	87,622
GTO*	—	—	—	52	4,200
Solstice	—	157	5,642	10,739	16,779
Sunfire	—	—	—	—	39
Vibe	—	97	33,842	46,551	37,170
Pontiac Total	**—**	**1,114**	**168,662**	**246,659**	**323,968**
Astra*	—	25	6,298	11,968	—
Aura	—	644	21,395	59,380	59,964
Ion	—	—	12	315	47,873
Saturn L	—	—	—	—	2
Sky	—	179	3,399	9,162	11,263
Saturn Total	**—**	**848**	**31,104**	**80,825**	**119,102**
GM TOTAL	**952,395**	**806,473**	**867,808**	**1,239,760**	**1,461,715**
NSX*	—	—	—	—	2
RL*	1,096	2,037	2,043	4,517	6,262
RSX*	—	—	—	1	296
TL	31,237	34,049	33,620	46,766	58,545
TSX*	30,935	32,076	28,650	31,998	33,037
Acura Total	**63,268**	**68,162**	**64,313**	**83,282**	**98,142**
Accord	235,621	282,360	273,466	309,461	355,767
Accord*	4	170	14,026	63,328	36,464
Civic	210,839	252,882	244,271	305,509	292,192
Civic*	10,396	7,336	15,451	33,780	38,903
CR-Z*	11,330	5,249	—	—	—
FCX*	—	—	—	—	10
FCX Clarity*	2	17	5	11	—
Fit*	59,235	54,354	67,315	79,794	56,432
Insight*	15,549	20,962	20,572	—	3
S2000*	5	85	795	2,538	4,302
Honda Total	**542,981**	**623,415**	**635,901**	**794,651**	**784,073**
HONDA TOTAL	**606,249**	**691,577**	**700,214**	**877,703**	**882,215**
Accent*	55,601	51,975	68,086	50,431	36,055
Azera*	1,524	3,051	3,808	14,461	21,948
Elantra	174,562	4,724	—	—	—
Elantra*	11,799	127,522	103,269	94,720	85,724
Equus*	3,193	196	—	—	—

U.S. Vehicle Sales by Model

U.S. VEHICLE SALES BY MODEL — continued

Model	2011	2010	2009	2008	2007
Genesis*	32,998	29,122	21,889	6,167	—
Sonata	225,961	196,623	120,028	117,357	145,568
Tiburon*	—	—	8,587	9,111	14,073
Veloster*	9,284	—	—	—	—
HYUNDAI TOTAL	**514,922**	**413,213**	**325,667**	**292,247**	**303,368**
Jaguar S-Type*	—	—	24	904	3,524
Jaguar Vanden Plas*	—	8	272	853	1,512
Jaguar X-Type*	—	—	9	431	3,198
Jaguar XF*	5,303	6,925	8,487	8,578	—
Jaguar XJ6/8*	5,235	4,267	872	1,471	2,638
Jaguar XJR*	—	3	17	128	324
Jaguar XK8*	1,738	2,137	2,274	2,459	4,487
JAGUAR LAND ROVER TOTAL	**12,276**	**13,340**	**11,955**	**14,824**	**15,683**
Amanti*	8	281	3,704	3,614	5,522
Forte*	76,295	68,500	26,328	—	—
Optima	27,255	—	—	—	—
Optima*	57,335	27,382	37,527	44,904	40,901
Rio*	20,111	24,619	34,666	36,532	33,370
Soul*	102,267	67,110	31,621	—	—
Spectra*	—	272	47,114	68,465	73,474
KIA TOTAL	**283,271**	**188,164**	**180,960**	**153,515**	**153,267**
Mazda2*	13,952	3,021	—	—	—
Mazda3*	102,417	106,353	96,466	109,957	120,291
Mazda6	35,711	35,662	34,866	52,590	57,575
MX-5 Miata*	5,674	6,370	7,917	10,977	15,075
RX-8*	759	1,134	2,217	3,368	5,767
MAZDA TOTAL	**158,513**	**152,540**	**141,466**	**176,892**	**198,708**
Eclipse	7,546	4,282	6,672	20,107	27,292
Galant	15,631	11,492	11,740	26,941	26,491
I*	80	—	—	—	—
Lancer*	19,874	21,416	20,117	27,861	31,376
MITSUBISHI TOTAL	**43,131**	**37,190**	**38,529**	**74,909**	**85,159**
G35/37*	58,246	58,143	47,174	64,181	71,811
M35/45*	10,818	14,618	8,501	15,618	21,885
Q45*	—	—	—	—	22
Infiniti Total	**69,064**	**72,761**	**55,675**	**79,799**	**93,718**
350Z*	—	—	3,875	10,337	18,957
370Z*	7,328	10,215	9,242	—	—
Altima	268,981	229,263	203,568	269,668	284,762
Cube*	14,459	22,968	21,471	—	—
GT-R*	1,294	877	1,534	1,730	—
Leaf*	9,674	19	—	—	—
Maxima	58,737	60,569	53,351	47,072	52,574
Sentra	114,991	94,065	82,706	99,797	106,522
Versa	99,730	99,705	82,906	85,182	79,443
Nissan Total	**575,194**	**517,681**	**458,653**	**513,786**	**542,258**
NISSAN TOTAL	**644,258**	**590,442**	**514,328**	**593,585**	**635,976**
911*	6,016	5,737	6,839	8,324	12,493
Boxster*	1,773	2,177	1,909	2,982	3,622
Carrera GT*	—	—	—	—	4
Cayman*	1,377	1,322	1,966	3,513	6,027
Panamera*	6,879	7,741	1,247	—	—
PORSCHE TOTAL	**16,045**	**16,977**	**11,961**	**14,819**	**22,146**
9-2X*	—	—	—	3	118
9-3*	3,847	4,533	5,428	15,167	22,979
9-5*	1,496	811	1,034	2,538	4,357
SAAB TOTAL	**5,343**	**5,344**	**6,462**	**17,708**	**27,454**
Impreza*	41,196	44,395	46,611	49,098	46,333
Legacy	42,401	38,725	30,974	22,614	22,349
SUBARU TOTAL	**83,597**	**83,120**	**77,585**	**71,712**	**68,682**
Aerio*	—	—	9	80	1,531
Forenza*	—	12	3,769	20,796	42,113
Kizashi*	6,944	6,138	71	—	—
SX4*	12,520	11,606	20,704	29,483	15,209
Verona*	—	—	1	3	315
SUZUKI TOTAL	**19,464**	**17,756**	**24,554**	**50,362**	**59,168**
CT*	14,381	—	—	—	—
ES*	40,873	48,652	48,485	64,135	82,867
GS*	3,746	7,059	7,430	15,759	23,381
HS*	2,864	10,663	6,699	—	—
IS*	29,669	34,129	38,077	49,432	54,933
LFA*	62	—	—	—	—

U.S. Vehicle Sales by Model

U.S. VEHICLE SALES BY MODEL — continued

Model	2011	2010	2009	2008	2007
LS*	9,568	12,275	11,334	20,255	35,226
SC*	18	328	720	1,986	3,927
Lexus Total	**101,181**	**113,106**	**112,745**	**151,567**	**200,334**
iQ*	248				
tC*	22,433	15,204	17,998	40,980	63,852
xA*	—	—	3	39	9,547
xB*	17,017	20,364	25,461	45,220	45,834
xD*	9,573	10,110	14,499	27,665	10,948
Scion Total	**49,271**	**45,678**	**57,961**	**113,904**	**130,181**
Avalon	28,925	28,390	26,935	42,790	72,945
Camry	307,447	324,756	346,957	428,841	418,757
Camry*	1,063	3,048	9,867	7,776	54,351
Celica*	—		1	1	4
Corolla/Matrix	175,995	228,165	265,440	252,877	348,016
Corolla*	64,264	37,917	31,434	98,130	23,374
Echo*	—		1		3
MR2 Spyder*	—	—	—	1	
Prius*	136,463	140,928	139,682	158,884	181,221
Yaris*	32,704	40,076	63,743	102,328	84,799
Toyota Total	**746,861**	**803,280**	**884,060**	**1,091,628**	**1,183,470**
TOYOTA TOTAL	**897,313**	**962,064**	**1,054,766**	**1,357,099**	**1,513,985**
Beetle	5,626	11,874	9,581	15,520	17,155
Beetle Cabrio	842	4,663	4,504	10,957	13,866
CC*	29,502	27,987	23,872	2,105	
Eos*	7,533	6,690	7,204	12,837	12,744
Golf*	17,839	13,426	1,211	—	25
GTI*	16,867	13,755	7,932	12,232	14,618
Jetta	177,360	123,213	108,427	97,461	98,951
Passat	22,615	—	—	—	—
Passat*	220	12,497	11,138	30,034	37,183
Phaeton*	—	—	—	—	17
R32*	—	—	139	3,106	1,756
Rabbit*	—	1,105	6,470	20,070	25,445
VOLKSWAGEN TOTAL	**278,404**	**215,210**	**180,478**	**204,322**	**221,760**
30-Series*	3,471	3,906	4,267	4,299	2,090
40-Series*	2,984	5,623	7,957	9,687	18,141
50-Series*	555	1,720	2,155	1,856	2,850
60-Series*	21,282	1,437	5,895	8,966	18,511
70-Series*	4,956	5,263	6,986	8,787	8,310
80-Series*	4,735	7,224	8,331	11,038	12,347
VOLVO TOTAL	**37,983**	**25,173**	**35,591**	**44,633**	**62,249**
TOTAL CARS	**6,089,422**	**5,635,433**	**5,400,890**	**6,769,107**	**7,562,334**
Q5*	24,908	23,518	13,790		
Q7*	8,998	7,976	7,299	13,209	20,695
AUDI TOTAL	**33,906**	**31,494**	**21,089**	**13,209**	**20,695**
X3	27,793	940	—		
X3*	—	5,135	6,067	17,622	28,058
X5	40,547	35,776	27,071	31,858	35,202
X6	6,192	6,257	4,787	4,548	—
BMW Total	**74,532**	**48,108**	**37,925**	**54,028**	**63,260**
Mini Countryman*	16,683	—	—	—	—
BMW TOTAL	**91,215**	**48,108**	**37,925**	**54,028**	**63,260**
Aspen	—	30	5,996	22,254	28,788
Pacifica	—	—	1,955	7,345	53,947
PT Cruiser	1,328	9,440	17,939	49,816	88,607
Town & Country	94,320	112,275	84,558	118,563	138,151
Chrysler Total	**95,648**	**121,745**	**110,448**	**197,978**	**309,493**
Caravan	110,862	103,323	90,666	123,749	176,150
Durango	51,697	572	3,521	21,420	45,503
Journey	55,155	48,577	53,826	47,097	—
Nitro	24,434	22,618	17,443	36,368	74,825
Dodge Total	**242,148**	**175,090**	**165,456**	**228,634**	**296,478**
Commander	105	8,115	12,655	27,694	63,027
Compass	47,709	15,894	11,739	25,349	39,491
Grand Cherokee	127,744	84,635	50,328	73,678	120,937
Liberty	66,684	49,564	43,503	66,911	92,105
Patriot	54,647	38,620	31,432	55,654	40,434
Wrangler	122,460	94,310	82,044	84,615	119,243
Jeep Total	**419,349**	**291,138**	**231,701**	**333,901**	**475,237**
Cargo Van	691	—	—	—	—
Dakota	12,156	13,047	10,690	26,044	50,702
Ram Pickup Light-Duty	237,236	194,175	173,066	240,454	357,707

U.S. Vehicle Sales by Model

U.S. VEHICLE SALES BY MODEL — continued

Model	2011	2010	2009	2008	2007
Sprinter Van*	—	248	6,819	13,505	14,869
Sprinter Wagon*	—	5	335	1,095	1,717
Ram Total	**250,083**	**207,475**	**190,910**	**281,098**	**424,995**
CHRYSLER TOTAL	**1,007,228**	**795,448**	**698,515**	**1,041,611**	**1,506,203**
G-Class*	1,191	919	662	931	1,152
GL	25,139	19,943	15,012	23,328	26,396
GLK*	24,310	20,946	21,944	—	—
M-Class	35,835	29,698	25,799	34,320	33,879
R-Class	2,385	2,937	2,825	7,733	13,031
Sprinter Van*	16,577	8,559	—	—	—
Mercedes Total	**105,437**	**83,002**	**66,242**	**66,312**	**74,458**
Mitsubishi Fuso Light-Duty*	221	311	275	202	52
Sterling Light-Duty*	—	1	103	12	—
DAIMLER TOTAL	**105,658**	**83,314**	**66,620**	**66,526**	**74,510**
Club Wagon	25,569	23,799	20,948	26,677	31,973
Econoline	91,305	84,459	64,787	97,919	136,749
Edge	121,702	118,637	88,548	110,798	130,125
Escape	254,293	191,026	173,044	156,544	165,596
Expedition	40,499	37,336	31,655	55,123	90,287
Explorer	135,704	60,687	52,190	78,439	137,817
F-Series Light-Duty	552,647	502,125	392,112	476,469	633,949
Flex	27,428	34,227	38,717	14,457	—
Freestar	—	—	—	—	2,390
Freestyle	—	—	—	—	23,765
Ranger	70,832	55,364	55,600	65,872	72,711
Taurus X	—	12	6,106	23,112	18,345
Transit Connect*	31,914	27,405	8,834	—	—
Ford Total	**1,351,893**	**1,135,077**	**932,541**	**1,105,410**	**1,443,707**
Mark LT	—	—	147	4,631	8,382
MKT	5,024	7,435	2,580	—	—
MKX	23,395	21,932	21,433	29,076	37,953
Navigator	8,018	8,245	8,057	14,836	24,050
Lincoln Total	**36,437**	**37,612**	**32,217**	**48,543**	**70,385**
Mariner	—	29,912	28,688	32,306	34,844
Monterey	—	—	—	—	700
Mountaineer	—	5,791	5,169	10,596	23,849
Mercury Total	**—**	**35,703**	**33,857**	**42,902**	**59,393**
FORD TOTAL	**1,388,330**	**1,208,392**	**998,615**	**1,196,855**	**1,573,485**
Enclave	58,392	55,426	43,150	44,706	29,286
Rainier	—	—	4	117	4,819
Rendezvous	—	—	9	27	15,295
Terraza	—	—	33	544	5,569
Buick Total	**58,392**	**55,426**	**43,196**	**45,394**	**54,969**
Escalade	15,079	16,118	16,873	23,947	36,654
Escalade ESV	8,388	8,674	6,588	11,054	16,370
Escalade EXT	2,036	2,082	2,423	4,709	7,967
SRX	56,905	51,094	20,237	16,156	22,543
Cadillac Total	**82,408**	**77,968**	**46,121**	**55,866**	**83,534**
Astro	—	—	—	—	25
Avalanche	20,088	20,515	16,432	35,003	55,550
Captiva Sport	7,038	—	—	—	—
Colorado	31,026	24,642	32,413	54,346	75,716
Equinox	193,274	149,979	86,148	67,447	89,552
Express	71,943	59,753	54,302	86,986	114,730
HHR	37,012	75,401	70,842	96,053	105,175
S Blazer	—	—	—	—	7
Silverado	415,130	370,135	316,544	465,065	618,257
SSR	—	—	—	13	244
Suburban	49,427	45,152	41,055	54,058	83,673
Tahoe	80,527	75,675	73,254	91,578	146,256
TrailBlazer	33	218	8,829	74,878	134,626
Traverse	107,131	106,744	91,074	9,456	—
Uplander	—	76	1,758	40,456	69,885
Venture	—	—	—	—	25
W4 Tiltmaster	—	54	142	293	432
W4 Tiltmaster*	—	28	62	144	379
Chevrolet Total	**1,012,629**	**928,372**	**792,855**	**1,075,776**	**1,494,532**
Acadia	79,288	68,295	53,820	66,440	72,765
Canyon	9,590	7,992	10,107	14,974	20,888
Envoy	5	84	4,857	23,876	48,586
Safari	—	—	—	—	13
Savana	17,268	13,942	12,164	22,437	25,706
Sierra	149,170	129,794	111,842	168,544	208,243

SALES

U.S. Vehicle Sales by Model

U.S. VEHICLE SALES BY MODEL — continued

Model	2011	2010	2009	2008	2007
Terrain	83,179	60,519	14,033	—	—
W4 Forward	—	47	139	364	504
W4 Forward*	—	42	145	240	624
Yukon	34,250	28,781	29,411	39,064	63,428
Yukon XL	25,223	23,797	16,819	26,404	45,303
GMC Total	**397,973**	**333,293**	**253,337**	**362,343**	**486,060**
H1	—	—	—	17	125
H2	—	108	1,147	4,793	9,897
H2 SUT	—	43	366	1,302	2,534
H3	—	2,713	5,487	20,681	43,430
H3T	—	948	2,046	692	—
Hummer Total	**—**	**3,812**	**9,046**	**27,485**	**55,986**
Aztek	—	—	—	—	25
Montana	—	—	—	—	26
Montana SV6	—	—	—	64	1,359
Torrent	—	68	9,638	20,625	32,644
Pontiac Total	**—**	**68**	**9,638**	**20,689**	**34,054**
Outlook	—	2,649	13,115	25,340	34,748
Relay	—	—	12	163	1,474
Vue	—	3,201	28,429	81,676	84,767
Saturn Total	**—**	**5,850**	**41,556**	**107,179**	**120,989**
GM TOTAL	**1,551,402**	**1,404,789**	**1,195,749**	**1,694,732**	**2,330,124**
MDX	43,271	47,210	31,178	45,377	58,606
RDX	15,196	14,975	10,153	15,845	23,356
ZDX	1,564	3,259	79	—	—
Acura Total	**60,031**	**65,444**	**41,410**	**61,222**	**81,962**
CR-V	175,596	166,334	153,431	90,480	26,130
CR-V*	42,777	37,380	37,783	106,799	193,030
Crosstour	17,974	28,851	2,564	—	—
Element	11,534	14,247	14,884	26,447	35,218
Odyssey	107,068	108,182	100,133	135,493	173,046
Pilot	116,297	102,323	83,901	96,746	117,146
Ridgeline	9,759	16,142	16,464	33,875	42,795
Honda Total	**481,005**	**473,459**	**409,160**	**489,840**	**587,365**
HONDA TOTAL	**541,036**	**538,903**	**450,570**	**551,062**	**669,327**
Entourage*	—	—	3,433	8,470	17,155
Santa Fe	74,391	76,680	80,343	70,994	92,421
Tucson*	47,232	39,594	15,411	19,027	41,476
Veracruz*	9,146	8,741	10,210	11,004	12,589
HYUNDAI TOTAL	**130,769**	**125,015**	**109,397**	**109,495**	**163,641**
International Truck Light-Duty	845	1,008	374	704	—
INTERNATIONAL TOTAL	**845**	**1,008**	**374**	**704**	**—**
Ascender	—	—	68	1,760	2,948
Axiom	—	—	—	—	8
i-Series	—	—	97	2,998	4,138
Rodeo	—	—	—	—	4
Isuzu Total	**—**	**—**	**165**	**4,758**	**7,098**
Isuzu Truck Light-Duty	370	608	666	1,034	1,153
Isuzu Truck Light-Duty*	1,470	1,082	807	1,534	3,197
ISUZU TOTAL	**1,840**	**1,690**	**1,638**	**7,326**	**11,448**
Land Rover Evoque*	2,244	—	—	—	—
Land Rover Freelander*	—	—	—	—	1
Land Rover LR2*	2,778	3,649	4,433	5,618	9,205
Land Rover LR3*	—	—	2,330	4,039	11,039
Land Rover LR4*	7,983	7,122	867	—	—
Land Rover Range Rover*	9,761	8,746	7,312	8,393	12,316
Land Rover Range Rover Sport*	15,333	12,347	11,364	11,668	16,989
JAGUAR LAND ROVER TOTAL	**38,099**	**31,864**	**26,306**	**29,718**	**49,550**
Borrego*	429	9,835	10,530	1,869	—
Rondo*	47	3,588	14,206	28,645	26,020
Sedona*	24,047	21,823	27,398	26,915	40,493
Sorento	130,235	108,202	—	—	—
Sorento*	—	783	24,460	29,699	36,300
Sportage*	47,463	23,873	42,509	32,754	49,393
KIA TOTAL	**202,221**	**168,104**	**119,103**	**119,882**	**152,206**
B-Series	—	10	573	1,319	2,657
CX-7*	35,641	28,788	20,583	26,811	41,659
CX-9*	34,421	28,908	21,132	26,100	25,566
Mazda5*	19,155	15,683	18,488	22,021	13,718
MPV*	—	—	—	—	122
Tribute	2,696	3,637	5,525	10,806	13,680
MAZDA TOTAL	**91,913**	**77,026**	**66,301**	**87,057**	**97,402**
Endeavor	9,658	4,294	3,228	5,938	11,886

U.S. Vehicle Sales by Model

U.S. VEHICLE SALES BY MODEL — continued

Model	2011	2010	2009	2008	2007
Montero*	—	—	2	4	401
Outlander*	9,788	12,500	10,283	13,471	23,285
Outlander Sport*	16,443	1,690	—	—	—
Raider	—	9	1,944	2,935	8,262
MITSUBISHI TOTAL	**35,889**	**18,493**	**15,457**	**22,348**	**43,834**
EX*	6,030	8,312	7,950	12,873	305
FX*	9,939	10,420	11,024	12,660	20,727
QX56	—	5,064	6,440	7,657	12,288
QX56*	13,428	6,854	—	—	—
Infiniti Total	**29,397**	**30,650**	**25,414**	**33,190**	**33,320**
Armada	18,331	19,344	9,903	15,685	31,632
Frontier	51,700	40,427	28,415	44,997	64,397
Juke*	35,886	8,639	—	—	—
Murano*	53,626	53,999	52,546	71,401	76,358
NV	6,444	—	—	—	—
Pathfinder	25,935	21,438	18,341	33,555	63,056
Quest	—	177	8,437	18,252	28,590
Quest*	12,199	—	—	—	—
Rogue*	124,543	99,515	77,222	73,053	17,808
Titan	21,994	23,416	19,042	34,053	65,746
Xterra	18,221	20,523	16,455	33,579	51,355
Nissan Total	**368,879**	**287,478**	**230,361**	**324,575**	**398,942**
NISSAN TOTAL	**398,276**	**318,128**	**255,775**	**357,765**	**432,262**
Cayenne*	12,978	8,343	7,735	11,216	12,547
PORSCHE TOTAL	**12,978**	**8,343**	**7,735**	**11,216**	**12,547**
9-4X	267	—	—	—	—
9-7X	—	102	2,218	3,660	5,257
SAAB TOTAL	**267**	**102**	**2,218**	**3,660**	**5,257**
Baja	—	—	—	2	1,127
Forester*	76,196	85,080	77,781	60,748	44,530
Outback	104,405	93,148	55,356	44,262	56,079
Tribeca	2,791	2,472	5,930	10,975	16,790
SUBARU TOTAL	**183,392**	**180,700**	**139,067**	**115,987**	**118,526**
Equator	2,127	1,447	2,221	13	—
Vitara*	4,980	4,478	7,557	11,936	19,540
XL7	48	313	4,357	22,554	22,722
XL7*	—	—	—	—	454
SUZUKI TOTAL	**7,155**	**6,238**	**14,135**	**34,503**	**42,716**
GX*	11,609	16,450	6,235	16,424	23,035
LX*	3,167	3,983	3,616	7,915	2,468
RX	64,993	72,556	63,593	63,610	74,351
RX*	17,602	23,234	29,786	20,571	28,989
Lexus Total	**97,371**	**116,223**	**103,230**	**108,520**	**128,843**
4Runner*	44,316	46,531	19,675	47,878	87,718
FJ Cruiser*	13,541	14,959	11,941	28,668	55,170
Highlander	95,906	70,767	10,948	—	—
Highlander*	5,346	21,354	72,170	104,661	127,878
Land Cruiser*	1,662	1,807	2,261	3,801	3,251
RAV4	110,584	101,850	46,360	157	—
RAV4*	21,653	69,027	102,728	136,863	172,752
Sequoia	13,022	13,848	16,387	30,693	23,273
Sienna	111,429	98,337	84,064	115,944	138,162
Tacoma	110,705	106,198	111,824	144,655	173,238
Tundra	82,908	93,309	79,385	137,249	196,555
Venza	38,904	47,321	54,410	1,474	—
Toyota Total	**649,976**	**685,308**	**612,153**	**752,043**	**977,997**
TOYOTA TOTAL	**747,347**	**801,531**	**715,383**	**860,563**	**1,106,840**
Routan	12,473	15,961	14,681	3,387	—
Tiguan*	25,990	20,946	13,903	8,664	—
Touareg*	7,535	4,713	4,392	6,755	8,812
VOLKSWAGEN TOTAL	**45,998**	**41,620**	**32,976**	**18,806**	**8,812**
XC60*	12,932	12,030	9,262	—	—
XC70*	5,716	6,626	5,825	9,489	12,628
XC90*	10,609	10,119	10,757	18,980	31,336
VOLVO TOTAL	**29,257**	**28,775**	**25,844**	**28,469**	**43,964**
UD Trucks Light-Duty*	—	—	—	112	279
VOLVO TRUCK TOTAL	**—**	**—**	**—**	**112**	**279**
TOTAL LIGHT TRUCKS	**6,645,021**	**5,919,085**	**5,000,792**	**6,425,634**	**8,526,888**
TOTAL LIGHT VEHICLES	**12,734,443**	**11,554,518**	**10,401,682**	**13,194,741**	**16,089,222**
TOTAL MED./HVY. TRUCKS	**306,189**	**217,702**	**199,686**	**298,424**	**371,093**
TOTAL VEHICLES	**13,040,632**	**11,772,220**	**10,601,368**	**13,493,165**	**16,460,315**

*Units imported from outside North America.
SOURCE: Ward's AutoInfoBank.

U.S. Sales of Vehicles by Source, Market Class and Purchasing Sector

U.S. LIGHT VEHICLE SALES BY COUNTRY OF ORIGIN

	2011	2010	2009	2008	2007	2006	2005	2004	2003	2002
Germany	522,096	482,148	407,487	506,736	581,905	574,683	534,287	541,940	543,823	546,654
Japan	806,213	798,706	829,496	1,141,768	1,183,144	1,154,455	922,934	810,004	830,355	930,253
South Korea	399,016	448,679	435,108	404,564	420,523	435,925	524,496	550,314	447,660	485,061
Others	122,571	114,023	171,191	225,203	179,491	179,701	204,816	246,801	261,213	263,616
Imported Totals	**1,849,896**	**1,843,556**	**1,843,282**	**2,278,271**	**2,365,063**	**2,344,764**	**2,186,533**	**2,149,059**	**2,083,051**	**2,225,584**
North America (Domestic)	4,239,526	3,791,877	3,557,608	4,490,836	5,197,271	5,416,828	5,473,450	5,333,496	5,472,500	5,816,671
TOTAL CARS	**6,089,422**	**5,635,433**	**5,400,890**	**6,769,107**	**7,562,334**	**7,761,592**	**7,659,983**	**7,482,555**	**7,555,551**	**8,042,255**
Germany	112,298	87,278	68,918	41,235	37,945	42,696	53,748	60,890	41,829	12,680
Japan	615,639	601,055	592,155	806,902	983,295	855,396	699,706	751,219	821,678	796,007
South Korea	128,364	108,237	148,157	158,383	223,426	227,661	258,510	232,668	198,309	165,254
Others	126,142	102,074	75,012	89,949	143,419	220,997	203,351	201,481	165,364	92,434
Imported Totals	**982,443**	**898,644**	**884,242**	**1,096,469**	**1,388,085**	**1,346,750**	**1,215,315**	**1,246,258**	**1,227,180**	**1,066,375**
North America (Domestic)	5,662,578	5,020,441	4,116,550	5,329,165	7,138,803	7,396,058	8,072,456	8,138,107	7,856,322	7,707,738
TOTAL LIGHT TRUCKS	**6,645,021**	**5,919,085**	**5,000,792**	**6,425,634**	**8,526,888**	**8,742,808**	**9,287,771**	**9,384,365**	**9,083,502**	**8,774,113**
Germany	634,394	569,426	476,405	547,971	619,850	617,379	588,035	602,830	585,652	559,334
Japan	1,421,852	1,399,761	1,421,651	1,948,670	2,166,439	2,009,851	1,622,640	1,561,223	1,652,033	1,726,260
South Korea	527,380	556,916	583,265	562,947	643,949	663,586	783,006	782,982	645,969	650,315
Others	248,713	216,097	246,203	315,152	322,910	400,698	408,167	448,282	426,577	356,050
Imported Totals	**2,832,339**	**2,742,200**	**2,727,524**	**3,374,740**	**3,753,148**	**3,691,514**	**3,401,848**	**3,395,317**	**3,310,231**	**3,291,959**
North America (Domestic)	9,902,104	8,812,318	7,674,158	9,820,001	12,336,074	12,812,886	13,545,906	13,471,603	13,328,822	13,524,409
TOTAL LIGHT VEHICLES	**12,734,443**	**11,554,518**	**10,401,682**	**13,194,741**	**16,089,222**	**16,504,400**	**16,947,754**	**16,866,920**	**16,639,053**	**16,816,368**

NOTE: North America is U.S., Canada, Mexico. Light vehicles are cars and light trucks (GVW Classes 1-3, under 14,001 lbs.).
SOURCE: *WardsAuto InfoBank*.

U.S. LIGHT VEHICLE SALES BY SEGMENT GROUP

Year	Small Car	Middle Car	Large Car	Luxury Car	Cross Utility	Sport Utility	Van	Pickup	Comm. Chassis	Total
2011	18.3	19.9	1.9	7.8	24.6	7.8	5.8	14.0	—	100.0
2010	17.8	20.5	2.9	7.6	24.5	6.9	5.9	13.9	—	100.0
2009	19.6	21.7	3.1	7.5	22.3	6.9	5.6	13.3	—	100.0
2008	19.0	21.0	3.5	7.8	18.4	9.0	6.4	14.8	—	100.0
2007	15.8	19.3	4.3	7.6	17.3	12.1	7.0	16.6	—	100.0
2006	15.3	19.3	4.8	7.7	14.4	13.2	8.0	17.2	—	100.0
2005	14.2	18.8	4.7	7.6	12.9	14.5	8.7	18.8	0.1	100.0
2004	13.6	19.6	3.5	7.6	11.4	16.8	8.6	18.8	—	100.0
2003	14.1	20.5	2.9	7.9	10.2	17.4	8.4	18.6	—	100.0
2002	14.7	21.8	3.0	8.4	7.7	17.7	8.7	18.0	—	100.0

SOURCE: *WardsAuto InfoBank*.

U.S. CAR SALES BY SECTOR

Year	Consumer	Business	Government	Total	Consumer	Business	Year	Consumer	Business	Government	Total	Consumer	Business
	Units by Consuming Sector (000)				% of Total Sales			Units by Consuming Sector (000)				% of Total Sales	
2011	3,325	2,723	41	6,089	54.6	44.7	2000	4,678	3,950	150	8,778	53.3	45.0
2010	2,944	2,621	70	5,635	52.2	46.5	1999	4,388	4,076	174	8,638	50.8	47.2
2009	3,228	2,042	131	5,401	59.8	37.8	1998	3,981	3,943	161	8,085	49.2	48.8
2008	3,759	2,821	189	6,769	55.5	41.7	1997	3,908	4,166	143	8,217	47.6	50.7
2007	4,113	3,255	194	7,562	54.4	43.0	1996	4,079	4,273	176	8,527	47.8	50.1
2006	4,330	3,239	193	7,762	55.8	41.7	1995	4,351	4,186	151	8,687	50.1	48.2
2005	4,335	3,169	156	7,660	56.6	41.4	1994	4,600	4,268	124	8,991	51.2	47.5
2004	4,275	3,078	130	7,483	57.1	41.1	1993	4,657	3,748	113	8,518	54.7	44.0
2003	4,341	3,074	141	7,556	57.5	40.7	1992	4,566	3,529	119	8,214	55.6	43.0
2002	4,523	3,374	145	8,042	56.2	42.0	1991	4,424	3,648	103	8,175	54.1	44.6
2001	4,629	3,570	153	8,352	55.4	42.7							

SOURCE: U.S. Department of Commerce, Bureau of Economic Analysis.

U.S. Sales of Trucks by Manufacturer, Gross Vehicle Weight Rating, and Source

U.S. TRUCK SALES BY GVW CLASS AND SOURCE, 2011

	Gross Vehicle Weight Rating (Pounds)								
	6,000 & Less	6,001- 10,000	10,001- 14,000	14,001- 16,000	16,001- 19,500	19,501- 26,000	26,001- 33,000	33,001 & Over	Total
DOMESTIC*									
BMW	74,532	—	—	—	—	—	—	—	74,532
Chrysler	718,295	192,744	96,189	—	7,527	—	—	—	1,014,755
Ford	633,354	661,721	61,341	1,784	27,310	5,176	3,705	—	1,394,391
Freightliner/Sterling/Western Star	—	—	—	1,319	226	13,757	14,931	54,367	84,600
General Motors	680,416	836,126	34,860	10	5	7	1	—	1,551,425
Hino	—	—	—	1	14	3,952	1,111	—	5,078
Honda	498,259	—	—	—	—	—	—	—	498,259
Hyundai	74,391	—	—	—	—	—	—	—	74,391
International	—	7	838	594	3,831	16,201	15,537	35,928	72,936
Isuzu	—	—	370	862	—	—	7	—	1,239
Kenworth	—	—	—	—	18	850	2,666	22,577	26,111
Kia	130,235	—	—	—	—	—	—	—	130,235
Mack	—	—	—	—	—	—	—	12,928	12,928
Mazda	2,696	—	—	—	—	—	—	—	2,696
Mercedes-Benz	63,359	—	—	—	—	—	—	—	63,359
Mitsubishi	9,658	—	—	—	—	—	—	—	9,658
Nissan	114,187	28,438	—	—	—	—	—	—	142,625
Peterbilt	—	—	—	—	32	168	2,945	24,583	27,728
Saab	267	—	—	—	—	—	—	—	267
Subaru	107,196	—	—	—	—	—	—	—	107,196
Suzuki	2,175	—	—	—	—	—	—	—	2,175
Toyota	628,451	—	—	—	—	—	—	—	628,451
Volkswagen	12,473	—	—	—	—	—	—	—	12,473
Volvo Truck	—	—	—	—	—	—	—	20,955	20,955
Other Domestic	—	—	—	—	—	—	—	20	20
Total Domestic	**3,749,944**	**1,719,036**	**193,598**	**4,570**	**38,963**	**40,111**	**40,903**	**171,358**	**5,958,483**
IMPORT									
Audi	33,906	—	—	—	—	—	—	—	33,906
BMW	16,683	—	—	—	—	—	—	—	16,683
Ford	31,914	—	—	—	—	—	—	—	31,914
Honda	42,777	—	—	—	—	—	—	—	42,777
Hyundai	56,378	—	—	—	—	—	—	—	56,378
Isuzu	—	—	1,470	4,376	2,989	—	—	—	8,835
Kia	71,986	—	—	—	—	—	—	—	71,986
Land Rover	38,099	—	—	—	—	—	—	—	38,099
Mazda	89,217	—	—	—	—	—	—	—	89,217
Mercedes-Benz	25,501	16,577	—	—	—	—	—	—	42,078
Mitsubishi	26,231	—	—	—	—	—	—	—	26,231
Mitsubishi Fuso	—	—	221	1,500	439	138	23	—	2,321
Nissan	255,651	—	—	—	—	—	—	—	255,651
Porsche	12,978	—	—	—	—	—	—	—	12,978
Subaru	76,196	—	—	—	—	—	—	—	76,196
Suzuki	4,980	—	—	—	—	—	—	—	4,980
Toyota	118,896	—	—	—	—	—	—	—	118,896
UD Trucks	—	—	—	13	92	428	286	—	819
Volkswagen	33,525	—	—	—	—	—	—	—	33,525
Volvo	29,257	—	—	—	—	—	—	—	29,257
Total Import	**964,175**	**16,577**	**1,691**	**5,889**	**3,520**	**566**	**309**	**—**	**992,727**
Total Trucks	**4,714,119**	**1,735,613**	**195,289**	**10,459**	**42,483**	**40,677**	**41,212**	**171,358**	**6,951,210**

*Units produced in the United States, Canada and Mexico.
SOURCE: *WardsAuto InfoBank.*

U.S. Sales of Trucks by Gross Vehicle Weight Rating and Body Type

U.S. LIGHT TRUCK SALES BY GVW AND BODY TYPE

GVWR/Body type	2011	2010	2009	2008	2007
0-6,000 Lbs.					
Utility	3,810,770	3,383,837	2,794,008	3,255,649	4,131,827
Mini Van	472,398	460,154	415,173	592,000	793,335
Passenger Carrier	2,999	3,158	2,695	3,670	1,939
Van	47,149	37,918	19,573	20,800	35,065
Compact Pickup	297,895	266,226	272,394	392,735	516,875
Conventional Pickup	82,908	93,309	79,424	137,744	259,372
Total 0-6,000 lbs.	**4,714,119**	**4,244,602**	**3,583,267**	**4,402,598**	**5,738,413**
6,001-10,000 Lbs.					
Utility	320,168	254,048	239,745	370,507	607,973
Passenger Carrier	37,321	33,427	29,637	40,060	50,397
Van	129,673	106,984	83,012	129,688	170,677
Van Cutaway	44,576	36,716	33,305	54,496	67,666
Conventional Pickup	1,203,875	1,081,866	920,122	1,293,446	1,725,866
Total 6,001-10,000 lbs.	**1,735,613**	**1,513,041**	**1,305,821**	**1,888,197**	**2,622,579**
10,001-14,000 lbs.					
Conventional Pickup	192,390	158,294	109,024	130,278	159,151
Other Body Types	2,899	3,148	2,680	4,561	6,745
Total 10,001-14,000 lbs.	**195,289**	**161,442**	**111,704**	**134,839**	**165,896**
Total Light Trucks	**6,645,021**	**5,919,085**	**5,000,792**	**6,425,634**	**8,526,888**

SOURCE: *WardsAuto InfoBank.*

U.S. TRUCK SALES BY COUNTRY OF ORIGIN

	2011	2010	2009	2008	2007	2006	2005	2004	2003	2002
Germany	112,298	87,278	68,918	41,235	37,945	42,696	53,748	60,890	41,829	12,680
Japan	615,639	601,055	592,155	806,902	983,295	855,396	699,706	751,219	821,678	796,007
South Korea	128,364	108,237	148,157	158,383	223,426	227,661	258,510	232,668	198,309	165,254
Others	126,142	102,074	75,012	89,949	143,419	220,997	203,351	201,481	165,364	92,434
Imported Totals	**982,443**	**898,644**	**884,242**	**1,096,469**	**1,388,085**	**1,346,750**	**1,215,315**	**1,246,258**	**1,227,180**	**1,066,375**
North America (Domestic)	5,662,578	5,020,441	4,116,550	5,329,165	7,138,803	7,396,058	8,072,456	8,138,107	7,856,322	7,707,738
TOTAL LIGHT TRUCKS	**6,645,021**	**5,919,085**	**5,000,792**	**6,425,634**	**8,526,888**	**8,742,808**	**9,287,771**	**9,384,365**	**9,083,502**	**8,774,113**
Japan	10,284	9,554	6,753	10,699	20,151	22,624	21,953	22,984	18,406	16,426
Others	—	—	—	—	—	—	—	21	454	699
Imported Totals	**10,284**	**9,554**	**6,753**	**10,699**	**20,151**	**22,624**	**21,953**	**23,005**	**18,860**	**17,125**
North America (Domestic)	295,905	208,148	192,933	287,725	350,942	521,957	474,622	408,648	309,529	305,159
TOTAL MED./HVY. TRUCKS	**306,189**	**217,702**	**199,686**	**298,424**	**371,093**	**544,581**	**496,575**	**431,653**	**328,389**	**322,284**
Germany	112,298	87,278	68,918	41,235	37,945	42,696	53,748	60,890	41,829	12,680
Japan	625,923	610,609	598,908	817,601	1,003,446	878,020	721,659	774,203	840,084	812,433
South Korea	128,364	108,237	148,157	158,383	223,426	227,661	258,510	232,668	198,309	165,254
Others	126,142	102,074	75,012	89,949	143,419	220,997	203,351	201,502	165,818	93,133
Imported Totals	**992,727**	**908,198**	**890,995**	**1,107,168**	**1,408,236**	**1,369,374**	**1,237,268**	**1,269,263**	**1,246,040**	**1,083,500**
North America (Domestic)	5,958,483	5,228,589	4,309,483	5,616,890	7,489,745	7,918,015	8,547,078	8,546,755	8,165,851	8,012,897
TOTAL TRUCKS	**6,951,210**	**6,136,787**	**5,200,478**	**6,724,058**	**8,897,981**	**9,287,389**	**9,784,346**	**9,816,018**	**9,411,891**	**9,096,397**

Note: North America is U.S., Canada, Mexico.
SOURCE: *WardsAuto InfoBank.*

Annual and Monthly Records for U.S. Production and Sales

RECORD U.S. PRODUCTION YEARS

Cars		Trucks	
Year	Units	Year	Units
1973	9,660,821	2004	7,794,429
1965	9,329,104	2005	7,680,781
1977	9,211,411	2003	7,633,659
1978	9,173,606	1999	7,447,229
1968	8,843,031	2002	7,322,205
1972	8,821,737	2000	7,302,797
1966	8,598,917	2006	6,948,581

RECORD U.S. SALES YEARS

Cars		Trucks	
Year	Units	Year	Units
1973	11,423,851	2004	9,816,018
1986	11,404,239	2005	9,784,346
1978	11,314,079	2003	9,411,891
1977	11,183,412	2006	9,287,389
1985	10,979,187	2001	9,120,378
1972	10,940,482	2002	9,096,397
1979	10,672,768	2000	9,033,950

RECORD U.S. PRODUCTION BY MONTH

Month	Year	Units
Cars		
January	1973	917,273
February	1973	856,117
March	1965	963,101
April	1978	870,689
May	1973	941,019
June	1977	949,440
July	1965	740,576
August	1950	684,970
September	1972	758,578
October	1973	951,434
November	1965	913,146
December	1964	866,632
Trucks		
January	2003	636,722
February	2004	678,010
March	2004	786,195
April	2004	693,282
May	2000	713,996
June	2005	706,460
July	2003	428,676
August	2005	732,841
September	2005	721,291
October	2003	757,513
November	2004	626,000
December	2003	594,003

RECORD U.S. SALES BY MONTH

Month	Year	Units
Cars		
January	1973	874,084
February	1973	918,681
March	1973	1,140,386
April	1978	1,043,341
May	1978	1,159,996
June	1978	1,138,504
July	1973	958,270
August	1985	994,926
September	1986	1,212,714
October	1972	1,068,400
November	1972	1,029,689
December	1986	987,744
Trucks		
January	2004	658,568
February	2000	775,789
March	2005	897,083
April	2005	827,851
May	2004	920,354
June	2005	1,015,406
July	2005	1,134,313
August	2003	924,067
September	2004	864,381
October	2001	946,182
November	2001	750,766
December	2004	931,903

U.S. PRODUCTION MILESTONES

Cars		Trucks		Total Vehicles	
Year	Units	Year	Units	Year	Units
2003	450 millionth	2005	200 millionth	2010	700 millionth
1994	400 millionth	1998	150 millionth	2001	600 millionth
1986	350 millionth	1988	100 millionth	1992	500 millionth
1979	300 millionth	1971	50 millionth	1982	400 millionth
1973	250 millionth	1965	40 millionth	1972	300 millionth
1967	200 millionth	1957	30 millionth	1962	200 millionth
1952	100 millionth	1949	20 millionth	1955	150 millionth
1935	50 millionth	1938	10 millionth	1948	100 millionth
1925	25 millionth	1929	5 millionth	1931	50 millionth
1920	10 millionth	1920	1 millionth	1920	10 millionth
1912	1 millionth	1915	100,000th	1912	1 millionth

SOURCE: *Ward's* Automotive Group

Top Selling Vehicles and Automotive Color Popularity

TOP 10 CARS SOLD IN THE U.S.

	2011			2010	
Rank	Model	Sales	Rank	Model	Sales
1	Toyota Camry	308,510	1	Toyota Camry	327,804
2	Nissan Altima	268,981	2	Honda Accord	282,530
3	Ford Fusion	248,067	3	Toyota Corolla/Matrix	266,082
4	Toyota Corolla/Matrix	240,259	4	Honda Civic	260,218
5	Honda Accord	235,625	5	Nissan Altima	229,263
6	Chevrolet Cruze	231,732	6	Ford Fusion	219,219
7	Hyundai Sonata	225,961	7	Chevrolet Malibu	198,770
8	Honda Civic	221,235	8	Hyundai Sonata	196,623
9	Chevrolet Malibu	204,808	9	Ford Focus	172,421
10	Hyundai Elantra	186,361	10	Chevrolet Impala	172,078

TOP 10 LIGHT TRUCKS SOLD IN THE U.S.

	2011			2010	
Rank	Model	Sales	Rank	Model	Sales
1	Ford F-Series	552,647	1	Ford F-Series	502,125
2	Chevrolet Silverado	415,130	2	Chevrolet Silverado	370,135
3	Ford Escape	254,293	3	Honda CR-V	203,714
4	Ram Pickup	237,236	4	Ram Pickup	194,175
5	Honda CR-V	218,373	5	Ford Escape	191,026
6	Chevrolet Equinox	193,274	6	Toyota RAV4	170,877
7	GMC Sierra	149,170	7	Chevrolet Equinox	149,979
8	Ford Explorer	135,704	8	GMC Sierra	129,794
9	Toyota RAV4	132,237	9	Ford Edge	118,637
10	Kia Sorento	130,235	10	Chrysler Town & Country	112,275

SOURCE: *WardsAuto InfoBank.*

AUTOMOTIVE PAINT COLOR POPULARITY BY VEHICLE TYPE, 2011 MODEL YEAR

Luxury Cars/Luxury SUV		Intermediate Cars/CUV		Compact/Sports Cars		Light Trucks	
Color	Percent	Color	Percent	Color	Percent	Color	Percent
Black/Black Effect	27%	White/White Pearl	18%	Silver	20%	White/White Pearl	29%
White/White Pearl	22%	Black/Black Effect	18%	Black/Black Effect	19%	Black/Black Effect	17%
Silver	15%	Silver	17%	White/White Pearl	18%	Silver	14%
Red	10%	Gray	16%	Gray	17%	Red	11%
Gray	8%	Blue	10%	Red	10%	Gray	11%
Beige/Brown	8%	Red	10%	Blue	9%	Blue	8%
Yellow/Gold	5%	Beige/Brown	6%	Beige/Brown	5%	Beige/Brown	4%
Blue	4%	Yellow/Gold	4%	Green	1%	Green	3%
Green	<1%	Green	1%	Yellow/Gold	<1%	Yellow/Gold	3%
Other	<1%	Other	<1%	Other	<1%	Other	<1%

SOURCE: Du Pont Automotive Products.

Canada Vehicle Sales and Registrations

CANADA VEHICLE SALES BY SOURCE

Year	Cars			Commercial Vehicles			Total Vehicles
	Domestic[(1)]	Imports	Total	Domestic[(1)]	Imports	Total	
2011	436,070	245,886	681,956	794,827	143,438	938,265	1,620,221
2010	399,330	295,019	694,349	766,826	122,213	889,039	1,583,388
2009	427,930	301,093	729,023	636,568	116,641	753,209	1,482,232
2008	547,321	325,399	872,720	664,145	136,657	800,802	1,673,522
2007	552,838	288,747	841,585	723,401	125,359	848,760	1,690,345
2006	578,491	280,335	858,826	674,514	132,668	807,182	1,666,008
2005	572,202	275,234	847,436	668,342	114,364	782,706	1,630,142
2004	545,767	275,783	821,550	649,525	103,728	753,253	1,574,803
2003	603,444	261,545	864,989	654,112	105,949	760,061	1,625,050
2002	651,703	282,354	934,057	700,427	97,339	797,766	1,731,823
2001	620,162	248,026	868,188	651,952	77,735	729,687	1,597,875
2000	640,916	208,216	849,132	673,631	63,320	736,951	1,586,083
1999	620,233	186,207	806,440	676,107	57,832	733,939	1,540,379
1998	590,041	150,775	740,816	629,720	56,056	685,776	1,426,592
1997	628,739	109,816	738,555	628,124	56,315	684,439	1,422,994
1996	572,001	88,803	660,804	516,288	25,302	541,590	1,202,394
1995	554,878	116,103	670,981	470,147	23,470	493,617	1,164,598
1994	584,985	165,343	750,328	478,826	27,828	506,654	1,256,982
1993	511,611	229,257	740,868	407,864	41,850	449,714	1,190,582
1992	511,220	289,107	800,327	369,896	54,155	424,051	1,224,378

(1) Units produced in the United States, Canada and Mexico.
SOURCE: *WardsAuto InfoBank.*

CANADA TOTAL REGISTRATIONS BY PROVINCE, 2009

Province	Total Vehicle Registrations by Weight			
	less than 9,000 lbs.	over 9,000 lbs.	Buses	Total
Alberta	2,605,008	222,468	15,201	2,842,677
British Columbia	2,561,329	148,027	9,557	2,718,913
Manitoba	670,511	29,537	3,939	703,987
New Brunswick	489,507	12,305	3,086	504,898
Newfoundland	297,249	8,323	1,242	306,814
Northwest Territories	21,539	2,184	142	23,865
Nova Scotia	541,748	16,733	1,962	560,443
Nunavut	3,752	524	31	4,307
Ontario	7,243,898	216,157	28,649	7,488,704
Prince Edward Island	81,699	4,241	132	86,072
Quebec	4,613,923	94,379	17,409	4,725,711
Saskatchewan	719,577	71,147	3,884	794,608
Yukon Territory	27,244	3,660	341	31,245
Total	**19,876,984**	**829,685**	**85,575**	**20,792,244**

SOURCE: Statistics Canada.

CANADA TOTAL REGISTRATIONS

Year	Cars (000)	Commercial Vehicles (000)	Total (000)
2011	20,352	959	21,311
2010	20,121	933	21,054
2009	19,877	915	20,792
2008	19,613	907	20,520
2007	19,199	872	20,071
2006	18,739	841	19,580
2005	18,124	786	18,910
2004	17,920	745	18,665
2003	17,755	741	18,496
2002	17,544	723	18,267
2001	17,055	728	17,783
2000	16,832	739	17,571
1999	16,538	2,679	19,217
1998	13,887	3,694	17,581
1997	13,487	3,591	17,078
1996	13,217	3,644	16,861
1994	13,122	3,466	16,588
1992	12,781	3,413	16,194
1990	12,622	3,931	16,553

NOTE: 2010 and 2011 estimated by Ward's. Beginning in 2000, data excludes farm tractors and off-road vehicles.
SOURCE: Statistics Canada.

Canada Vehicle Sales

CANADA VEHICLE SALES BY MODEL

Model	2011	2010	2009	2008	2007
A3*	1,289	1,322	1,245	1,351	1,175
A4*	5,480	5,211	4,224	4,480	4,334
A5*	1,948	2,309	1,520	400	35
A6*	669	596	579	795	769
A7*	606	—	—	—	—
A8*	211	132	96	161	234
R8*	147	137	152	155	34
TT*	450	319	406	660	414
AUDI TOTAL	**10,800**	**10,026**	**8,222**	**8,002**	**6,995**
1-Series*	1,556	1,764	2,533	2,212	—
3-Series*	11,226	14,009	12,610	11,754	13,102
5-Series*	2,963	2,382	1,619	2,042	2,651
6-Series*	205	61	165	286	371
7-Series*	532	741	638	424	467
Z4	—	—	7	249	390
Z4*	345	376	479	—	—
BMW Total	**16,827**	**19,333**	**18,051**	**16,967**	**16,981**
Mini Cooper*	3,592	4,501	4,251	4,905	3,703
BMW TOTAL	**20,419**	**23,834**	**22,302**	**21,872**	**20,684**
200 Series	7,170	1	—	—	—
300 Series	3,045	4,180	5,234	7,443	10,210
Crossfire*	—	—	3	119	75
PT Cruiser Convertible	—	—	—	19	739
Sebring Convertible	164	1,180	866	2,404	1,325
Sebring Sedan	140	2,160	3,966	7,600	8,250
Chrysler Total	**10,519**	**7,521**	**10,069**	**17,585**	**20,599**
Avenger	4,680	3,495	5,533	7,873	7,067
Caliber	4,919	7,275	9,802	19,544	18,553
Challenger	2,350	3,097	2,660	1,631	—
Charger	4,137	4,662	4,861	6,675	7,858
Magnum	—	—	13	585	2,494
Viper	33	54	71	157	27
Dodge Total	**16,119**	**18,583**	**22,940**	**36,465**	**35,999**
Fiat 500	5,392	—	—	—	—
CHRYSLER TOTAL	**32,030**	**26,104**	**33,009**	**54,050**	**56,598**
B-Class*	2,440	2,994	2,865	3,207	3,035
C-Class*	9,447	8,151	7,589	7,966	5,066
E-Class*	3,898	3,914	2,819	2,161	2,267
S-Class*	743	763	748	1,026	1,320
SL*	192	230	268	398	286
SLK*	375	324	371	519	—
SLR*	—	7	4	11	11
SLS*	110	111	—	—	—
Maybach*	2	3	3	5	6
Mercedes Total	**17,207**	**16,497**	**14,667**	**15,293**	**11,991**
Smart Fortwo*	1,851	2,019	2,667	3,749	2,433
DAIMLER TOTAL	**19,058**	**18,516**	**17,334**	**19,042**	**14,424**
Crown Victoria	2,575	2,243	2,429	2,938	2,809
Fiesta	13,064	4,423	—	—	—
Five Hundred	—	—	—	—	1,045
Focus	25,736	23,452	21,831	23,654	24,013
Ford GT	—	—	—	—	95
Fusion	18,404	19,364	16,526	13,326	15,882
Mustang	4,433	5,232	5,200	6,261	7,987
Taurus	3,264	3,847	2,035	2,064	1,513
Ford Total	**67,476**	**58,561**	**48,021**	**48,243**	**53,344**
MKS	630	980	1,142	615	—
MKZ	1,500	1,493	1,508	1,358	1,585
Town Car	310	233	447	652	883
Lincoln Total	**2,440**	**2,706**	**3,097**	**2,625**	**2,468**
Mercury Grand Marquis	—	48	126	305	335
FORD TOTAL	**69,916**	**61,315**	**51,244**	**51,173**	**56,147**
Allure	—	—	2,025	9,200	8,741
LaCrosse	2,839	3,947	810	—	—
Lucerne	2,239	2,367	1,749	2,872	2,948
Regal	753	—	—	—	—
Regal*	2,093	820	—	—	—
Verano	32	—	—	—	—
Buick Total	**7,956**	**7,134**	**4,584**	**12,072**	**11,689**
CTS	3,048	2,974	2,488	4,223	3,839
Deville	—	—	—	—	6
DTS	227	278	355	704	959
STS	13	46	74	279	505
XLR	—	1	16	30	59
Cadillac Total	**3,288**	**3,299**	**2,933**	**5,236**	**5,368**
Aveo	6,228	6,653	4,577	121	—
Aveo*	3	305	2,909	10,532	11,082

Canada Vehicle Sales

CANADA VEHICLE SALES BY MODEL — continued

Model	2011	2010	2009	2008	2007
Camaro	3,750	4,113	2,554	—	—
Caprice*	4	—	—	—	—
Cobalt	360	25,957	14,350	33,754	32,613
Corvette	352	364	307	596	787
Cruze	33,900	3,184	—	—	—
Epica*	—	—	—	6	46
Impala	9,287	11,434	12,292	14,913	16,326
Malibu	10,913	13,092	12,427	17,596	9,857
Monte Carlo	—	—	2	37	802
Optra*	—	—	1	76	4,148
Sonic	1,241	—	—	—	—
Volt	275	—	—	—	—
Chevrolet Total	**66,313**	**65,102**	**49,419**	**77,631**	**75,661**
Bonneville	—	—	—	—	1
G5	2	2,834	10,085	26,436	25,211
G6	5	307	3,891	13,640	11,848
G8*	1	1	2,171	691	—
Grand Am	—	—	—	—	2
Grand Prix	—	—	12	333	13,086
Solstice	7	46	443	899	1,816
Vibe	20	1,559	11,537	17,335	12,915
Wave	5	1,740	3,074	106	—
Wave*	2	241	2,612	8,426	8,711
Pontiac Total	**42**	**6,728**	**33,825**	**67,866**	**73,590**
Astra*	—	2	4,066	7,536	1
Aura	—	—	1,156	2,587	3,165
Ion	—	—	3	445	13,932
Saturn L	—	—	—	—	1
Sky	—	—	169	409	613
Saturn Total	**—**	**2**	**5,394**	**10,977**	**17,712**
GM TOTAL	**77,599**	**82,265**	**96,155**	**173,782**	**184,020**
CSX	1,795	2,064	2,526	2,998	3,729
RL*	56	64	94	157	158
RSX*	—	—	—	5	12
TL	3,229	2,895	3,577	4,019	3,995
TSX*	1,659	2,297	2,020	3,118	2,104
Acura Total	**6,739**	**7,320**	**8,217**	**10,297**	**9,998**
Accord	7,818	12,483	16,017	22,623	22,102
Civic	55,028	56,838	61,810	70,270	68,470
Civic*	62	663	844	2,193	2,368
CR-Z*	517	325	—	—	—
Fit*	2,835	7,900	9,553	14,836	13,507
Insight*	242	1,136	668	1	2
S2000*	1	21	49	65	123
Honda Total	**66,503**	**79,366**	**88,941**	**109,988**	**106,572**
HONDA TOTAL	**73,242**	**86,686**	**97,158**	**120,285**	**116,570**
Accent*	22,280	24,017	25,220	29,751	16,390
Azera*	—	3	176	369	762
Elantra	31,845	201	—	—	—
Elantra*	13,125	34,355	30,675	11,814	14,327
Equus*	116	—	—	—	—
Genesis*	3,625	3,924	3,438	342	—
Sonata	16,343	13,792	8,587	9,320	8,633
Sonata*	—	64	388	978	2,401
Tiburon*	—	2	890	1,996	1,429
Veloster*	1,902	—	—	—	—
HYUNDAI TOTAL	**89,236**	**76,358**	**69,374**	**54,570**	**43,942**
Jaguar S-Type*	—	—	—	32	132
Jaguar X-Type*	—	—	—	80	208
Jaguar XF*	401	449	604	536	—
Jaguar XJ6/8*	227	189	77	133	156
Jaguar XK8*	148	117	123	148	242
JAGUAR LAND ROVER TOTAL	**776**	**755**	**804**	**929**	**738**
Amanti*	—	37	111	158	142
Forte*	13,984	13,578	5,734	—	—
Magentis*	62	574	1,033	1,975	2,021
Optima*	2,125	—	—	—	—
Rio*	6,849	7,887	10,287	9,742	7,236
Soul*	11,651	9,857	8,489	—	—
Spectra*	—	13	2,027	5,030	6,602
KIA TOTAL	**34,671**	**31,946**	**27,681**	**16,905**	**16,001**
Mazda2*	9,020	2,868	—	—	—
Mazda3*	37,224	47,740	46,943	50,317	48,236
Mazda6	3,676	6,092	6,614	6,561	8,451
MX-5 Miata*	612	736	850	1,407	1,814
RX-8*	165	111	310	543	659
MAZDA TOTAL	**50,697**	**57,547**	**54,717**	**58,828**	**59,160**

Canada Vehicle Sales

CANADA VEHICLE SALES BY MODEL — continued

Model	2011	2010	2009	2008	2007
Eclipse	590	851	802	1,675	1,951
Galant	40	362	463	902	553
I*	23	—	—	—	—
Lancer*	6,632	8,765	9,446	9,157	7,192
MITSUBISHI TOTAL	**7,285**	**9,978**	**10,711**	**11,734**	**9,696**
G35/37*	3,603	4,408	3,998	4,286	4,908
M35/45*	408	550	217	410	550
Infiniti Total	**4,011**	**4,958**	**4,215**	**4,696**	**5,458**
350Z*	—	—	112	311	469
370Z*	453	899	455	—	—
Altima	12,537	13,425	13,853	16,676	17,126
Cube*	459	2,864	2,416	—	—
GT-R*	72	62	133	137	—
Leaf*	170	—	—	—	—
Maxima	2,069	2,266	1,642	1,475	1,304
Sentra	12,880	14,651	13,431	11,000	8,563
Versa	14,497	15,743	20,097	21,845	21,940
Nissan Total	**43,137**	**49,910**	**52,139**	**51,444**	**49,402**
NISSAN TOTAL	**47,148**	**54,868**	**56,354**	**56,140**	**54,860**
911*	475	525	495	463	660
Boxster*	151	166	208	272	282
Cayman*	124	119	154	169	222
Panamera*	359	387	114	—	—
PORSCHE TOTAL	**1,109**	**1,197**	**971**	**904**	**1,164**
9-2X*	—	—	—	1	19
9-3*	115	2	627	1,254	1,575
9-5*	52	—	92	197	327
SAAB TOTAL	**167**	**2**	**719**	**1,452**	**1,921**
Impreza*	7,664	8,658	9,126	8,555	7,480
Legacy	3,115	3,269	2,612	4,089	4,919
SUBARU TOTAL	**10,779**	**11,927**	**11,738**	**12,644**	**12,399**
Aerio*	—	—	2	1	303
Kizashi*	734	688	—	—	—
Swift+*	18	473	988	1,828	2,593
SX4*	2,969	4,970	7,079	7,833	4,424
Verona*	—	—	15	—	—
SUZUKI TOTAL	**3,721**	**6,131**	**8,084**	**9,662**	**7,320**
CT*	1,350	—	—	—	—
ES*	1,892	2,688	2,999	3,634	4,251
GS*	128	251	336	511	596
HS*	308	746	269	—	—
IS*	2,235	2,233	2,617	3,600	2,792
LFA*	4	—	—	—	—
LS*	156	226	256	311	588
SC*	3	29	44	80	109
Lexus Total	**6,076**	**6,173**	**6,521**	**8,136**	**8,336**
iQ*	8	—	—	—	—
tC*	2,045	233	—	—	—
xB*	1,529	367	—	—	—
xD*	1,138	79	—	—	—
Scion Total	**4,720**	**679**	**—**	**—**	**—**
Avalon	496	502	280	380	1,010
Camry	12,334	12,251	15,600	24,814	28,785
Camry*	—	—	—	2	173
Corolla	36,663	38,680	53,933	57,736	40,474
Matrix	14,895	19,093	22,526	23,549	21,369
Prius*	2,134	2,967	4,610	4,458	2,585
Yaris*	7,968	13,817	23,773	40,602	34,424
Toyota Total	**74,490**	**87,310**	**120,722**	**151,541**	**128,820**
TOYOTA TOTAL	**85,286**	**94,162**	**127,243**	**159,677**	**137,156**
Beetle	269	395	499	869	928
Beetle Cabrio	111	404	438	737	779
CC*	1,043	1,620	1,577	237	—
Eos*	708	774	802	1,121	1,013
Golf*	12,163	15,868	8,698	9,259	7,839
GTI*	1,756	2,135	1,045	1,406	1,614
Jetta	26,749	14,758	13,970	13,915	14,665
Passat	1,649	—	—	—	—
Passat*	317	2,024	1,559	2,352	3,093
Rabbit*	—	83	4,027	7,660	6,324
VOLKSWAGEN TOTAL	**44,765**	**38,061**	**32,615**	**37,556**	**36,255**
30-Series*	682	755	906	1,142	1,143
40-Series*	478	818	758	683	1,099
50-Series*	94	260	264	353	606
60-Series*	1,519	208	145	541	1,425
70-Series*	158	269	265	551	719
80-Series*	321	361	250	243	543

Canada Vehicle Sales

CANADA VEHICLE SALES BY MODEL — continued

Model	2011	2010	2009	2008	2007
VOLVO TOTAL	**3,252**	**2,671**	**2,588**	**3,513**	**5,535**
TOTAL CARS	**681,956**	**694,349**	**729,023**	**872,720**	**841,585**
Q5*	4,502	3,060	1,942	—	—
Q7*	1,565	1,247	1,146	1,269	1,235
AUDI TOTAL	**6,067**	**4,307**	**3,088**	**1,269**	**1,235**
X1*	2,980	—	—	—	—
X3	4,671	—	—	—	—
X3*	—	2,840	2,236	2,296	2,975
X5	4,155	4,012	3,410	3,255	4,075
X6	1,140	1,017	1,027	726	—
BMW Total	**12,946**	**7,869**	**6,673**	**6,277**	**7,050**
Mini Countryman*	1,563	—	—	—	—
BMW TOTAL	**14,509**	**7,869**	**6,673**	**6,277**	**7,050**
Aspen	—	15	411	1,719	1,535
Pacifica	—	—	2	290	2,016
PT Cruiser	—	1,020	2,534	2,615	5,058
Town & Country	4,536	4,175	3,165	4,865	1,531
Chrysler Total	**4,536**	**5,210**	**6,112**	**9,489**	**10,140**
Caravan	53,406	55,306	40,283	39,780	55,041
Durango	2,549	6	97	1,115	1,634
Journey	29,021	23,785	15,390	11,817	—
Nitro	465	1,103	2,348	5,831	8,793
Dodge Total	**85,441**	**80,200**	**58,118**	**58,543**	**65,468**
Commander	—	650	627	793	1,147
Compass	6,619	4,610	5,176	9,423	10,229
Grand Cherokee	10,283	7,255	5,285	7,617	8,078
Liberty	1,950	2,993	3,824	6,904	8,776
Patriot	8,421	10,753	7,998	13,836	9,629
Wrangler	15,636	11,062	7,271	12,137	9,834
Jeep Total	**42,909**	**37,323**	**30,181**	**50,710**	**47,693**
Cargo Van	432	—	—	—	—
Dakota	1,347	1,715	3,161	4,982	8,425
Ram Pickup Light-Duty	62,929	53,386	30,621	41,320	42,296
Sprinter Van*	—	136	1,161	2,486	2,068
Ram Total	**64,708**	**55,237**	**34,943**	**48,788**	**52,789**
CHRYSLER TOTAL	**197,594**	**177,970**	**129,354**	**167,530**	**176,090**
G-Class*	74	37	26	21	83
GL	1,648	1,400	1,117	1,135	863
GLK*	5,294	5,852	5,012	—	—
M-Class	3,846	3,871	3,146	3,525	2,689
R-Class	515	408	308	394	488
Sprinter Van*	2,479	1,567	—	—	—
Mercedes Total	**13,856**	**13,135**	**9,609**	**5,075**	**4,123**
Mitsubishi Fuso Light-Duty*	15	14	23	21	2
Sterling Light-Duty*	—	1	19	14	—
DAIMLER TOTAL	**13,871**	**13,150**	**9,651**	**5,110**	**4,125**
Club Wagon	642	718	524	724	861
Econoline	8,329	8,323	5,438	7,659	8,778
Edge	15,633	17,040	12,060	11,834	10,349
Escape	44,248	43,038	36,980	32,898	31,643
Expedition	1,677	1,664	1,584	1,557	2,217
Explorer	9,406	4,292	4,121	4,486	7,583
F-Series Light-Duty	92,737	95,446	79,411	65,430	70,406
Flex	2,862	4,803	6,047	2,134	—
Freestar	—	—	—	—	883
Freestyle	—	—	—	—	2,848
Ranger	16,381	19,653	20,715	24,211	23,386
Taurus X	—	8	870	3,106	1,267
Transit Connect*	4,709	3,180	803	—	—
Ford Total	**196,624**	**198,165**	**168,553**	**154,039**	**160,221**
Mark LT	—	—	6	493	701
MKT	518	922	186	—	—
MKX	4,595	4,458	2,471	2,218	2,531
Navigator	609	544	414	384	961
Lincoln Total	**5,722**	**5,924**	**3,077**	**3,095**	**4,193**
FORD TOTAL	**202,346**	**204,089**	**171,630**	**157,134**	**164,414**
Enclave	3,696	4,135	3,854	4,994	2,557
Rainier	—	—	—	5	74
Rendezvous	—	—	—	5	1,112
Terraza	—	—	—	2	467
Buick Total	**3,696**	**4,135**	**3,854**	**5,006**	**4,210**
Escalade	652	713	512	848	1,083
Escalade ESV	223	264	127	208	303
Escalade EXT	217	204	162	270	336
SRX	3,197	2,918	990	1,045	1,503
Cadillac Total	**4,289**	**4,099**	**1,791**	**2,371**	**3,225**

Canada Vehicle Sales

CANADA VEHICLE SALES BY MODEL — continued

Model	2011	2010	2009	2008	2007
Astro	—	—	—	—	3
Avalanche	3,667	3,670	2,775	3,875	4,958
Colorado	2,694	3,961	2,838	4,586	6,239
Equinox	22,468	19,261	11,759	11,946	13,205
Express	4,875	4,422	4,494	5,271	7,237
HHR	1,214	1,783	2,862	4,916	5,026
Orlando*	1,128	—	—	—	—
Silverado	40,523	41,737	36,428	34,685	40,066
SSR	—	—	—	7	11
Suburban	1,302	1,492	1,059	1,118	1,460
Tahoe	1,197	1,522	1,048	1,874	2,211
TrailBlazer	—	7	254	2,206	2,778
Traverse	5,143	6,307	4,351	263	—
Uplander	16	30	10,433	16,133	18,999
Venture	—	—	—	—	7
Chevrolet Total	**84,227**	**84,192**	**78,301**	**86,880**	**102,200**
Acadia	5,207	5,047	4,197	5,844	6,067
Canyon	2,293	3,411	2,041	3,602	4,816
Envoy	—	13	223	2,083	1,962
Savana	4,631	4,649	4,259	4,640	7,687
Sierra	46,680	45,457	37,316	34,555	40,606
Terrain	11,817	10,148	2,252	—	—
W4 Forward*	—	12	67	112	410
Yukon	1,172	1,914	1,227	1,585	2,197
Yukon XL	1,189	1,088	664	842	1,218
GMC Total	**72,989**	**71,739**	**52,246**	**53,263**	**64,963**
H2	—	—	29	131	219
H2 SUT	—	2	12	36	58
H3	2	86	178	583	992
H3T	—	80	275	62	—
Hummer Total	**2**	**168**	**494**	**812**	**1,269**
Montana	—	—	—	—	3
Montana SV6	13	57	9,687	14,953	19,169
Torrent	—	16	6,112	10,465	11,799
Pontiac Total	**13**	**73**	**15,799**	**25,418**	**30,971**
Outlook	—	1	708	1,739	2,072
Relay	—	—	—	6	227
Vue	—	8	2,657	6,007	5,799
Saturn Total	**—**	**9**	**3,365**	**7,752**	**8,098**
GM TOTAL	**165,216**	**164,415**	**155,850**	**181,502**	**214,936**
MDX	5,334	5,994	5,994	5,514	6,017
RDX	3,070	3,163	2,869	3,573	4,104
ZDX	129	863	8	—	—
Acura Total	**8,533**	**10,020**	**8,871**	**9,087**	**10,121**
CR-V	25,076	24,930	18,554	20,488	20,915
CR-V*	—	—	—	12	65
Crosstour	951	2,176	—	—	—
Element	180	380	976	1,810	1,764
Odyssey	9,060	8,616	6,449	10,125	12,025
Pilot	4,366	5,062	4,452	5,564	4,328
Ridgeline	1,713	3,200	3,546	3,987	4,519
Honda Total	**41,346**	**44,364**	**33,977**	**41,986**	**43,616**
HONDA TOTAL	**49,879**	**54,384**	**42,848**	**51,073**	**53,737**
Entourage*	49	111	380	1,400	2,383
Santa Fe	24,121	27,882	24,676	14,401	15,389
Santa Fe*	—	—	—	—	40
Tucson*	14,309	12,923	7,278	8,711	12,008
Veracruz*	1,525	1,233	1,525	1,550	1,243
HYUNDAI TOTAL	**40,004**	**42,149**	**33,859**	**26,062**	**31,063**
Isuzu Truck Light-Duty	—	—	10	5	—
Isuzu Truck Light-Duty*	41	19	17	2	—
ISUZU TOTAL	**41**	**19**	**27**	**7**	**—**
Land Rover Evoque*	412	—	—	—	—
Land Rover LR2*	343	426	549	840	1,054
Land Rover LR3*	—	—	254	544	694
Land Rover LR4*	579	522	73	—	—
Land Rover Range Rover*	419	431	293	244	381
Land Rover Range Rover Sport*	1,475	1,168	837	665	834
JAGUAR LAND ROVER TOTAL	**3,228**	**2,547**	**2,006**	**2,293**	**2,963**
Borrego*	137	302	528	187	—
Rondo*	6,154	6,307	9,835	9,906	7,682
Sedona*	1,290	1,615	2,135	3,615	3,171
Sorento	15,105	10,214	—	—	—
Sorento*	—	—	879	1,398	1,573
Sportage*	7,766	3,498	5,060	5,509	6,393
KIA TOTAL	**30,452**	**21,936**	**18,437**	**20,615**	**18,819**
B-Series	661	2,545	1,638	3,464	4,297

Canada Vehicle Sales

CANADA VEHICLE SALES BY MODEL — continued

Model	2011	2010	2009	2008	2007
CX-7*	6,710	4,466	2,806	3,576	4,729
CX-9*	1,283	1,282	1,021	1,725	2,117
Mazda5*	6,084	7,532	8,638	11,944	11,690
Tribute	3,751	5,290	4,852	5,437	4,666
MAZDA TOTAL	**18,489**	**21,115**	**18,955**	**26,146**	**27,499**
Endeavor	451	382	545	398	826
Montero*	—	—	—	—	10
Outlander*	5,711	8,343	8,530	6,507	6,227
RVR*	7,064	801	—	—	—
MITSUBISHI TOTAL	**13,226**	**9,526**	**9,075**	**6,905**	**7,063**
EX*	1,521	1,925	1,785	2,300	—
FX*	934	1,085	919	1,003	1,094
QX56	—	211	162	160	204
QX56*	470	54	—	—	—
Infiniti Total	**2,925**	**3,275**	**2,866**	**3,463**	**1,298**
Armada	611	413	196	100	153
Frontier	2,512	2,272	1,649	1,608	2,162
Juke*	4,586	825	—	—	—
Murano*	4,862	3,798	3,691	4,557	4,159
NV	569	—	—	—	—
Pathfinder	1,880	1,400	815	1,196	1,944
Quest	—	20	402	904	1,341
Quest*	1,022	—	—	—	—
Rogue*	14,191	13,199	11,054	13,163	2,924
Titan	3,103	1,903	1,377	1,520	1,894
X-Trail*	—	—	—	—	4,579
Xterra	1,258	1,040	613	800	1,469
Nissan Total	**34,594**	**24,870**	**19,797**	**23,848**	**20,625**
NISSAN TOTAL	**37,519**	**28,145**	**22,663**	**27,311**	**21,923**
Cayenne*	1,105	839	718	778	823
PORSCHE TOTAL	**1,105**	**839**	**718**	**778**	**823**
9-7X	—	—	58	116	288
SAAB TOTAL	**—**	**—**	**58**	**116**	**288**
Baja	—	—	—	1	1
Forester*	8,673	8,941	8,638	6,322	3,303
Outback	7,072	6,401	2,070	—	—
Tribeca	460	536	588	925	801
SUBARU TOTAL	**16,205**	**15,878**	**11,296**	**7,248**	**4,105**
Equator	—	155	294	32	—
Vitara*	1,904	2,842	3,333	3,296	3,331
XL7	—	—	592	452	1,336
XL7*	—	—	—	—	14
SUZUKI TOTAL	**1,904**	**2,997**	**4,219**	**3,780**	**4,681**
GX*	414	513	198	291	342
LX*	114	180	255	353	45
RX	4,748	4,679	5,235	2,766	2,162
RX*	2,012	2,704	3,593	3,455	2,503
Lexus Total	**7,288**	**8,076**	**9,281**	**6,865**	**5,052**
4Runner*	2,580	2,820	680	725	1,530
FJ Cruiser*	639	797	899	2,630	4,901
Highlander	4,736	3,344	410	—	—
Highlander*	838	859	4,421	6,486	5,052
Land Cruiser*	158	93	158	261	262
RAV4	21,190	22,025	23,237	445	—
RAV4*	360	785	2,547	20,077	16,329
Sequoia	733	912	800	842	195
Sienna	10,835	9,960	6,345	7,000	9,820
Tacoma	7,711	8,111	9,082	9,673	9,477
Tundra	6,747	7,560	7,637	9,477	11,552
Venza	13,159	12,468	12,375	—	—
Toyota Total	**69,686**	**69,734**	**68,591**	**57,616**	**59,118**
TOYOTA TOTAL	**76,974**	**77,810**	**77,872**	**64,481**	**64,170**
Routan	842	1,010	1,489	355	—
Tiguan*	5,379	5,611	5,075	1,412	—
Touareg*	1,618	706	880	703	654
VOLKSWAGEN TOTAL	**7,839**	**7,327**	**7,444**	**2,470**	**654**
XC60*	1,865	1,540	1,211	—	—
XC70*	942	1,145	1,287	1,492	1,416
XC90*	756	1,194	1,456	1,502	1,923
VOLVO TOTAL	**3,563**	**3,879**	**3,954**	**2,994**	**3,339**
TOTAL LIGHT TRUCKS	**900,031**	**860,351**	**729,677**	**761,101**	**808,977**
TOTAL LIGHT VEHICLES	**1,581,987**	**1,554,700**	**1,458,700**	**1,633,821**	**1,650,562**
TOTAL MED./HVY. TRUCKS	**38,234**	**28,688**	**23,532**	**39,701**	**39,783**
TOTAL VEHICLES	**1,620,221**	**1,583,388**	**1,482,232**	**1,673,522**	**1,690,345**

*Units imported from outside North America.
SOURCE: WardsAuto InfoBank.

Mexico Vehicle Sales

MEXICO VEHICLE SALES BY MODEL

Model	2011	2010	2009	2008	2007
A1*	2,391	186	—	—	—
A3*	1,117	1,368	1,365	1,726	1,609
A4*	1,653	1,622	1,292	1,724	1,529
A5*	814	702	365	349	25
A6*	169	161	310	331	468
A7*	191	—	—	—	—
A8*	26	22	23	37	48
R8*	23	21	26	77	14
TT*	74	86	183	328	435
AUDI TOTAL[1]	**6,458**	**4,168**	**3,564**	**4,572**	**4,128**
1-Series*	813	922	1,055	1,168	977
3-Series*	2,527	2,255	2,247	2,855	3,429
5-Series*	638	518	382	636	755
6-Series*	19	9	21	33	48
7-Series*	62	72	65	63	71
Z4	—	—	35	145	145
Z4*	76	126	87	—	—
BMW Total	**4,135**	**3,902**	**3,892**	**4,900**	**5,425**
Mini Cooper*	2,452	2,093	1,786	2,015	2,070
BMW TOTAL[1]	**6,587**	**5,995**	**5,678**	**6,915**	**7,495**
200 Series	1,217	—	—	—	—
300 Series	308	218	196	412	660
Cirrus Coupe	2	6	16	47	40
Cirrus Sedan	43	344	423	1,012	2,772
Crossfire*	—	—	—	96	40
Neon	—	—	—	—	7
PT Cruiser Convertible	—	—	—	6	54
Chrysler Total	**1,570**	**568**	**635**	**1,573**	**3,573**
Atoz*	6,491	6,454	6,395	8,946	12,088
Attitude*	9,533	10,989	8,060	10,901	9,068
Avenger	3,871	4,375	4,362	8,091	7,798
Caliber	840	764	1,869	4,811	6,993
Challenger	209	233	270	233	—
Charger	742	687	589	3,283	990
I10*	2,682	—	—	—	—
Stratus Sedan	—	—	22	10	3,042
Verna*	—	—	4	5	31
Viper	9	6	5	13	3
Dodge Total	**24,377**	**23,508**	**21,576**	**36,293**	**40,013**
CHRYSLER TOTAL	**25,947**	**24,076**	**22,211**	**37,866**	**43,586**
B-Class*	302	384	304	469	552
C-Class*	3,603	2,579	2,049	2,901	2,657
CL*	2	1	11	19	34
CLK*	—	—	41	79	98
CLS*	37	18	69	114	144
E-Class*	940	700	617	537	713
S-Class*	71	48	65	94	147
SL*	1	12	19	20	26
SLK*	200	91	168	248	322
SLS*	19	40	—	—	—
Mercedes Total[1]	**5,175**	**3,873**	**3,343**	**4,481**	**4,693**
Forfour*	—	—	—	1	39
Fortwo*	1,470	936	678	786	515
Smart Total	**1,470**	**936**	**678**	**787**	**554**
DAIMLER TOTAL	**6,645**	**4,809**	**4,021**	**5,268**	**5,247**
159*	5	—	—	—	—
Giulietta*	13	—	—	—	—
MiTo*	12	—	—	—	—
Alfa Romeo Total	**30**	—	—	—	—
500	599	—	—	—	—
500*	534	278	340	124	—
Albea*	6	306	435	110	—
Bravo*	1	17	109	—	—
Grande Punto*	—	9	610	669	605
Linea*	380	10	—	—	—
Palio*	21	805	608	648	1,460
Panda*	468	179	464	445	330
Stilo*	—	—	29	90	116
Fiat Total	**2,009**	**1,604**	**2,595**	**2,086**	**2,511**
FIAT TOTAL	**2,039**	**1,604**	**2,595**	**2,086**	**2,511**
Crown Victoria	29	82	21	205	140
Fiesta	8,958	5,280	—	—	—
Fiesta*	2,990	5,245	7,394	13,861	18,870
Five Hundred	—	—	1	53	459
Focus	10,915	8,436	8,896	8,230	6,629
Fusion	2,670	3,833	3,718	5,476	5,853
Ikon	—	—	—	501	6,865

Mexico Vehicle Sales

MEXICO VEHICLE SALES BY MODEL — continued

Model	2011	2010	2009	2008	2007
Ikon*	2,307	—	—	—	—
Ka*	—	—	3	441	2,727
Mondeo*	—	—	—	115	824
Mustang	1,272	1,558	1,655	1,769	2,052
Ford Total	**29,141**	**24,434**	**21,688**	**30,651**	**44,419**
LS	—	—	—	—	6
MKS	120	199	222	261	—
MKZ	594	300	337	526	491
Town Car	—	—	—	5	67
Lincoln Total	**714**	**499**	**559**	**792**	**564**
Milan	—	5	10	357	520
Montego	—	—	1	15	83
Mercury Total	**—**	**5**	**11**	**372**	**603**
FORD TOTAL	**29,855**	**24,938**	**22,258**	**31,815**	**45,586**
LaCrosse	224	351	—	—	—
Buick Total	**224**	**351**	**—**	**—**	**—**
BLS*	—	—	2	152	204
CTS	214	238	257	658	323
STS	—	5	14	31	52
XLR	—	—	—	—	1
Cadillac Total	**214**	**243**	**273**	**841**	**580**
Astra*	—	8	250	2,384	2,654
Aveo	36,972	29,409	24,157	14,083	—
Aveo*	—	—	49	5,788	—
Camaro	768	1,079	1,263	—	—
Chevy	38,914	43,964	36,320	56,142	59,621
Corsa*	—	—	6	6,277	20,800
Corvette	3	6	10	22	37
Cruze*	10,838	10,919	2,878	—	—
Epica*	2	152	610	106	—
Impala	—	—	—	1	6
Malibu	2,000	3,123	3,073	5,691	5,988
Meriva*	—	1	134	1,618	3,632
Optra*	24	2,954	10,518	16,828	21,798
Sonic	6,664	—	—	—	—
Spark*	15,718	6,129	—	—	—
Vectra*	—	—	7	117	589
Chevrolet Total	**111,903**	**97,744**	**79,275**	**109,057**	**115,125**
G3	2	13	2,985	1,783	—
G3*	—	4	26	5,784	7,520
G5	—	9	768	2,426	2,592
G6	—	5	124	557	595
Matiz*	12,305	6,315	5,193	9,721	9,587
Solstice	1	25	237	377	458
Pontiac Total	**12,308**	**6,371**	**9,333**	**20,648**	**20,752**
GM TOTAL	**124,649**	**104,709**	**88,881**	**130,546**	**136,457**
RL*	11	21	31	57	92
TL	443	445	656	397	543
TSX*	405	378	366	546	—
Acura Total	**859**	**844**	**1,053**	**1,000**	**635**
Accord	4,396	5,339	6,466	11,828	9,572
City*	3,221	5,949	2,428	—	—
Civic	6,187	5,186	6,295	13,643	13,319
Fit*	2,107	2,658	3,466	3,327	4,745
Honda Total	**15,911**	**19,132**	**18,655**	**28,798**	**27,636**
HONDA TOTAL	**16,770**	**19,976**	**19,708**	**29,798**	**28,271**
Jaguar S-Type*	—	2	6	11	60
Jaguar X-Type*	—	—	—	21	105
Jaguar XF*	41	73	131	175	—
Jaguar XJ*	10	17	6	13	8
Jaguar XK8*	3	4	16	17	26
JAGUAR LAND ROVER TOTAL	**54**	**96**	**159**	**237**	**199**
Mazda2*	2,005	—	—	—	—
Mazda3*	13,559	13,213	9,217	9,502	6,939
Mazda6	2,170	3,216	2,193	2,241	980
MX-5 Miata*	176	149	119	179	261
MAZDA TOTAL	**17,910**	**16,578**	**11,529**	**11,922**	**8,180**
Eclipse	132	161	247	326	729
Galant	—	4	452	356	572
Lancer*	3,522	4,277	5,585	5,525	7,253
MITSUBISHI TOTAL	**3,654**	**4,442**	**6,284**	**6,207**	**8,554**
G35/37*	102	—	—	—	—
M35/45*	54	—	—	—	—
Q45*	—	—	1	—	1
Infiniti Total	**156**	**—**	**1**	**—**	**1**
350Z*	—	—	4	25	40

Mexico Vehicle Sales

MEXICO VEHICLE SALES BY MODEL — continued

Model	2011	2010	2009	2008	2007
370Z*	24	44	69	—	—
Almera*	—	—	—	—	1
Altima	3,263	4,207	3,003	5,213	7,127
Aprio*	39	4,006	4,632	12,140	6,374
Leaf*	3	—	—	—	—
March	18,995	—	—	—	—
Maxima*	114	187	442	367	172
Micra*	—	—	—	120	501
Platina	27	584	2,316	6,288	15,687
Sentra	20,309	19,836	14,318	17,859	22,309
Tiida	41,131	40,091	22,982	24,030	26,424
Tsuru	55,741	61,147	54,463	68,874	63,461
Versa	20,894	—	—	—	—
Nissan Total	**160,540**	**130,102**	**102,229**	**134,916**	**142,096**
NISSAN TOTAL	**160,696**	**130,102**	**102,230**	**134,916**	**142,097**
206*	—	—	53	2,970	6,010
207*	3,046	3,712	4,861	1,892	178
307*	2	47	394	1,525	3,255
308*	154	179	155	129	—
407*	—	2	65	185	447
607*	—	—	—	—	14
Grand Raid*	794	475	532	1,144	1,989
Partner*	800	872	816	1,463	1,694
RCZ*	70	22	—	—	—
PEUGEOT TOTAL	**4,866**	**5,309**	**6,876**	**9,308**	**13,587**
911*	81	95	116	183	165
Boxster*	45	51	61	65	74
Cayman*	44	36	74	93	110
Panamera*	28	45	22	—	—
PORSCHE TOTAL[1]	**198**	**227**	**273**	**341**	**349**
Clio	—	3	4,114	8,098	9,019
Clio*	—	—	19	411	911
Fluence*	4,772	958	—	—	—
Laguna*	—	—	—	5	24
Megane*	—	65	1,723	2,948	3,429
Safrane*	460	776	487	—	—
Sandero*	7,940	8,979	—	—	—
Scala*	5,310	3,018	—	—	—
RENAULT TOTAL	**18,482**	**13,799**	**6,343**	**11,462**	**13,383**
9-3*	1	8	93	247	228
9-5*	—	—	—	3	27
SAAB TOTAL	**1**	**8**	**93**	**250**	**255**
Impreza*	202	152	313	333	116
Legacy	126	93	70	133	136
SUBARU TOTAL	**328**	**245**	**383**	**466**	**252**
Aerio*	—	—	—	—	600
Kizashi*	598	666	48	—	—
SX4*	6,240	4,859	4,515	4,675	1,668
SUZUKI TOTAL	**6,838**	**5,525**	**4,563**	**4,675**	**2,268**
Avanza*	3,672	3,082	3,021	2,825	1,307
Camry	4,167	3,717	3,836	4,980	6,872
Corolla	10,870	8,349	9,249	9,850	9,316
Matrix	10	185	634	1,024	1,033
Prius*	247	168	—	—	—
Yaris*	3,713	5,883	8,934	13,357	11,762
TOYOTA TOTAL	**22,679**	**21,384**	**25,674**	**32,036**	**30,290**
Altea*	842	742	391	87	241
Cordoba*	—	—	3,549	3,535	4,552
Exeo*	228	—	—	—	—
Ibiza*	15,233	11,243	10,216	8,334	9,573
Leon*	1,812	1,395	1,428	1,077	1,119
Toledo*	—	—	—	29	159
SEAT Total	**18,115**	**13,380**	**15,584**	**13,062**	**15,644**
Beetle	2,421	2,445	2,552	3,657	4,365
Beetle Cabrio	1	17	37	47	51
Bora	985	16,447	20,137	23,263	25,104
Derby*	—	—	90	3,008	4,207
Eos*	1	136	74	—	—
Gol*	21,781	24,294	23,699	2,672	—
Golf*	529	508	325	728	1,129
Jetta	83,828	51,847	32,585	41,783	44,395
Lupo*	—	—	99	826	1,934
Passat	1,708	—	—	—	—
Passat*	1,181	1,727	2,170	1,719	2,072
Pointer*	—	—	1,829	25,279	28,300

Mexico Vehicle Sales

MEXICO VEHICLE SALES BY MODEL — continued

Model	2011	2010	2009	2008	2007
Polo*	—	—	—	33	899
Sport Van*	—	54	1,591	2,799	3,650
Volkswagen Total	**112,435**	**97,475**	**85,188**	**105,814**	**116,106**
VOLKSWAGEN TOTAL	**130,550**	**110,855**	**100,772**	**118,876**	**131,750**
30-Series*	208	287	154	376	346
40-Series*	177	315	361	834	1,112
50-Series*	—	—	—	—	8
60-Series*	432	38	9	50	189
70-Series*	13	38	21	44	106
80-Series*	20	44	39	108	186
VOLVO TOTAL	**850**	**722**	**584**	**1,412**	**1,947**
TOTAL CARS	**586,056**	**499,567**	**434,679**	**580,974**	**626,392**
Q5*	1,164	907	877	—	—
Q7*	436	415	429	666	772
AUDI TOTAL[1]	**1,600**	**1,322**	**1,306**	**666**	**772**
X1*	617	526	—	—	—
X3	932	—	—	—	—
X3*	—	191	456	781	1,187
X5	693	759	789	1,008	1,220
X6	257	354	392	211	—
BMW Total	**2,499**	**1,830**	**1,637**	**2,000**	**2,407**
Mini Countryman*	551	—	—	—	—
BMW TOTAL[1]	**3,050**	**1,830**	**1,637**	**2,000**	**2,407**
Aspen	—	4	245	772	982
Pacifica	—	—	6	71	447
PT Cruiser	27	312	887	1,571	2,478
Town & Country	3,122	2,942	2,226	3,154	2,822
Voyager	—	—	8	1,394	8,505
Chrysler Total	**3,149**	**3,258**	**3,372**	**6,962**	**15,234**
Durango	1,345	2	582	2,074	2,880
Journey	12,321	12,879	13,491	10,711	—
Nitro	435	661	1,058	3,000	6,779
Dodge Total	**14,101**	**13,542**	**15,131**	**15,785**	**9,659**
Commander	—	23	79	238	558
Compass	4,083	1,565	2,130	2,960	4,367
Grand Cherokee	5,337	3,742	1,623	2,856	3,250
Liberty	1,706	2,204	2,156	3,726	6,988
Patriot	7,904	7,066	7,676	11,516	10,950
Wrangler	2,143	2,054	1,312	2,345	2,653
Jeep Total	**21,173**	**16,654**	**14,976**	**23,641**	**28,766**
Dakota	2,936	3,778	3,760	5,431	4,283
H100*	1,866	3,373	4,082	6,505	8,008
Ram 1000*	—	9	1,236	1,115	225
Ram Pickup	12,900	13,884	17,569	18,832	18,780
Ram Total	**17,702**	**21,044**	**26,647**	**31,883**	**31,296**
CHRYSLER TOTAL	**56,125**	**54,498**	**60,126**	**78,271**	**84,955**
Mercedes G-Class*	36	46	54	26	4
Mercedes GL	140	149	157	183	263
Mercedes GLK*	624	626	675	162	—
Mercedes M-Class	224	433	451	636	729
Mercedes R-Class	120	36	21	40	64
Mercedes Sprinter Van*	1,333	788	498	1,515	1,844
Mercedes Sprinter Wagon*	53	115	106	175	173
Mercedes Vito Cargo*	49	78	15	—	—
Mercedes Vito Passenger*	69	61	19	—	—
DAIMLER TOTAL[1]	**2,648**	**2,332**	**1,996**	**2,737**	**3,077**
Ducato*	534	352	127	182	1
Idea*	—	6	296	507	407
Strada*	37	540	490	429	381
FIAT TOTAL	**571**	**898**	**913**	**1,118**	**789**
Courier*	2,523	3,020	2,839	4,426	4,910
Econoline	912	972	1,130	1,785	1,800
Ecosport*	1,916	3,774	4,599	9,446	13,909
Edge	3,379	2,817	2,405	3,103	2,710
Escape	10,938	8,916	8,281	12,260	10,857
Expedition	1,109	1,653	2,112	3,135	3,535
Explorer	4,311	3,043	2,783	3,676	3,603
F-Series Light-Duty	16,440	20,733	24,875	37,461	40,030
Freestar	—	—	—	8	160
Ranger	10,528	13,049	13,449	14,826	17,669
Transit*	3,110	2,432	2,211	1,638	215
Ford Total	**55,166**	**60,409**	**64,684**	**91,764**	**99,398**
Mark LT	497	755	541	1,189	1,544
MKX	511	375	263	513	677
Navigator	294	326	342	465	625

Mexico Vehicle Sales

MEXICO VEHICLE SALES BY MODEL — continued

Model	2011	2010	2009	2008	2007
Lincoln Total	**1,302**	**1,456**	**1,146**	**2,167**	**2,846**
Mariner	—	730	660	921	1,024
Mercury Total	**—**	**730**	**660**	**921**	**1,024**
FORD TOTAL	**56,468**	**62,595**	**66,490**	**94,852**	**103,268**
Enclave	879	745	57	—	—
Buick Total	**879**	**745**	**57**	**—**	**—**
Escalade	218	230	178	257	325
Escalade ESV	297	319	252	338	379
Escalade EXT	76	128	133	277	395
SRX	609	708	216	2	2
Cadillac Total	**1,200**	**1,385**	**779**	**874**	**1,101**
Avalanche	184	437	697	1,007	1,915
Captiva Sport*	7,670	8,156	7,739	7,615	274
Colorado	2,295	2,680	2,805	4,389	4,462
Equinox	—	1	72	1,876	5,402
Express	1,464	1,708	1,504	2,687	3,349
HHR	1	4	147	1,132	3,254
Silverado	13,106	16,634	17,395	27,152	28,246
Sonora	—	—	—	—	16
Suburban	1,951	2,413	2,114	3,583	4,431
Tahoe	889	1,030	1,257	2,103	3,249
Tornado*	8,034	8,727	7,158	12,704	14,677
Tracker	—	—	30	2,677	5,093
TrailBlazer	—	—	2	195	1,320
Traverse	1,772	2,061	1,668	—	—
Uplander	—	8	404	2,467	3,821
Zafira*	—	—	—	1	434
Chevrolet Total	**37,366**	**43,859**	**42,992**	**69,588**	**79,943**
Acadia	1,431	1,925	1,979	2,601	2,048
Canyon	556	605	502	587	618
Sierra	911	1,293	828	1,678	1,739
Terrain	983	—	—	—	—
Yukon	523	647	646	1,013	1,268
GMC Total	**4,404**	**4,470**	**3,955**	**5,879**	**5,673**
H2	—	3	32	84	132
H2 SUT	1	—	70	206	262
H3	3	153	341	1,005	1,472
H3T	—	240	739	368	—
Hummer Total	**4**	**396**	**1,182**	**1,663**	**1,866**
Montana SV6	—	—	15	329	581
Torrent	—	16	491	1,340	1,969
Pontiac Total	**—**	**16**	**506**	**1,669**	**2,550**
GM TOTAL	**43,853**	**50,871**	**49,471**	**79,673**	**91,133**
MDX	617	719	593	743	761
RDX	297	293	296	389	455
ZDX	10	20	—	—	—
Acura Total	**924**	**1,032**	**889**	**1,132**	**1,216**
CR-V	10,346	12,650	11,211	16,929	3,941
CR-V*	—	—	5	172	14,134
Crosstour	87	407	112	—	—
Odyssey	5,410	3,029	2,457	4,264	4,391
Pilot	2,333	2,368	2,375	3,244	1,937
Ridgeline	339	404	430	725	912
Honda Total	**18,515**	**18,858**	**16,590**	**25,334**	**25,315**
HONDA TOTAL	**19,439**	**19,890**	**17,479**	**26,466**	**26,531**
Isuzu Truck Light-Duty*	1,629	1,337	972	787	171
ISUZU TOTAL	**1,629**	**1,337**	**972**	**787**	**171**
Land Rover Defender*	57	26	—	—	—
Land Rover Freelander*	—	—	—	—	4
Land Rover LR2*	114	150	170	309	367
Land Rover LR3*	—	—	60	99	179
Land Rover LR4*	85	80	18	—	—
Land Rover Range Rover*	39	34	30	39	82
Land Rover Range Rover Sport*	318	209	154	279	277
JAGUAR LAND ROVER TOTAL	**613**	**499**	**432**	**726**	**909**
CX-7*	9,249	5,420	5,204	7,014	6,089
CX-9*	1,915	2,573	1,661	2,204	1,614
Mazda5*	786	545	520	857	721
MAZDA TOTAL	**11,950**	**8,538**	**7,385**	**10,075**	**8,424**
Endeavor	1,073	1,106	934	1,219	2,039
Grandis*	—	55	343	489	579
L200*	2,234	1,891	2,007	1,672	—
Montero*	362	368	120	400	188
Montero Sport*	413	536	339	152	518
Outlander*	2,760	4,135	4,293	6,665	5,788
MITSUBISHI TOTAL	**6,842**	**8,091**	**8,036**	**10,597**	**9,112**

Mexico Vehicle Sales

MEXICO VEHICLE SALES BY MODEL — continued

Model	2011	2010	2009	2008	2007
FX*	48	—	—	—	—
QX56*	27	—	—	—	—
Infiniti Total	**75**	**—**	**—**	**—**	**—**
Armada	93	94	141	321	445
Cabstar*	193	131	988	1,696	468
Frontier	4,235	1,994	1,052	4,309	5,188
Juke*	503	—	—	—	—
Murano*	318	605	611	1,307	680
Nissan Chassis	23,935	21,044	18,429	25,782	24,187
Nissan Pickup	16,687	14,837	14,324	16,365	17,092
Pathfinder	470	496	512	826	1,345
Quest	—	2	295	1,012	1,414
Quest*	2	—	—	—	—
Rogue*	5,219	5,690	3,765	4,632	892
Titan	146	59	118	435	830
Urvan*	7,202	8,174	8,063	11,057	9,852
X-Trail*	4,966	6,290	5,657	9,347	9,567
Xterra	—	—	1	17	64
Nissan Total	**63,969**	**59,416**	**53,956**	**77,106**	**72,024**
NISSAN TOTAL	**64,044**	**59,416**	**53,956**	**77,106**	**72,024**
3008*	678	400	—	—	—
Expert*	2	177	111	62	—
Manager*	250	308	257	146	—
PEUGEOT TOTAL	**930**	**885**	**368**	**208**	**—**
Cayenne*	341	213	262	414	424
PORSCHE TOTAL[1]	**341**	**213**	**262**	**414**	**424**
Kangoo*	2,273	1,902	2,540	3,171	4,391
Koleos*	1,839	1,979	1,866	590	—
Scenic*	—	—	27	134	344
Trafic*	538	366	724	703	495
RENAULT TOTAL	**4,650**	**4,247**	**5,157**	**4,598**	**5,230**
Forester*	189	165	271	355	207
Outback	40	30	7	18	11
Tribeca	30	60	91	237	233
SUBARU TOTAL	**259**	**255**	**369**	**610**	**451**
Vitara*	2,341	2,407	2,482	3,114	3,220
XL7	—	—	50	215	212
SUZUKI TOTAL	**2,341**	**2,407**	**2,532**	**3,329**	**3,432**
4Runner*	—	—	14	172	576
FJ Cruiser*	233	596	1,234	2,824	2,032
Hiace*	3,575	2,573	3,552	3,679	3,141
Highlander*	2,126	1,767	1,354	1,493	1,293
Hilux	3,523	4,779	4,146	6,162	4,914
Land Cruiser*	30	65	73	148	147
RAV4*	4,684	5,323	5,958	7,491	11,948
Rush*	—	—	649	—	—
Sequoia	373	528	543	267	—
Sienna	7,215	5,619	3,303	4,363	6,580
Tacoma	3,861	3,432	4,129	4,154	4,886
Tundra	290	703	1,362	517	401
TOYOTA TOTAL	**25,910**	**25,385**	**26,317**	**31,270**	**35,918**
Alhambra*	—	—	—	4	25
SEAT Total	**—**	**—**	**—**	**4**	**25**
Amarok*	1,493	581	—	—	—
Crafter*	457	611	636	688	93
Crossfox*	3,484	3,251	3,074	4,953	8,294
Eurovan*	—	299	1,921	3,955	5,299
Pointer Pickup*	—	245	3,686	2,585	2,167
Routan	350	501	1,139	114	—
Saveiro*	3,833	3,223	—	—	—
Sharan*	—	—	—	381	593
Tiguan*	2,994	2,673	1,539	53	—
Touareg*	430	249	323	857	688
Transporter*	1,355	1,224	—	—	—
Volkswagen Total	**14,396**	**12,857**	**12,318**	**13,586**	**17,134**
VOLKSWAGEN TOTAL	**14,396**	**12,857**	**12,318**	**13,590**	**17,159**
XC60*	422	492	181	—	—
XC70*	—	—	—	—	4
XC90*	62	79	170	425	770
VOLVO TOTAL	**484**	**571**	**351**	**425**	**774**
TOTAL LIGHT TRUCKS	**318,143**	**318,937**	**317,873**	**439,518**	**466,960**
TOTAL LIGHT VEHICLES	**904,199**	**818,504**	**752,552**	**1,020,492**	**1,093,352**
TOTAL MED./HVY. TRUCKS	**30,894**	**28,377**	**20,833**	**48,244**	**50,953**
TOTAL VEHICLES	**935,093**	**846,881**	**773,385**	**1,068,736**	**1,144,305**

(1) Models estimated from brand totals for October-December 2011.
*Units imported from outside North America.
SOURCE: WardsAuto InfoBank.

Car, Truck and Bus Registrations by State

U.S. TOTAL VEHICLE REGISTRATIONS BY STATE

State	Cars 2010	Cars 2009	Trucks and Buses 2010	Trucks and Buses 2009	Total 2010	Total 2009
Alabama	2,211,550	2,171,584	2,442,288	2,439,261	4,653,838	4,610,845
Alaska	228,407	236,223	482,037	459,059	710,444	695,282
Arizona	2,201,251	2,228,172	2,118,759	2,129,462	4,320,010	4,357,634
Arkansas	945,198	947,406	1,128,213	1,089,995	2,073,411	2,037,401
California	17,977,605	19,972,837	13,036,523	14,460,369	31,014,128	34,433,206
Colorado	1,890,748	2,345,502	2,289,550	2,927,972	4,180,298	5,273,474
Connecticut	1,985,500	1,983,114	1,096,511	1,088,461	3,082,011	3,071,575
Delaware	434,037	463,779	364,975	379,578	799,012	843,357
Dist. of Columbia	160,090	166,519	51,563	51,129	211,653	217,648
Florida	7,295,121	7,597,789	7,077,686	7,716,968	14,372,807	15,314,757
Georgia	3,738,952	4,134,274	3,962,990	4,373,019	7,701,942	8,507,293
Hawaii	450,398	448,535	454,069	446,801	904,467	895,336
Idaho	541,038	563,021	783,947	811,946	1,324,985	1,374,967
Illinois	5,772,947	5,824,074	4,305,671	4,066,798	10,078,618	9,890,872
Indiana	2,986,033	3,082,306	2,711,980	2,722,693	5,698,013	5,804,999
Iowa	1,691,090	1,736,330	1,621,615	1,626,778	3,312,705	3,363,108
Kansas	880,308	874,869	1,555,938	1,550,394	2,436,246	2,425,263
Kentucky	1,890,079	1,952,420	1,699,039	1,632,081	3,589,118	3,584,501
Louisiana	1,917,283	1,940,586	2,168,845	2,092,825	4,086,128	4,033,411
Maine	518,779	538,469	535,063	517,451	1,053,842	1,055,920
Maryland	2,590,777	2,597,592	1,966,229	1,886,006	4,557,006	4,483,598
Massachusetts	3,144,691	3,128,371	2,189,224	2,133,432	5,333,915	5,261,803
Michigan	5,135,712	4,371,772	4,150,355	3,541,352	9,286,067	7,913,124
Minnesota	2,459,074	2,506,177	2,388,897	2,289,918	4,847,971	4,796,095
Mississippi	1,143,527	1,155,792	872,388	869,898	2,015,915	2,025,690
Missouri	2,578,536	2,559,639	2,574,889	2,344,562	5,153,425	4,904,201
Montana	351,574	370,107	574,280	554,843	925,854	924,950
Nebraska	773,080	784,194	1,029,418	1,008,829	1,802,498	1,793,023
Nevada	690,124	706,912	671,547	690,429	1,361,671	1,397,341
New Hampshire	618,598	639,635	584,376	572,858	1,202,974	1,212,493
New Jersey	3,971,896	3,705,322	2,656,184	2,408,485	6,628,080	6,113,807
New Mexico	702,897	698,100	909,594	922,604	1,612,491	1,620,704
New York	7,950,192	8,725,551	2,304,907	2,519,657	10,255,099	11,245,208
North Carolina	3,281,831	3,451,087	2,460,998	2,596,152	5,742,829	6,047,239
North Dakota	340,756	347,356	394,888	374,715	735,644	722,071
Ohio	5,614,698	6,318,803	4,186,235	4,703,326	9,800,933	11,022,129
Oklahoma	1,581,768	1,670,353	1,775,696	1,726,042	3,357,464	3,396,395
Oregon	1,488,595	1,439,985	1,561,659	1,606,388	3,050,254	3,046,373
Pennsylvania	5,682,239	5,818,056	4,308,702	4,039,255	9,990,941	9,857,311
Rhode Island	478,624	481,905	303,814	306,718	782,438	788,623
South Carolina	2,030,632	1,974,494	1,630,246	1,639,906	3,660,878	3,614,400
South Dakota	406,531	401,661	519,017	524,507	925,548	926,168
Tennessee	2,734,382	2,854,803	2,379,531	2,284,859	5,113,913	5,139,662
Texas	8,331,127	8,680,858	8,862,432	9,414,100	17,193,559	18,094,958
Utah	1,316,966	1,217,120	1,337,749	1,236,759	2,654,715	2,453,879
Vermont	293,084	292,317	273,566	265,053	566,650	557,370
Virginia	3,510,417	3,732,468	2,638,377	2,569,367	6,148,794	6,301,835
Washington	2,599,791	3,101,571	2,082,999	2,479,097	4,682,790	5,580,668
West Virginia	702,587	700,103	732,936	712,375	1,435,523	1,412,478
Wisconsin	2,461,343	2,526,673	2,506,434	2,347,643	4,967,777	4,874,316
Wyoming	209,777	214,199	453,476	438,125	663,253	652,324
Total	**130,892,240**	**136,380,785**	**111,168,305**	**113,590,300**	**242,060,545**	**249,971,085**

NOTE: Registrations include both privately and publicly owned motor vehicles, except those owned by the military.
SOURCE: U.S. Department of Transportation, Federal Highway Administration.

Truck Registrations by State and Type

U.S. TOTAL TRUCK REGISTRATIONS BY STATE AND TYPE, 2010

State	Pickups	Vans	Sport Utilities	Other Light	Truck Tractors	Other Med./Hvy.	Total
Alabama	1,260,770	266,457	778,595	—	90,446	37,207	2,433,475
Alaska	219,405	50,280	185,401	3,977	4,394	15,785	479,242
Arizona	834,774	296,219	870,482	9,251	22,867	80,088	2,113,681
Arkansas	585,574	121,246	386,330	4,698	19,523	2,976	1,120,347
California	4,886,255	2,292,101	5,643,778	56,419	78,300	24,138	12,980,991
Colorado	272,253	87,699	372,357	3,096	8,921	1,535,881	2,280,207
Connecticut	289,519	199,971	554,108	5,281	2,420	34,148	1,085,447
Delaware	51,609	27,707	75,759	2,781	1,534	203,332	362,722
Dist. of Columbia	4,894	8,481	23,816	336	231	11,027	48,785
Florida	1,851,181	1,042,685	2,649,489	23,165	241,681	1,216,973	7,025,174
Georgia	1,650,460	589,620	1,650,300	18,248	22,300	8,480	3,939,408
Hawaii	179,741	71,651	181,426	2,307	1,218	12,977	449,320
Idaho	392,740	70,786	223,769	3,338	32,126	57,350	780,109
Illinois	1,164,887	940,641	1,935,434	15,724	70,750	159,342	4,286,778
Indiana	1,065,965	526,225	984,164	9,833	58,316	34,088	2,678,591
Iowa	704,378	262,392	449,841	5,319	49,410	143,285	1,614,625
Kansas	636,856	331,644	381,091	8,541	28,263	165,627	1,552,022
Kentucky	790,121	232,983	555,405	6,294	27,415	72,099	1,684,317
Louisiana	1,082,660	203,239	738,293	7,440	42,815	71,690	2,146,137
Maine	239,715	70,427	186,861	2,146	3,624	28,690	531,463
Maryland	541,051	391,986	951,240	9,916	17,101	42,706	1,954,000
Massachusetts	555,709	404,337	1,130,705	10,965	13,142	62,394	2,177,252
Michigan	1,151,811	753,201	1,454,566	11,075	17,211	734,117	4,121,981
Minnesota	834,629	437,880	811,330	11,313	35,733	239,469	2,370,354
Mississippi	458,884	86,563	272,144	3,782	8,776	32,662	862,811
Missouri	1,072,767	407,015	911,884	9,603	53,902	108,634	2,563,805
Montana	263,629	50,024	158,958	1,845	19,667	77,789	571,912
Nebraska	413,234	140,111	328,695	3,819	36,305	99,570	1,021,734
Nevada	226,536	70,579	272,177	1,999	7,846	89,529	668,666
New Hampshire	212,940	84,823	251,534	3,135	5,815	24,106	582,353
New Jersey	502,103	554,549	1,435,928	16,425	13,808	109,183	2,631,996
New Mexico	419,190	87,464	288,523	3,260	13,177	94,650	906,264
New York	506,959	513,781	1,184,101	14,481	7,136	9,368	2,235,826
North Carolina	940,225	342,702	880,311	10,262	46,434	206,684	2,426,618
North Dakota	175,825	44,988	98,749	1,297	9,961	61,584	392,404
Ohio	1,438,500	860,305	1,700,300	17,152	41,809	81,264	4,139,330
Oklahoma	835,971	179,829	494,098	6,793	13,110	225,767	1,755,568
Oregon	626,041	215,523	551,308	6,913	21,385	124,429	1,545,599
Pennsylvania	1,245,420	739,156	1,894,208	15,407	71,377	309,666	4,275,234
Rhode Island	84,044	57,919	145,817	1,211	3,472	9,583	302,046
South Carolina	665,268	221,657	636,441	7,024	21,631	58,798	1,610,819
South Dakota	232,509	67,983	151,481	1,973	19,609	43,140	516,695
Tennessee	1,026,938	320,547	867,700	8,309	64,921	69,576	2,357,991
Texas	3,912,100	985,300	3,750,631	31,017	72,100	14,538	8,765,686
Utah	536,807	175,876	525,629	5,940	63,468	28,645	1,336,365
Vermont	111,515	34,192	109,679	989	2,943	12,226	271,544
Virginia	880,650	441,278	1,146,760	10,628	42,258	100,980	2,622,554
Washington	936,400	330,200	760,777	12,666	24,600	6,248	2,070,891
West Virginia	332,196	78,759	255,249	2,157	11,582	50,301	730,244
Wisconsin	849,823	496,554	884,471	8,448	53,538	198,149	2,490,983
Wyoming	218,626	30,611	130,444	1,772	4,411	64,024	449,888
Total	**40,372,057**	**17,298,146**	**43,262,537**	**439,770**	**1,644,782**	**7,304,962**	**110,322,254**

NOTE: The registrations given in this table are as reported by the states in most instances, but have been supplemented in some cases by estimates by USDOT based on data from other sources.
SOURCE: U.S. Department of Transportation, Federal Highway Administration.

Bus Registrations by State

U.S. TOTAL BUS REGISTRATIONS BY STATE, 2010

State	Private and Commercial		Publicly Owned		Total Privately and Publicly Owned		
	Commercial Buses[1]	School and Other[2]	Federal	School[3]	Commercial and Federal	School	Total Buses
Alabama	2,159	218	45	6,391	2,204	6,609	8,813
Alaska	1,709	603	86	397	1,795	1,000	2,795
Arizona	1,210	242	430	3,196	1,640	3,438	5,078
Arkansas	52	1,611	33	6,170	85	7,781	7,866
California	27,955	9,296	532	17,749	28,487	27,045	55,532
Colorado	2,022	2,954	49	4,318	2,071	7,272	9,343
Connecticut	3,109	7,027	14	914	3,123	7,941	11,064
Delaware	478	1,091	6	678	484	1,769	2,253
District of Columbia	2,229	117	313	119	2,542	236	2,778
Florida	3,747	1,266	236	47,263	3,983	48,529	52,512
Georgia	1,609	3,288	120	18,565	1,729	21,853	23,582
Hawaii	2,328	886	32	1,503	2,360	2,389	4,749
Idaho	642	713	170	2,313	812	3,026	3,838
Illinois	5,824	12,722	97	250	5,921	12,972	18,893
Indiana	4,366	5,165	63	23,795	4,429	28,960	33,389
Iowa	1,372	303	15	5,300	1,387	5,603	6,990
Kansas	348	1,008	14	2,546	362	3,554	3,916
Kentucky	557	824	180	13,161	737	13,985	14,722
Louisiana	1,170	14,511	28	6,999	1,198	21,510	22,708
Maine	151	352	14	3,083	165	3,435	3,600
Maryland	2,943	3,874	172	5,240	3,115	9,114	12,229
Massachusetts	3,769	7,492	94	617	3,863	8,109	11,972
Michigan	2,436	9,000	88	16,850	2,524	25,850	28,374
Minnesota	2,315	5,287	8	10,933	2,323	16,220	18,543
Mississippi	962	2,660	89	5,866	1,051	8,526	9,577
Missouri	800	2,896	41	7,347	841	10,243	11,084
Montana	393	609	22	1,344	415	1,953	2,368
Nebraska	616	864	11	6,193	627	7,057	7,684
Nevada	2,406	180	161	134	2,567	314	2,881
New Hampshire	377	1,259	3	384	380	1,643	2,023
New Jersey	4,925	14,366	65	4,832	4,990	19,198	24,188
New Mexico	410	1,701	351	868	761	2,569	3,330
New York	15,344	9,700	252	43,785	15,596	53,485	69,081
North Carolina	2,639	8,024	63	23,654	2,702	31,678	34,380
North Dakota	179	685	75	1,545	254	2,230	2,484
Ohio	19,236	2,377	96	25,196	19,332	27,573	46,905
Oklahoma	366	1,912	156	17,694	522	19,606	20,128
Oregon	1,699	3,245	79	11,037	1,778	14,282	16,060
Pennsylvania	10,223	20,750	140	2,355	10,363	23,105	33,468
Rhode Island	324	1,431	6	7	330	1,438	1,768
South Carolina	1,187	4,679	37	13,524	1,224	18,203	19,427
South Dakota	415	443	135	1,329	550	1,772	2,322
Tennessee	2,670	1,578	91	17,201	2,761	18,779	21,540
Texas	3,328	15,635	286	77,497	3,614	93,132	96,746
Utah	393	143	43	805	436	948	1,384
Vermont	102	556	5	1,359	107	1,915	2,022
Virginia	2,152	243	278	13,150	2,430	13,393	15,823
Washington	978	2,070	225	8,835	1,203	10,905	12,108
West Virginia	734	63	51	1,844	785	1,907	2,692
Wisconsin	1,574	8,967	27	4,883	1,601	13,850	15,451
Wyoming	892	129	11	2,556	903	2,685	3,588
Total	**149,824**	**197,015**	**5,638**	**493,574**	**155,462**	**690,589**	**846,051**

SOURCE: U.S. Department of Transportation, Federal Highway Administration.
(1) Includes municipally owned transit buses.
(2) In some instances church, industrial and other private buses are included here; and in other instances privately-owned school buses could not be segregated from commercial buses, and are included with the latter.
(3) This column consists primarily of publicly owned school buses but includes a few privately owned school, institutional, and industrial buses registered free or at a reduced rate.

School Bus Ownership and Usage by State

U.S. SCHOOL BUS OWNERSHIP AND USAGE BY STATE, 2009-2010 SCHOOL YEAR

	Pupils Transported at Public Expense	Bus Ownership			Total Miles of Service	Total Expenditures for Pupil Transportation
		Publicly Owned	Contractor	Total		
Alabama	377,045	7,033	308	7,341	84,199,680	245,100,957
Alaska	NA	NA	820	820	NA	NA
Arizona	NA	8,050	450	8,500	NA	NA
Arkansas	257,604	4,794	183	4,977	47,929,860	—
California	976,135	16,009	8,788	24,797	242,053,356	—
Colorado	331,907	6,000	300	6,300	53,120,711	49,626,462
Connecticut	467,168	NA	NA	—	NA	NA
Delaware	107,800	541	1,199	1,740	23,000,000	85,300,000
Florida	1,014,346	13,877	1,111	14,988	264,853,115	NA
Georgia	1,052,706	NA	NA	—	145,592,280	130,310,693
Hawaii	40,000	—	824	824	31,000	—
Idaho	110,598	2,058	842	2,900	24,469,957	60,842,061
Illinois	1,201,290	NA	NA	—	245,432,107	NA
Indiana	NA	13,500	2,853	16,353	NA	—
Iowa	235,346	4,000	300	4,300	41,561,331	NA
Kansas	206,000	2,932	1,299	4,231	62,343,802	—
Kentucky	380,881	8,393	—	8,393	96,744,440	170,307,817
Louisiana	464,686	4,538	2,303	6,841	186,097	NA
Maine	152,000	2,079	NA	2,079	29,343,769	NA
Maryland	614,350	3,796	3,357	7,153	123,363,711	NA
Massachusetts	500,000	NA	NA	—	NA	NA
Michigan	741,308	15,315	1,282	16,597	171,193,112	NA
Minnesota	604,918	5,413	9,135	14,548	NA	NA
Mississippi	457,439	5,195	324	5,519	47,669,244	NA
Missouri	561,993	6,801	4,020	10,821	43,746,545	NA
Montana	57,367	1,240	1,596	2,836	17,911,845	—
Nebraska	77,885	2,107	1,128	3,235	28,724,458	89,182,881
Nevada	116,336	2,376	—	2,376	29,570,614	NA
New Hampshire	136,541	482	2,181	2,663	NA	NA
New Jersey	726,628	NA	NA	—	NA	NA
New Mexico	322,956	667	1,557	2,224	34,384,871	86,343,110
New York	1,942,503	24,439	20,000	44,439	215,321,369	NA
North Carolina	776,686	13,877	67	13,944	178,454,236	362,016,094
North Dakota	93,715	970	335	1,305	19,020,047	20,716,355
Ohio	898,363	13,540	1,374	14,914	167,234,940	445,135,558
Oklahoma	372,049	7,300	NA	7,300	NA	NA
Oregon	282,859	3,474	2,242	5,716	57,861,565	na
Pennsylvania	1,377,157	5,039	16,495	21,534	401,173,623	NA
Rhode Island	156,454	335	1,356	1,691	NA	NA
South Carolina	701,718	5,070	NA	5,070	80,677,774	109,121,287
South Dakota	51,856	NA	NA	—	13,903,935	—
Tennessee	638,758	7,402	1,502	8,904	55,993,320	NA
Texas	1,442,638	NA	NA	—	296,934,668	NA
Utah	191,759	2,655	40	2,695	25,444,228	63,062,465
Vermont	NA	NA	NA	—	NA	NA
Virginia	918,457	13,982	149	14,131	125,284,271	NA
Washington	445,635	8,794	1,334	10,128	92,434,139	253,470,334
West Virginia	222,798	3,168	—	3,168	36,675,000	217,510,000
Wisconsin	554,000	2,000	8,000	10,000	NA	NA
Wyoming	37,450	1,743	—	1,743	19,332,753	38,289,780
Total	**23,398,088**	**250,984**	**99,054**	**350,038**	**3,643,171,773**	**2,426,335,854**

NOTE: NA Not available.
SOURCE: Bobit Publishing Company, School Bus Fleet Fact Book.

Government Ownership of Vehicles by State

U.S. GOVERNMENT OWNERSHIP OF VEHICLES BY STATE, 2010

State	Federal[1] Cars	Trucks	Buses	Total	State, County and Municipal[2] Cars	Trucks	Buses	Total	Total Government Owned Vehicles
Alabama	1,703	5,427	45	7,175	15,843	22,770	6,391	45,004	52,179
Alaska	515	3,504	86	4,105	2,236	7,292	397	9,925	14,030
Arizona	2,278	10,180	430	12,888	15,896	9,858	3,196	28,950	41,838
Arkansas	950	3,037	33	4,020	9,031	8,830	6,170	24,031	28,051
California	12,953	49,298	532	62,783	199,027	273,341	17,749	490,117	552,900
Colorado	1,781	9,685	49	11,515	9,009	18,369	4,318	31,696	43,211
Connecticut	903	4,829	14	5,746	11,011	25,718	914	37,643	43,389
Delaware	278	852	6	1,136	6,869	2,320	678	9,867	11,003
Dist. of Columbia	2,596	4,139	313	7,048	1,793	2,899	119	4,811	11,859
Florida	4,830	16,508	236	21,574	116,427	160,377	47,263	324,067	345,641
Georgia	2,541	8,036	120	10,697	30,321	75,292	18,565	124,178	134,875
Hawaii	524	1,903	32	2,459	6,770	7,681	1,503	15,954	18,413
Idaho	676	5,421	170	6,267	5,674	9,170	2,313	17,157	23,424
Illinois	3,580	11,726	97	15,403	67,156	1,454	250	68,860	84,263
Indiana	1,408	4,892	63	6,363	24,335	41,643	23,795	89,773	96,136
Iowa	704	3,626	15	4,345	9,000	21,700	5,300	36,000	40,345
Kansas	812	3,492	14	4,318	7,301	16,383	2,546	26,230	30,548
Kentucky	1,614	4,813	180	6,607	25,662	4,210	13,161	43,033	49,640
Louisiana	1,655	5,327	28	7,010	61,280	22,865	6,999	91,144	98,154
Maine	437	1,333	14	1,784	5,963	13,432	3,083	22,478	24,262
Maryland	2,621	7,557	172	10,350	11,827	17,370	5,240	34,437	44,787
Massachusetts	2,708	7,542	94	10,344	19,739	41,329	617	61,685	72,029
Michigan	2,661	9,625	88	12,374	49,046	74,322	16,850	140,218	152,592
Minnesota	1,527	6,020	8	7,555	11,922	24,729	10,933	47,584	55,139
Mississippi	1,356	3,830	89	5,275	11,096	9,267	5,866	26,229	31,504
Missouri	3,098	5,193	41	8,332	5,010	14,444	7,347	26,801	35,133
Montana	894	5,434	22	6,350	5,965	14,893	1,344	22,202	28,552
Nebraska	1,090	3,010	11	4,111	14,636	21,021	6,193	41,850	45,961
Nevada	1,161	6,994	161	8,316	9,074	8,196	134	17,404	25,720
New Hampshire	601	1,199	3	1,803	3,884	11,638	384	15,906	17,709
New Jersey	2,231	11,157	65	13,453	43,416	96,697	4,832	144,945	158,398
New Mexico	1,374	7,362	351	9,087	15,297	18,362	868	34,527	43,614
New York	8,479	19,739	252	28,470	71,338	76,353	43,785	191,476	219,946
North Carolina	1,833	5,840	63	7,736	30,194	46,485	23,654	100,333	108,069
North Dakota	603	2,081	75	2,759	3,733	6,696	1,545	11,974	14,733
Ohio	3,129	9,777	96	13,002	72,086	83,665	25,196	180,947	193,949
Oklahoma	1,522	5,272	156	6,950	12,617	51,980	17,694	82,291	89,241
Oregon	1,385	9,778	79	11,242	29,971	25,782	11,037	66,790	78,032
Pennsylvania	5,104	13,761	140	19,005	39,162	58,341	2,355	99,858	118,863
Rhode Island	241	1,201	6	1,448	4,736	4,210	7	8,953	10,401
South Carolina	1,596	5,305	37	6,938	10,424	23,722	13,524	47,670	54,608
South Dakota	566	2,871	135	3,572	4,406	11,758	1,329	17,493	21,065
Tennessee	3,382	10,341	91	13,814	18,883	56,996	17,201	93,080	106,894
Texas	6,346	25,070	286	31,702	126,258	239,219	77,497	442,974	474,676
Utah	935	4,806	43	5,784	11,437	12,955	805	25,197	30,981
Vermont	335	519	5	859	3,011	6,416	1,359	10,786	11,645
Virginia	2,560	9,557	278	12,395	28,192	23,315	13,150	64,657	77,052
Washington	2,820	13,578	225	16,623	18,239	28,356	8,835	55,430	72,053
West Virginia	885	2,163	51	3,099	12,012	23,280	1,844	37,136	40,235
Wisconsin	1,113	5,152	27	6,292	16,260	45,357	4,883	66,500	72,792
Wyoming	390	3,139	11	3,540	6,629	13,566	2,556	22,751	26,291
Total	107,284	382,901	5,638	495,823	1,351,104	1,936,324	493,574	3,781,002	4,276,825

(1) Federal data is 2009. Vehicles of the civilian branches of the federal government are given in this table. Vehicles of the military services are not included. Distribution by state is estimated by the Federal Highway Administration.
(2) This information, compiled chiefly from reports of state authorities, is incomplete in many cases. Some states give state owned vehicles only; others exclude certain classes, such as fire apparatus and police vehicles. For the states not reporting state, county and municipal vehicles separately from private and commercial vehicles and those reporting unsegregated totals only, classification by vehicle type has been estimated on the basis of other available data.
SOURCE: U.S. Department of Transportation, Federal Highway Administration.

Vehicles in Operation by Year

U.S. VEHICLES IN OPERATION BY YEAR

Year	Cars	Trucks	Total	% Change	Truck % of Total
2011	127,576,670	121,354,963	248,931,633	0.3	48.8
2010	129,052,669	119,178,682	248,231,351	-0.3	48.0
2009	132,500,000	116,472,046	248,972,046	-0.3	46.8
2008	135,882,003	113,930,720	249,812,723	0.4	45.6
2007	135,222,259	113,478,738	248,700,997	1.7	45.6
2006	135,046,706	109,595,904	244,642,610	2.6	44.8
2005	132,908,828	105,475,340	238,384,168	2.7	44.2
2004	132,469,269	99,697,867	232,167,136	2.8	42.9
2003	131,072,466	94,809,637	225,882,103	2.2	42.0
2002	129,906,797	91,120,324	221,027,121	2.0	41.2
2001	128,714,022	87,968,915	216,682,937	1.6	40.6
2000	127,720,809	85,578,504	213,299,313	1.8	40.1
1999	126,868,744	82,640,417	209,509,161	2.2	39.4
1998	125,965,709	79,076,930	205,042,639	2.0	38.6
1997	124,672,920	76,397,477	201,070,397	1.4	38.0
1996	124,612,787	73,680,672	198,293,459	2.5	37.2
1995	123,241,881	70,198,512	193,440,393	2.5	36.3
1994	121,996,580	66,717,417	188,713,997	1.3	35.4
1993	121,055,398	65,260,066	186,315,464	2.6	35.0
1992	120,346,746	61,172,404	181,519,150	--	33.7
1991	123,327,046	58,178,883	181,505,929	1.2	32.1
1990	123,276,268	56,022,934	179,299,202	1.9	31.2
1989	122,758,378	53,201,657	175,960,035	2.5	30.2
1988	121,519,074	50,221,502	171,740,576	2.7	29.2
1987	119,848,769	47,344,319	167,193,088	3.1	28.3
1986	117,268,071	44,825,523	162,093,594	3.2	27.7
1985	114,662,333	42,386,882	157,049,215	3.2	27.0
1984	112,018,640	40,142,872	152,161,512	3.4	26.4
1983	108,961,215	38,143,304	147,104,519	2.3	25.9
1982	106,867,108	36,986,537	143,853,645	1.4	25.7
1981	105,838,582	36,069,197	141,907,779	1.5	25.4
1980	104,563,781	35,267,535	139,831,316	1.9	25.2
1979	104,676,507	32,582,991	137,259,498	2.8	23.7
1978	102,956,713	30,564,701	133,521,414	4.2	22.9
1977	99,903,594	28,221,661	128,125,255	3.0	22.0
1976	97,818,221	26,560,296	124,378,517	3.6	21.4
1975	95,240,602	24,812,843	120,053,445	3.6	20.7
1974	92,607,551	23,312,245	115,919,796	4.2	20.1
1973	89,805,159	21,411,931	111,217,090	4.7	19.3
1972	86,438,957	19,772,938	106,211,895	4.5	18.6
1971	83,137,324	18,462,287	101,599,611	3.5	18.2
1970	80,448,463	17,687,505	98,135,968	3.2	18.0
1969	78,494,938	16,586,368	95,081,306	4.4	17.4
1968	75,358,034	15,684,917	91,042,951	3.5	17.2
1967	72,967,686	14,988,491	87,956,177	2.7	17.0
1966	71,263,738	14,356,591	85,620,329	4.3	16.8
1965	68,939,770	13,126,579	82,066,349	4.5	16.0
1964	66,051,415	12,444,964	78,496,379	4.1	15.9
1963	63,493,277	11,902,039	75,395,316	4.2	15.8
1962	60,919,579	11,463,381	72,382,960	3.6	15.8
1961	58,854,380	11,042,770	69,897,150	2.9	15.8
1960	57,102,676	10,802,959	67,905,635	3.5	15.9
1959	55,086,761	10,532,145	65,618,906	4.9	16.1
1958	52,492,509	10,056,567	62,549,076	2.2	16.1

NOTE: Data as of July 1 each calendar year except 2009, which is Oct. 1. Beginning in 2010, data as of Dec. 31.
SOURCE: R.L. Polk Company.

U.S. Market Used Vehicle Sales

USED VEHICLE SALES (in Thousands)

Year	Franchised Dealers	Independent Dealers	Casual	Total
2011	13,845	13,765	11,182	38,792
2010	12,816	13,010	11,057	36,883
2009	12,820	11,712	10,960	35,492
2008	13,190	11,742	11,599	36,531
2007	14,285	13,077	14,056	41,418
2006	14,319	13,710	14,536	42,565
2005	16,450	14,210	13,478	44,138
2004	15,953	14,751	11,841	42,545
2003	16,171	13,732	13,668	43,571
2002	16,470	13,078	13,478	43,026
2001	15,945	14,416	12,263	42,624
2000	16,178	13,559	11,883	41,620
1999	16,504	12,786	11,448	40,738
1998	15,684	13,182	11,976	40,842
1997	15,796	12,685	12,757	41,238
1996	15,713	13,247	11,871	40,831

SOURCE: CNW Marketing Research, Inc.

AVERAGE USED VEHICLE TRANSACTION PRICES

Year	Franchised Dealers	Independent Dealers	Casual	Total
2011	$10,416	$9,062	$8,124	$9,275
2010	$10,345	$8,875	$6,874	$8,715
2009	$10,243	$8,459	$6,451	$8,483
2008	$9,643	$8,358	$5,725	$7,986
2007	$10,100	$8,650	$5,810	$8,186
2006	$9,750	$8,492	$5,838	$8,009
2005	$10,516	$8,545	$4,471	$8,036
2004	$11,414	$8,490	$4,263	$8,410
2003	$12,177	$7,632	$4,002	$8,180
2002	$12,537	$7,157	$3,688	$8,130
2001	$12,238	$8,275	$4,316	$8,618
2000	$12,748	$7,613	$4,539	$8,896
1999	$12,630	$7,590	$4,505	$8,828
1998	$12,165	$7,172	$4,190	$8,341
1997	$12,350	$7,155	$4,164	$8,399
1996	$12,256	$7,076	$4,283	$8,257

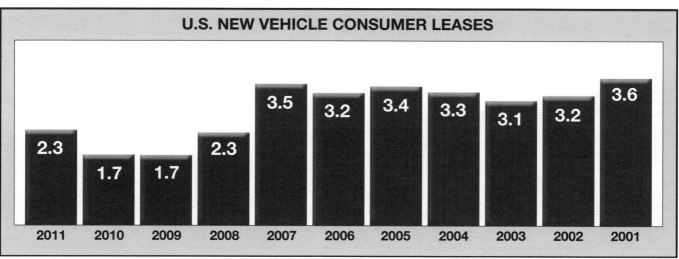

U.S. NEW VEHICLE CONSUMER LEASES

2011	2010	2009	2008	2007	2006	2005	2004	2003	2002	2001
2.3	1.7	1.7	2.3	3.5	3.2	3.4	3.3	3.1	3.2	3.6

NOTE: Units in thousands. SOURCE: CNW Marketing Research, Inc.

Light Vehicle Fleet Registrations

LIGHT VEHICLE FLEET REGISTRATIONS BY MODEL YEAR, 2011

Make	Commercial	Rental	Government	Total Fleet	Total Sales	Fleet % of Total Sales
Audi	1,381	3,402	15	4,798	81,165	5.9
BMW/Mini	1,959	2,154	37	4,150	221,456	1.9
Buick	1,324	16,113	90	17,527	116,380	15.1
Cadillac	971	8,402	18	9,391	66,874	14.0
Chevrolet	33,507	235,591	16,004	285,102	766,282	37.2
Chrysler	2,139	36,358	94	38,591	119,961	32.2
Dodge	8,677	76,768	7,358	92,803	211,020	44.0
Fiat	36	4,503	2	4,541	17,603	25.8
Ford	83,677	143,023	43,866	270,566	712,144	38.0
Honda/Acura	2,865	4,513	327	7,705	622,687	1.2
Hyundai/Kia	2,477	74,842	122	77,441	691,612	11.2
Jaguar	164	261	—	425	11,441	3.7
Lincoln/Mercury	2,073	7,555	32	9,660	49,397	19.6
Mazda	955	29,996	54	31,005	159,896	19.4
Mercedes-Benz	1,793	4,839	35	6,667	148,562	4.5
Mitsubishi	114	14,345	4	14,463	43,041	33.6
Nissan/Infiniti	11,271	124,286	750	136,307	624,653	21.8
Pontiac	1	1	—	2	13	15.4
Porsche	210	150	2	362	15,961	2.3
Saab	98	790	—	888	5,555	16.0
Smart	377	374	16	767	4,709	16.3
Subaru	2,035	4,208	49	6,292	184,161	3.4
Suzuki	108	1,212	5	1,325	19,339	6.9
Toyota/Lexus	11,818	103,057	1,098	115,973	865,602	13.4
Volkswagen	1,978	23,129	49	25,156	273,871	9.2
Volvo	816	5,411	5	6,232	36,827	16.9
Other	331	128	161	620	3,547	17.5
Total Cars	**173,155**	**925,411**	**70,193**	**1,168,759**	**6,073,759**	**19.2**
Audi	875	2,340	19	3,234	32,901	9.8
Azure	116	4	25	145	164	88.4
BMW	2,016	1,195	22	3,233	69,854	4.6
Buick	499	6,466	17	6,982	56,979	12.3
Cadillac	1,056	5,356	17	6,429	79,558	8.1
Chevrolet	114,373	150,952	30,402	295,727	1,029,879	28.7
Chrysler	685	28,510	65	29,260	95,358	30.7
Dodge	38,830	116,116	12,389	167,335	499,257	33.5
Ford	184,177	186,330	48,356	418,863	1,357,781	30.8
Freightliner	1,156	529	118	1,803	3,644	49.5
GMC	17,769	42,120	3,000	62,889	393,905	16.0
Honda/Acura	4,240	868	224	5,332	518,132	1.0
Hyundai/Kia	2,931	40,040	107	43,078	430,752	10.0
Jeep	7,806	59,410	1,417	68,633	413,196	16.6
Land Rover	1,023	428	4	1,455	35,730	4.1
Lincoln/Mercury	911	1,879	8	2,798	35,545	7.9
Mazda	557	17,462	68	18,087	91,021	19.9
Mercedes-Benz	7,153	2,682	80	9,915	95,540	10.4
Mitsubishi	194	7,520	14	7,728	35,245	21.9
Nissan/Infiniti	5,421	29,860	289	35,570	396,656	9.0
Porsche	395	255	5	655	12,731	5.1
Saab	2	5	0	7	243	2.9
Saturn	3	0	0	3	37	8.1
Subaru	659	1,437	25	2,121	78,034	2.7
Suzuki	124	406	0	530	6,768	7.8
Toyota/Lexus	15,720	20,318	812	36,850	747,223	4.9
Volkswagen	394	2,704	26	3,124	42,369	7.4
Volvo Truck	407	1,155	15	1,577	29,828	5.3
Total Light Trucks	**409,492**	**726,347**	**97,524**	**1,233,363**	**6,588,330**	**18.7**
Total Light Vehicles	**582,647**	**1,651,758**	**167,717**	**2,402,122**	**12,662,089**	**19.0**

NOTE: Total sales includes fleet plus retail.
SOURCE: Bobit Business Media, Automotive Fleet Fact Book 2012.

Total Vehicle Registrations by Country

VEHICLES IN OPERATION BY COUNTRY

Country	2010 Cars	2010 Commercial Vehicles	2010 Total	Population (000)	Persons Per Car	2009 Cars	2009 Commercial Vehicles	2009 Total
AFRICA								
Algeria	2,691,075	1,289,594	3,980,669	35,423	13.2	2,593,310	1,253,953	3,847,263
Angola	51,000	68,500	119,500	18,993	372.4	50,000	68,000	118,000
Benin	11,500	18,300	29,800	9,212	801.0	11,250	18,100	29,350
Botswana	135,000	124,500	259,500	1,978	14.7	127,634	117,805	245,439
Burkina Faso	115,500	50,500	166,000	16,287	141.0	110,931	48,994	159,925
Burundi	30,500	26,000	56,500	8,519	279.3	30,000	25,750	55,750
Cameroon	220,000	71,000	291,000	19,958	90.7	210,000	68,900	278,900
Central African Republic	2,300	2,050	4,350	4,506	1,959.1	2,250	2,000	4,250
Congo	44,200	20,400	64,600	3,759	85.0	43,500	19,500	63,000
Congo, Democratic Republic of	920,000	711,000	1,631,000	67,827	73.7	916,750	709,000	1,625,750
Egypt	2,820,242	1,042,180	3,862,422	84,474	30.0	2,437,543	995,020	3,432,563
Ethiopia	77,000	57,800	134,800	84,976	1,103.6	76,000	57,000	133,000
Ghana	115,000	61,000	176,000	24,333	211.6	113,750	60,500	174,250
Ivory Coast	22,200	97,500	119,700	21,571	971.7	22,000	96,500	118,500
Kenya	550,000	430,000	980,000	40,863	74.3	499,679	396,176	895,855
Liberia	14,000	38,200	52,200	4,102	293.0	13,500	37,900	51,400
Libya	448,000	410,000	858,000	6,546	14.6	441,000	400,000	841,000
Madagascar	78,250	53,500	131,750	20,146	257.5	77,500	53,000	130,500
Malawi	13,050	17,250	30,300	14,901	1,141.8	13,000	17,250	30,250
Mali	10,100	13,100	23,200	15,370	1,521.8	10,000	12,800	22,800
Mauritania	13,650	9,200	22,850	3,366	246.6	13,400	9,100	22,500
Mauritius	127,363	43,194	170,557	1,282	10.1	117,890	42,650	160,540
Morocco	1,430,000	455,000	1,885,000	32,381	22.6	1,395,600	445,000	1,840,600
Mozambique	34,500	32,000	66,500	23,406	678.4	34,000	31,750	65,750
Namibia	84,000	91,500	175,500	2,212	26.3	83,000	90,750	173,750
Niger	102,000	29,000	131,000	15,891	155.8	93,118	25,968	119,086
Nigeria	770,000	477,000	1,247,000	158,259	205.5	763,500	476,000	1,239,500
Reunion	239,200	97,000	336,200	840	3.5	237,750	96,250	334,000
Sierra Leone	21,000	9,700	30,700	5,836	277.9	20,650	9,550	30,200
South Africa	5,099,891	2,790,086	7,889,977	49,962	9.8	5,050,364	2,771,394	7,821,758
Sudan	41,100	52,500	93,600	43,552	1,059.7	41,000	51,500	92,500
Tanzania	24,250	53,500	77,750	45,040	1,857.3	24,000	52,500	76,500
Togo	107,500	49,500	157,000	6,780	63.1	106,000	49,000	155,000
Tunisia	670,000	330,000	1,000,000	10,535	15.7	660,000	322,500	982,500
Uganda	57,400	47,000	104,400	33,796	588.8	56,900	46,500	103,400
Zambia	174,000	101,100	275,100	12,926	74.3	171,350	99,500	270,850
Zimbabwe	400,000	69,000	469,000	12,644	31.6	394,000	68,000	462,000
Total Africa	**17,764,771**	**9,338,654**	**27,103,425**	**962,450**	**54.2**	**17,062,119**	**9,146,060**	**26,208,179**
AMERICA, Caribbean								
Bahamas	91,750	31,700	123,450	300	3.3	91,200	31,300	122,500

Total Vehicle Registrations by Country

VEHICLES IN OPERATION BY COUNTRY — continued

Country	2010 Cars	2010 Commercial Vehicles	2010 Total	Population (000)	Persons Per Car	2009 Cars	2009 Commercial Vehicles	2009 Total
Barbados	81,000	18,300	99,300	278	3.4	79,750	17,900	97,650
Bermuda	22,315	4,677	26,992	65	2.9	22,626	4,802	27,428
Cuba	210,000	225,000	435,000	11,309	53.9	205,500	221,500	427,000
Dominican Republic	661,747	670,648	1,332,395	8,951	13.5	645,158	629,394	1,274,552
Haiti	36,500	36,000	72,500	8,109	222.2	35,000	35,000	70,000
Jamaica	137,000	36,000	173,000	2,712	19.8	134,500	35,750	170,250
Netherlands Antilles	—	—	—	—	—	109,000	26,500	135,500
Puerto Rico	1,075,000	465,000	1,540,000	3,895	3.6	1,065,000	458,500	1,523,500
Trinidad and Tobago	320,000	41,250	361,250	1,084	3.4	317,000	41,000	358,000
Virgin Islands (US)	37,000	20,500	57,500	109	2.9	36,500	20,000	56,500
Total Caribbean	**2,672,312**	**1,549,075**	**4,221,387**	**37,030**	**13.9**	**2,741,234**	**1,521,646**	**4,262,880**
AMERICA, Central & South								
Argentina	7,604,921	2,511,097	10,116,018	39,145	5.1	6,706,101	2,248,774	8,954,875
Belize	13,300	15,900	29,200	274	20.6	13,100	15,650	28,750
Bolivia	220,000	310,000	530,000	8,724	39.7	217,900	307,500	525,400
Brazil	25,540,696	6,524,254	32,064,950	184,101	7.2	23,612,000	6,031,000	29,643,000
Chile	1,978,018	1,074,719	3,052,737	15,824	8.0	1,816,143	1,018,496	2,834,639
Colombia	1,100,000	640,000	1,740,000	42,311	38.5	1,018,000	624,000	1,642,000
Costa Rica	585,000	190,000	775,000	3,957	6.8	565,364	185,150	750,514
Ecuador	340,000	450,000	790,000	13,213	38.9	329,184	440,341	769,525
El Salvador	88,000	115,000	203,000	6,588	74.9	86,000	113,500	199,500
Guatemala	149,000	156,000	305,000	11,940	80.1	146,500	154,000	300,500
Guyana	32,100	15,500	47,600	763	23.8	31,500	15,250	46,750
Honduras	32,500	94,000	126,500	7,007	215.6	31,600	93,000	124,600
Nicaragua	77,000	115,000	192,000	5,360	69.6	75,000	113,000	188,000
Panama	286,000	185,500	471,500	3,090	10.8	283,000	183,000	466,000
Paraguay	97,250	93,000	190,250	6,191	63.7	95,500	91,500	187,000
Peru	809,967	734,154	1,544,121	27,544	34.0	766,742	694,541	1,461,283
Suriname	77,500	33,600	111,100	455	5.9	77,000	33,000	110,000
Uruguay	650,000	75,500	725,500	3,399	5.2	600,191	68,414	668,605
Venezuela	1,900,000	1,280,000	3,180,000	25,017	13.2	1,840,000	1,260,000	3,100,000
Total Central & South America	**41,581,252**	**14,613,224**	**56,194,476**	**404,904**	**9.7**	**38,310,825**	**13,690,116**	**52,000,941**
AMERICA, North								
Canada	20,121,339	932,655	21,053,994	32,508	1.6	19,876,990	915,274	20,792,264
Mexico	20,973,153	9,453,773	30,426,926	104,960	5.0	20,523,704	9,179,909	29,703,613
United States	118,946,744	120,865,240	239,811,984	293,028	2.5	119,291,910	119,770,033	239,061,943
Total North America	**160,041,236**	**131,251,668**	**291,292,904**	**430,495**	**2.7**	**159,692,604**	**129,865,216**	**289,557,820**
ASIA, Far East								
Afghanistan	621,937	241,318	863,255	28,514	45.8	558,495	221,940	780,435
Bangladesh	40,500	74,500	115,000	141,340	3,489.9	40,000	73,500	113,500
Brunei	90,000	20,500	110,500	365	4.1	88,500	20,000	108,500

Total Vehicle Registrations by Country

VEHICLES IN OPERATION BY COUNTRY — continued

Country	2010 Cars	2010 Commercial Vehicles	2010 Total	Population (000)	Persons Per Car	2009 Cars	2009 Commercial Vehicles	2009 Total
Burma	9,600	19,000	28,600	46,118	4,804.0	9,250	18,750	28,000
China	34,430,000	43,590,000	78,020,000	1,298,848	37.7	25,300,500	35,875,000	61,175,500
Hong Kong	415,000	153,000	568,000	6,855	16.5	394,000	151,000	545,000
India	13,300,000	9,500,000	22,800,000	1,075,473	80.9	12,365,806	8,885,694	21,251,500
Indonesia	8,891,041	6,937,898	15,828,939	226,004	25.4	7,910,407	6,659,144	14,569,551
Japan	58,347,387	15,511,896	73,859,283	127,333	2.2	58,019,853	15,789,222	73,809,075
Korea, South	13,631,754	4,309,602	17,941,356	48,426	3.6	13,023,803	4,301,407	17,325,210
Malaysia	9,114,920	1,138,287	10,253,207	23,522	2.6	8,506,080	1,098,531	9,604,611
Pakistan	1,726,347	537,791	2,264,138	159,196	92.2	1,657,860	512,570	2,170,430
Philippines	808,583	2,314,844	3,123,427	86,242	106.7	780,252	2,210,473	2,990,725
Singapore	584,399	199,923	784,322	4,354	7.5	566,608	198,932	765,540
Sri Lanka	355,000	413,000	768,000	20,303	57.2	353,000	409,000	762,000
Taiwan	5,642,969	1,022,580	6,665,549	22,750	4.0	5,704,312	1,014,434	6,718,746
Thailand	4,600,697	6,241,796	10,842,493	63,731	13.9	4,462,231	5,721,804	10,184,035
Vietnam	163,000	182,000	345,000	82,663	507.1	160,100	178,500	338,600
Total Far East	**152,773,134**	**92,407,935**	**245,181,069**	**3,462,038**	**22.7**	**139,901,057**	**83,339,901**	**223,240,958**
ASIA, Middle East								
Azerbaijan	815,683	148,029	963,712	7,968	9.8	759,203	147,363	906,566
Bahrain	320,500	143,000	463,500	678	2.1	317,000	141,000	458,000
Cyprus	452,000	165,000	617,000	776	1.7	447,605	162,357	609,962
Iran	3,100,000	805,000	3,905,000	64,326	20.8	3,065,000	794,000	3,859,000
Iraq	885,000	158,000	1,043,000	25,375	28.7	878,000	156,500	1,034,500
Israel	2,002,774	397,023	2,399,797	6,199	3.1	1,912,288	402,326	2,314,614
Jordan	408,000	138,000	546,000	5,611	13.8	391,000	136,000	527,000
Kuwait	940,000	240,000	1,180,000	2,258	2.4	925,000	237,000	1,162,000
Lebanon	450,000	96,000	546,000	3,777	8.4	445,000	94,000	539,000
Oman	315,000	127,500	442,500	2,903	9.2	309,500	125,500	435,000
Qatar	190,000	99,100	289,100	840	4.4	187,500	97,000	284,500
Saudi Arabia	3,470,000	1,955,000	5,425,000	25,796	7.4	3,400,000	1,920,000	5,320,000
Syria	741,260	747,246	1,488,506	18,017	24.3	637,604	680,831	1,318,435
Turkey	7,544,871	3,720,880	11,265,751	68,894	9.1	7,093,964	3,517,339	10,611,303
United Arab Emirates	330,000	97,000	427,000	2,524	7.6	322,000	93,500	415,500
Yemen	305,000	345,000	650,000	20,025	65.7	302,000	341,000	643,000
Total Middle East	**22,270,088**	**9,381,778**	**31,651,866**	**255,967**	**11.5**	**21,392,664**	**9,045,716**	**30,438,380**
EUROPE, East								
Belarus	2,501,200	153,196	2,654,396	9,856	3.9	2,339,800	132,863	2,472,663
Bulgaria	2,602,400	357,914	2,960,314	7,518	2.9	2,502,000	342,899	2,844,899
Croatia	1,515,449	162,608	1,678,057	4,497	3.0	1,532,549	169,832	1,702,381
Czech Republic	4,496,232	701,193	5,197,425	10,246	2.3	4,435,052	704,863	5,139,915
Hungary	2,984,063	434,313	3,418,376	10,032	3.4	3,013,719	437,136	3,450,855
Poland	17,240,000	3,079,000	20,319,000	38,580	2.2	16,494,650	2,892,182	19,386,832
Romania	4,320,000	793,000	5,113,000	22,356	5.2	4,245,000	703,000	4,948,000

Total Vehicle Registrations by Country

VEHICLES IN OPERATION BY COUNTRY — continued

Country	2010 Cars	Commercial Vehicles	Total	Population (000)	Persons Per Car	2009 Cars	Commercial Vehicles	Total
Russian Federation	34,797,488	6,427,425	41,224,913	143,507	4.1	33,186,915	6,322,625	39,509,540
Serbia & Montenegro	1,567,192	170,833	1,738,025	10,826	6.9	1,650,477	180,660	1,831,137
Slovak Republic	1,671,368	302,348	1,973,716	5,424	3.2	1,615,855	297,675	1,913,530
Slovenia	1,068,932	77,521	1,146,453	2,011	1.9	1,065,927	77,143	1,143,070
Ukraine	7,848,900	1,569,292	9,418,192	47,305	6.0	7,684,500	1,538,000	9,222,500
Total Eastern Europe	**82,613,224**	**14,228,643**	**96,841,867**	**312,159**	**3.8**	**79,766,444**	**13,798,878**	**93,565,322**
EUROPE, West								
Austria	4,441,027	406,436	4,847,463	8,175	1.8	4,359,944	397,571	4,757,515
Belgium	5,279,110	809,137	6,088,247	10,348	2.0	5,160,257	792,706	5,952,963
Denmark	2,163,676	499,662	2,663,338	5,413	2.5	2,120,322	522,370	2,642,692
Finland	2,858,244	473,426	3,331,670	5,215	1.8	2,758,291	452,574	3,210,865
France	31,300,000	6,444,000	37,744,000	60,424	1.9	31,050,000	6,388,000	37,438,000
Germany	42,301,563	2,959,625	45,261,188	82,425	1.9	41,737,627	2,895,281	44,632,908
Greece	5,216,873	1,346,079	6,562,952	10,648	2.0	5,131,960	1,329,754	6,461,714
Iceland	204,736	32,353	237,089	294	1.4	205,338	32,811	238,149
Ireland	1,890,110	411,945	2,302,055	3,970	2.1	1,914,924	423,713	2,338,637
Italy	36,751,311	4,898,566	41,649,877	58,057	1.6	36,371,790	4,840,741	41,212,531
Latvia	636,664	76,952	713,616	2,306	3.6	904,308	130,258	1,034,566
Luxembourg	337,251	40,043	377,294	463	1.4	331,513	39,138	370,651
Malta	233,622	49,044	282,666	397	1.7	227,264	48,646	275,910
Netherlands	7,904,583	1,100,730	9,005,313	16,318	2.1	7,800,123	1,120,094	8,920,217
Norway	2,308,548	547,389	2,855,937	4,575	2.0	2,244,039	545,625	2,789,664
Portugal	4,480,000	1,352,600	5,832,600	10,524	2.3	4,457,000	1,352,500	5,809,500
Spain	22,147,455	5,365,911	27,513,366	40,281	1.8	21,983,485	5,405,607	27,389,092
Sweden	4,335,182	540,314	4,875,496	8,986	2.1	4,300,752	527,983	4,828,735
Switzerland	4,075,825	387,951	4,463,776	7,451	1.8	4,009,602	378,483	4,388,085
United Kingdom	31,258,197	4,220,455	35,478,652	60,271	1.9	31,035,791	4,181,519	35,217,310
Total Western Europe	**210,123,977**	**31,962,618**	**242,086,595**	**396,540**	**1.9**	**208,104,330**	**31,805,374**	**239,909,704**
PACIFIC								
Australia	12,269,305	3,083,182	15,352,487	19,913	1.6	12,023,098	2,980,713	15,003,811
Fiji	89,422	58,432	147,854	881	9.9	87,249	57,404	144,653
French Polynesia	45,000	24,000	69,000	266	5.9	44,600	23,750	68,350
Guam	71,093	34,232	105,325	166	2.3	69,454	33,445	102,899
New Caledonia	65,600	29,600	95,200	214	3.3	65,000	29,300	94,300
New Zealand	2,599,568	499,355	3,098,923	3,994	1.5	2,574,589	498,217	3,072,806
Papua New Guinea	38,300	93,000	131,300	5,420	141.5	38,000	92,500	130,500
Samoa (American)	7,400	7,600	15,000	58	7.8	7,300	7,550	14,850
Vanuatu	9,200	5,150	14,350	203	22.1	9,100	5,050	14,150
Total Pacific	**15,194,888**	**3,834,551**	**19,029,439**	**31,115**	**2.0**	**14,918,390**	**3,727,929**	**18,646,319**
WORLD TOTAL	**705,034,882**	**308,568,146**	**1,013,603,028**	**6,143,989**	**8.7**	**681,889,667**	**295,940,836**	**977,830,503**

SOURCE: International Road Federation, VDA, World Bank and *WardsAuto* estimates.

U.S. Vehicle Exports by Country of Destination and Vehicle Type

U.S. EXPORTS BY COUNTRY OF DESTINATION AND VEHICLE TYPE, 2011

	Cars		Trucks		Buses		Total	
COUNTRY	Units	Value ($000)	Units	Value ($000)	Units	Value ($000)	Units	Value ($000)
Afghanistan	623	47,982	7,516	1,127,827	14	292	8,153	1,176,101
Albania	164	3,293	—	—	1	70	165	3,363
Algeria	30	499	126	7,839	—	—	156	8,338
Angola	1,148	27,777	122	5,596	5	325	1,275	33,698
Anguilla	24	428	21	361	—	—	45	789
Antigua Barbuda	25	471	13	331	—	—	38	802
Argentina	2,334	54,375	190	12,235	1	21	2,525	66,631
Aruba	246	5,100	34	1,950	—	—	280	7,050
Australia	25,406	726,027	2,883	268,274	43	851	28,332	995,152
Austria	851	23,428	2	35	—	—	853	23,463
Azerbaijan	181	5,206	20	2,868	—	—	201	8,074
Bahamas	569	12,332	513	9,757	6	143	1,088	22,232
Bahrain	4,118	103,160	183	13,806	7	173	4,308	117,139
Bangladesh	—	—	25	1,640	—	—	25	1,640
Barbados	29	669	39	2,727	—	—	68	3,396
Belarus	159	5,553	—	—	—	—	159	5,553
Belgium	1,854	49,808	132	5,110	3	125	1,989	55,043
Belize	59	1,011	138	1,853	1	11	198	2,875
Benin	4,728	62,591	43	1,252	10	179	4,781	64,022
Bermuda	81	1,474	41	971	—	—	122	2,445
Bolivia	483	10,859	287	7,171	—	—	770	18,030
Brazil	8,053	206,949	367	21,811	2	79	8,422	228,839
British Virgin Islands	324	5,477	46	1,056	3	80	373	6,613
Brunei	90	2,294	—	—	—	—	90	2,294
Bulgaria	30	872	12	779	—	—	42	1,651
Burkina Faso	3	49	40	1,390	1	28	44	1,467
Burma (Myanmar)	113	2,564	1	80	—	—	114	2,644
Cambodia	145	2,536	23	845	1	13	169	3,394
Cameroon	129	2,320	16	757	1	32	146	3,109
Canada	476,755	11,033,130	318,967	11,145,946	13,456	502,968	809,178	22,682,044
Cape Verde	56	1,020	—	—	—	—	56	1,020
Cayman Islands	370	8,462	67	1,371	4	95	441	9,928
Chile	13,738	319,434	6,630	292,478	27	677	20,395	612,589
China	125,699	4,013,910	780	60,521	41	1,011	126,520	4,075,442
Colombia	4,454	104,236	1,211	70,250	7	226	5,672	174,712
Congo (ROC)	140	2,633	69	2,982	1	22	210	5,637
Costa Rica	1,609	42,514	635	12,690	57	984	2,301	56,188
Cote d'Ivoire	112	2,086	10	181	3	52	125	2,319
Croatia	37	730	13	2,363	—	—	50	3,093
Curacao	203	4,056	17	575	14	378	234	5,009
Czech Republic	373	10,796	1	54	1	67	375	10,917
Denmark	27	487	173	4,607	—	—	200	5,094
Dominica Islands	18	374	60	1,126	—	—	78	1,500

U.S. Vehicle Exports by Country of Destination and Vehicle Type

U.S. EXPORTS BY COUNTRY OF DESTINATION AND VEHICLE TYPE, 2011 — continued

COUNTRY	Cars Units	Cars Value ($000)	Trucks Units	Trucks Value ($000)	Buses Units	Buses Value ($000)	Total Units	Total Value ($000)
Dominican Republic	4,558	86,064	934	25,982	66	1,551	5,558	113,597
Ecuador	2,692	51,637	2,343	95,228	6	219	5,041	147,084
Egypt	495	16,264	335	29,894	3	47	833	46,205
El Salvador	280	6,595	482	3,383	5	154	767	10,132
Equatorial Guinea	82	1,918	14	381	—	—	96	2,299
Estonia	208	5,105	22	586	—	—	230	5,691
Finland	841	23,173	281	7,234	26	661	1,148	31,068
France	3,772	98,527	45	3,249	—	—	3,817	101,776
French Polynesia	110	2,561	80	2,078	—	—	190	4,639
Gabon	137	3,186	47	4,610	7	172	191	7,968
Gambia	30	541	8	94	—	—	38	635
Georgia	1,830	32,735	19	2,146	—	—	1,849	34,881
Germany	145,512	5,016,225	492	26,163	23	642	146,027	5,043,030
Ghana	3,292	46,376	267	41,210	7	265	3,566	87,851
Greece	111	2,318	19	809	1	38	131	3,165
Grenada	17	418	10	179	—	—	27	597
Guatemala	1,381	33,612	2,588	21,703	13	348	3,982	55,663
Guinea	129	2,257	32	1,077	2	61	163	3,395
Guyana	106	2,131	168	4,052	1	16	275	6,199
Haiti	169	3,571	151	7,457	4	67	324	11,095
Honduras	555	13,116	904	11,306	3	46	1,462	24,468
Hong Kong	3,119	98,352	44	1,664	10	224	3,173	100,240
Hungary	52	1,584	14	2,244	—	—	66	3,828
Iceland	112	2,912	—	—	—	—	112	2,912
India	1,027	37,436	51	4,067	—	—	1,078	41,503
Indonesia	920	25,367	40	2,739	—	—	960	28,106
Iraq	3,068	67,459	521	76,459	7	161	3,596	144,079
Ireland	64	1,578	2	27	—	—	66	1,605
Israel	6,194	151,213	2,289	85,359	44	1,375	8,527	237,947
Italy	10,552	281,372	55	3,985	9	173	10,616	285,530
Jamaica	305	9,126	85	4,130	1	15	391	13,271
Japan	13,058	308,588	359	20,786	25	768	13,442	330,142
Jordan	2,207	41,353	208	11,999	61	1,084	2,476	54,436
Kazakhstan	264	6,264	97	4,564	—	—	361	10,828
Kenya	98	1,589	137	9,111	2	29	237	10,729
Korea	12,777	322,859	581	16,112	115	3,240	13,473	342,211
Kuwait	22,288	540,577	5,040	99,918	125	3,739	27,453	644,234
Laos	20	527	5	199	—	—	25	726
Latvia	34	1,112	—	—	2	54	36	1,166
Lebanon	3,579	62,387	67	6,319	130	2,386	3,776	71,092
Liberia	151	2,599	37	939	4	60	192	3,598
Libya	255	3,040	67	7,292	52	727	374	11,059
Lithuania	127	2,599	—	—	1	24	128	2,623
Luxembourg	62	1,771	2	101	—	—	64	1,872

U.S. Vehicle Exports by Country of Destination and Vehicle Type

U.S. EXPORTS BY COUNTRY OF DESTINATION AND VEHICLE TYPE, 2011 — continued

COUNTRY	Cars Units	Cars Value ($000)	Trucks Units	Trucks Value ($000)	Buses Units	Buses Value ($000)	Total Units	Total Value ($000)
Macao	69	1,177	1	125	14	439	84	1,741
Madagascar	46	1,868	1	188	—	—	47	2,056
Malawi	1	36	36	683	—	—	37	719
Malaysia	44	1,114	17	2,011	—	—	61	3,125
Mali	8	149	8	261	6	120	22	530
Mauritania	18	135	17	3,455	9	226	44	3,816
Mexico	135,200	2,858,876	16,410	441,370	756	24,422	152,366	3,324,668
Mongolia	366	9,994	42	2,435	86	2,738	494	15,167
Montenegro	37	537	—	—	3	66	40	603
Morocco	129	3,275	417	27,094	5	120	551	30,489
Mozambique	2	34	1,694	32,986	5	75	1,701	33,095
Namibia	96	2,242	951	13,808	—	—	1,047	16,050
Netherlands	1,661	40,713	179	5,810	3	72	1,843	46,595
Netherlands Antilles	220	4,341	55	3,045	12	339	287	7,725
New Caledonia	156	4,251	381	10,476	—	—	537	14,727
New Zealand	1,834	54,942	535	30,772	2	30	2,371	85,744
Nicaragua	253	6,403	327	5,534	3	82	583	12,019
Nigeria	8,497	149,828	5,502	127,634	289	5,810	14,288	283,272
Norway	515	12,998	85	4,937	—	—	600	17,935
Oman	8,571	222,334	436	26,550	21	521	9,028	249,405
Pakistan	366	4,258	43	12,367	—	—	409	16,625
Panama	2,423	63,806	1,504	58,057	40	798	3,967	122,661
Paraguay	627	14,289	68	3,614	—	—	695	17,903
Peru	3,944	93,313	604	42,875	1	32	4,549	136,220
Philippines	1,799	46,997	232	5,139	—	—	2,031	52,136
Poland	719	18,693	17	1,037	—	—	736	19,730
Portugal	345	9,472	3	74	—	—	348	9,546
Qatar	6,500	180,842	962	33,198	115	3,407	7,577	217,447
Reunion	23	531	—	—	—	—	23	531
Romania	86	2,222	18	2,717	—	—	104	4,939
Russia	7,544	235,324	1,553	70,484	3	104	9,100	305,912
Saudi Arabia	97,588	2,777,764	8,426	228,400	240	5,845	106,254	3,012,009
Senegal	366	7,252	46	1,161	2	43	414	8,456
Serbia	68	1,688	1	103	—	—	69	1,791
Sierra Leone	158	2,782	21	489	8	313	187	3,584
Singapore	172	4,985	265	15,418	7	166	444	20,569
Sint Maarten	207	4,420	40	1,498	—	—	247	5,918
Slovak Republic	77	2,395	12	362	—	—	89	2,757
Slovenia	37	823	1	242	—	—	38	1,065
South Africa	9,638	238,199	1,772	166,190	2	55	11,412	404,444
Spain	2,394	66,273	38	1,531	7	264	2,439	68,068
Sri Lanka	18	791	—	—	—	—	18	791
St. Kitts-Nevis	38	869	16	428	1	18	55	1,315
St. Lucia Islands	23	461	15	465	1	18	39	944

U.S. Vehicle Exports by Country of Destination and Vehicle Type

U.S. EXPORTS BY COUNTRY OF DESTINATION AND VEHICLE TYPE, 2011 — continued

	Cars		Trucks		Buses		Total	
COUNTRY	Units	Value ($000)	Units	Value ($000)	Units	Value ($000)	Units	Value ($000)
St. Vincent & Grenadines	15	365	20	495	—	—	35	860
Suriname	113	3,015	14	384	1	46	128	3,445
Sweden	1,177	23,311	98	4,654	24	670	1,299	28,635
Switzerland	2,242	60,959	1,422	39,162	6	159	3,670	100,280
Taiwan	1,130	27,616	31	2,974	2	108	1,163	30,698
Tanzania	27	512	34	1,617	1	17	62	2,146
Thailand	221	6,004	22	2,842	4	149	247	8,995
Togo	780	11,370	48	1,152	5	98	833	12,620
Trinidad & Tobago	36	993	69	4,087	5	167	110	5,247
Tunisia	41	798	1	146	—	—	42	944
Turkey	1,559	42,667	58	6,158	1	21	1,618	48,846
Turks & Caicos Islands	54	1,233	36	630	1	28	91	1,891
Uganda	14	345	7	1,233	1	16	22	1,594
Ukraine	872	22,651	49	6,057	1	25	922	28,733
United Arab Emirates	37,997	972,314	3,474	128,966	196	5,035	41,667	1,106,315
United Kingdom	34,961	1,160,589	198	19,202	3	92	35,162	1,179,883
Uruguay	207	5,891	119	7,074	—	—	326	12,965
Venezuela	574	14,436	768	46,478	47	1,774	1,389	62,688
Vietnam	1,997	59,810	693	22,710	8	360	2,698	82,880
Yemen	725	15,420	10	130	1	33	736	15,583
Zambia	5	134	97	1,492	—	—	102	1,626
Zimbabwe	14	534	634	13,762	1	12	649	14,308
Other	201	4,356	76	4,125	11	873	288	9,354
Total	**1,300,075**	**33,917,985**	**411,137**	**15,440,853**	**16,425**	**583,054**	**1,727,637**	**49,941,892**

SOURCE: Compiled from official statistics of the U.S. Department of Commerce.

U.S. EXPORTS BY COUNTRY OF DESTINATION

Year	Canada	France	Germany	Japan	Kuwait	Mexico	Saudi Arabia	Taiwan	Other Countries	Total Exports
2011	809,178	3,817	146,027	13,442	27,453	152,366	106,254	1,163	467,937	1,727,637
2010	780,392	1,751	98,029	7,338	23,256	133,840	91,870	4,145	361,254	1,501,875
2009	620,735	774	112,364	6,370	15,095	104,766	44,266	501	202,107	1,106,978
2008	1,006,832	5,281	182,336	15,297	27,344	233,152	88,310	452	407,168	1,966,172
2007	969,484	11,841	173,863	18,683	25,497	307,509	101,187	1,166	786,337	2,395,567
2006	905,284	5,757	145,997	17,889	26,929	304,580	100,556	1,506	546,194	2,054,692
2005	892,368	3,154	120,585	26,285	38,986	348,980	127,836	9,287	496,718	2,064,199
2004	851,630	3,456	129,931	27,044	26,372	314,308	79,928	3,734	357,242	1,793,645
2003	851,034	2,213	131,186	25,734	22,654	266,099	49,832	3,151	262,036	1,613,939
2002	938,455	1,669	97,433	25,619	16,893	301,008	58,099	3,079	216,267	1,658,522
2001	822,280	5,958	77,628	29,159	8,384	266,534	36,755	4,742	210,898	1,462,338
2000	844,977	3,166	49,635	34,809	4,432	214,886	14,762	11,126	120,382	1,298,175
1999	817,527	3,307	43,210	40,670	2,789	140,117	9,648	8,398	153,511	1,219,177
1998	772,766	3,174	46,618	50,202	4,750	127,488	19,098	9,893	213,825	1,247,814
1997	921,174	2,986	62,604	81,961	5,389	152,114	20,316	25,510	318,939	1,590,993

NOTE: Data include used vehicles prior to 2008.
SOURCE: Compiled from official statistics of the U.S. Department of Commerce.

U.S. Vehicle Imports by Country of Origin and Vehicle Type

U.S. IMPORTS BY COUNTRY OF ORIGIN AND VEHICLE TYPE, 2011

Country of Origin	Cars Units	Cars Value ($000)	Trucks Units	Trucks Value ($000)	Buses Units	Buses Value ($000)	Total Units	Total Value ($000)
Australia	2,328	50,504	11	942	1	7	2,340	51,453
Austria	24,954	581,419	—	—	6	25	24,960	581,444
Belgium	41,513	1,159,700	3	141	334	141,474	41,850	1,301,315
Brazil	287	5,349	68	4,958	2	227	357	10,534
Canada	1,831,084	38,283,614	14,251	1,007,845	1,819	375,720	1,847,154	39,667,179
China	194,108	257,902	1,496	2,884	30	2,116	195,634	262,902
Finland	938	70,890	26	7,945	—	—	964	78,835
France	565	27,243	18	1,012	—	—	583	28,255
Germany	680,204	20,824,188	1,836	63,872	137	41,242	682,177	20,929,302
Hungary	2,223	73,255	—	—	106	9,959	2,329	83,214
Italy	5,016	676,590	138	4,317	—	—	5,154	680,907
Japan	2,376,388	31,342,690	14,064	431,130	—	—	2,390,452	31,773,820
Korea, South	826,904	8,994,667	1	150	—	—	826,905	8,994,817
Mexico	952,088	15,157,371	472,053	15,489,322	402	38,473	1,424,543	30,685,166
Portugal	9,184	237,279	—	—	—	—	9,184	237,279
Slovak Republic	17,533	669,722	—	—	—	—	17,533	669,722
South Africa	67,727	2,052,821	14	416	—	—	67,741	2,053,237
Sweden	26,711	857,978	13	294	3	382	26,727	858,654
Taiwan	44,766	1,343	—	—	—	—	44,766	1,343
Turkey	33,050	482,803	27	1,011	53	13,095	33,130	496,909
United Kingdom	97,098	3,745,958	93	1,264	16	940	97,207	3,748,162
Other	184	3,925	115	10,229	4	63	303	14,217
Total	**7,234,853**	**125,557,211**	**504,227**	**17,027,732**	**2,913**	**623,723**	**7,741,993**	**143,208,666**

SOURCE: Compiled from official statistics of the U.S. Department of Commerce.

U.S. IMPORTS OF NEW ASSEMBLED CARS BY COUNTRY OF ORIGIN

Year	Canada	Germany	Japan	South Korea	Mexico	Sweden	United Kingdom	Other	Total Imports
2011	1,831,084	680,204	2,376,388	826,904	952,088	26,711	97,098	444,376	7,234,853
2010	1,737,543	624,913	2,433,340	800,474	890,100	38,150	96,738	206,965	6,828,223
2009	1,161,188	526,570	2,029,754	730,848	641,089	26,691	77,973	172,290	5,366,403
2008	1,598,115	679,624	3,119,746	800,447	912,841	59,172	111,880	254,744	7,536,569
2007	1,907,775	753,898	3,504,443	891,237	875,417	91,788	112,399	302,423	8,439,380
2006	1,927,382	695,364	3,693,385	888,256	945,726	80,380	147,403	254,459	8,632,355
2005	1,955,072	544,971	1,628,313	730,431	692,659	92,617	184,138	144,056	5,972,257
2004	2,004,890	545,634	1,538,805	860,057	650,400	97,992	185,059	190,114	6,072,951
2003	1,751,958	560,381	1,575,599	690,885	677,771	119,833	205,937	174,990	5,757,354
2002	1,815,323	571,164	1,827,434	623,810	838,829	89,347	156,258	157,992	6,080,157
2001	1,809,236	492,177	1,616,950	631,945	853,264	89,412	81,261	178,380	5,752,625
2000	2,076,181	489,086	1,661,906	560,728	927,574	85,713	79,639	125,007	6,005,834
1999	2,125,876	456,246	1,560,857	369,264	637,486	82,808	67,689	99,590	5,399,816
1998	1,817,836	372,632	1,317,702	207,165	586,973	84,404	49,037	65,690	4,501,439
1997	1,722,199	298,032	1,383,519	222,535	539,384	79,725	43,726	68,100	4,357,220
1996	1,688,123	234,480	1,190,581	225,613	550,622	86,595	43,616	44,817	4,064,447
1995	1,678,276	206,892	1,387,193	216,618	463,305	82,634	42,176	36,823	4,113,917
1994	1,591,326	187,999	1,593,169	217,962	360,370	63,867	28,239	54,082	4,097,014
1993	1,468,272	184,356	1,597,391	126,576	299,634	58,742	20,048	53,441	3,808,460
1990	1,220,221	245,286	1,867,794	201,475	215,986	93,084	27,271	73,485	3,944,602
1985	1,144,805	473,110	2,527,467	—	13,647	142,640	24,474	71,536	4,397,679
1980	594,770	338,711	1,991,502	—	—	61,496	32,517	97,451	3,116,448
1975	733,766	370,012	695,573	—	—	51,993	67,106	156,203	2,074,653
1970	692,783	674,945	381,338	—	—	57,844	76,257	130,253	2,013,420

NOTE: Figures include imports into Puerto Rico and do not include automobiles assembled in U.S. foreign trade zones.
SOURCE: Compiled from official statistics of the U.S. Department of Commerce.

World Trade in Vehicles

EXPORTS AND IMPORTS OF VEHICLES FOR SELECTED COUNTRIES, 2010

Country	Exports Cars	Exports Commercial Vehicles	Exports Total	Imports Cars	Imports Commercial Vehicles	Imports Total
Argentina	344,918	161,797	506,715	12,604	15,250	27,854
Austria	129,661	21,513	151,174	407,901	40,298	448,199
Brazil	401,194	140,374	541,568	578,931	279,096	858,027
Czech Republic	1,331,973	6,867	1,338,840	NA	NA	NA
Finland	—	—	—	126,123	18,302	144,425
France	4,336,759	556,356	4,893,115	NA	NA	NA
Germany	4,518,973	307,960	4,826,933	1,792,585	NA	1,792,585
Italy	203,769	249039	452,808	1,230,302	80,410	1,310,712
Japan	3,929,904	534,509	4,464,413	260,707	14,937	275,644
Korea, South	2,980,659	171,049	3,151,708	105,037	12,555	117,592
Mexico	1,372,391	771,488	2,143,879	259,327	213,987	473,314
Portugal	140,352	48,690	189,042	NA	NA	NA
Romania	282,191	22,733	304,924	66,287	13,474	79,761
Spain	1,642,578	478,490	2,121,068	607,755	88,021	695,776
Switzerland	—	—	—	318,958	36,298	355,256
Turkey	442,674	348,292	790,966	414,031	124,596	538,627
United Kingdom	1,124,676	69,376	1,194,052	NA	NA	NA
United States	1,300,075	427,562	1,727,637	7,234,853	507,140	7,741,993
Total	**24,482,747**	**4,316,095**	**28,798,842**	**14,406,313**	**2,097,019**	**16,503,332**

NA - Not available.
SOURCE: Compiled by *Ward's* Automotive Group from various sources.

WORLD VEHICLE EXPORTS

Vehicle Exports by Country of Origin (In Thousands)

Year	World Total[1]	Belgium	Canada	France	Germany	Italy	Japan	Sweden	United Kingdom	United States
2011	28,798.8	NA	NA	4,893.1	4,826.9	452.8	4,464.4	NA	1,194.1	1,727.6
2010	27,190.9	504.9	NA	4,785.5	4,480.9	436.7	4,370.8	NA	1,047.0	1,501.9
2009	22,106.2	505.1	NA	3,885.5	3,583.7	382.6	3,616.2	367.7	838.6	1,107.0
2008	30,034.1	652.9	NA	4,322.2	4,500.8	561.0	6,727.1	558.9	1,256.4	1,966.2
2007	31,496.6	758.3	NA	4,696.7	4,664.3	650.5	6,550.2	750.8	1,317.0	2,395.6
2006	27,821.9	848.2	NA	3,126.0	4,182.7	596.0	5,966.7	643.9	1,242.2	2,054.7
2005	27,533.7	868.8	NA	4,319.4	4,080.6	497.6	5,053.1	628.4	1,316.5	2,064.2
2004	26,962.8	870.8	NA	4,268.9	3,924.1	595.7	4,957.7	648.4	1,307.9	1,793.6
2003	24,999.7	871.9	NA	4,045.6	3,935.9	703.6	4,756.3	565.3	1,246.7	1,613.9
2002	26,765.7	1,014.6	2,373.0	3,916.7	3,875.1	733.7	4,698.2	546.3	1,161.0	1,658.5
2001	25,577.3	1,140.8	2,023.3	3,734.7	3,915.8	813.7	4,166.2	575.4	991.8	1,462.3
2000	25,886.6	993.7	2,323.0	3,619.0	3,722.8	911.6	4,454.9	453.5	1,127.9	1,298.2
1999	24,241.3	983.0	2,331.8	3,255.5	3,675.8	797.8	4,408.9	221.0	1,213.5	1,219.2
1998	24,145.6	1,026.3	2,220.5	3,122.8	3,510.9	812.4	4,528.9	425.9	1,123.6	1,247.8
1997	23,620.8	1,050.8	2,220.5	2,822.5	3,035.6	739.3	4,553.2	416.6	1,065.3	1,591.0
1996	21,691.1	1,192.7	2,134.8	2,272.0	2,841.8	799.2	3,711.7	194.5	1,073.3	1,289.6
1995	20,142.7	1,218.8	1,908.6	2,261.2	2,639.5	806.5	3,790.8	206.3	837.0	1,243.6

Percent of World Vehicle Exports

Year		Belgium	Canada	France	Germany	Italy	Japan	Sweden	United Kingdom	United States
2011	100.0	NA	NA	17.0	16.8	1.6	15.5	NA	4.1	6.0
2010	100.0	1.9	NA	17.6	16.5	1.6	16.1	NA	3.9	5.5
2009	100.0	2.3	NA	17.6	16.2	1.7	16.4	1.7	3.8	5.0
2008	100.0	2.2	NA	14.4	15.0	1.9	22.4	1.9	4.2	6.5
2007	100.0	2.4	NA	14.9	14.8	2.1	20.8	2.4	4.2	7.6
2006	100.0	3.0	NA	11.2	15.0	2.1	21.4	2.3	4.5	7.4
2005	100.0	3.2	NA	15.7	14.8	1.8	18.4	2.3	4.8	7.5
2004	100.0	3.2	NA	15.8	14.6	2.2	18.4	2.4	4.9	6.7
2003	100.0	3.5	NA	16.2	15.7	2.8	19.0	2.3	5.0	6.5
2002	100.0	3.8	8.9	14.6	14.5	2.7	17.6	2.0	4.3	6.2
2001	100.0	4.5	7.9	14.6	15.3	3.2	16.3	2.2	3.9	5.7
2000	100.0	3.8	9.0	14.0	14.4	3.5	17.2	1.8	4.4	5.0
1999	100.0	4.1	9.6	13.4	15.2	3.3	18.2	1.0	5.0	5.4
1998	100.0	4.3	9.2	12.9	14.5	3.4	18.8	1.8	4.7	5.2
1997	100.0	4.4	9.4	11.9	12.9	3.1	19.3	1.8	4.5	6.7
1996	100.0	5.5	9.8	10.5	13.1	3.7	17.1	0.9	4.9	5.9
1995	100.0	6.1	9.5	11.2	13.1	4.0	18.8	1.0	4.2	6.2

(1) World total includes countries with vehicle exports not shown separately. NA - Not available.
SOURCE: Compiled by *Ward's* Data Group from various sources.

Material Usage by the Automotive Industry

AUTOMOTIVE CONSUMPTION OF MATERIALS BY TYPE

Material	U.S. Total Consumption	Automotive Consumption	Automotive Percentage	Material	U.S. Total Consumption	Automotive Consumption	Automotive Percentage
COPPER AND COPPER ALLOY (Thousands of Pounds)				**ALUMINUM (Thousands of Pounds)**			
2011	5,420,000	705,000	13.0	2011	14,600,000	3,650,000	25.0
2010	5,350,000	689,000	12.9	2010	13,950,000	3,350,000	24.0
2009	4,884,000	578,000	11.8	2009	14,750,000	3,317,000	22.5
2008	5,855,000	647,000	11.1	2008	18,595,000	4,473,000	24.1
2007	6,617,000	737,000	11.1	2007	21,415,000	5,923,000	27.7
2006	7,279,000	778,000	10.7	2006	23,151,000	6,397,000	27.6
2005	7,786,000	794,400	10.2	2005	23,113,000	6,529,000	28.2
GRAY IRON (Tons)				**ALLOY STEEL (Tons)**			
2011	2,750,000	413,000	15.0	2011	3,894,614	485,623	12.5
2010	2,700,000	411,000	15.2	2010	3,542,538	467,615	13.2
2009	3,357,000	594,000	17.7	2009	2,592,638	339,630	13.1
2008	4,158,000	793,000	19.1	2008	5,403,008	694,867	12.9
2007	4,440,000	915,000	20.6	2007	5,159,400	670,722	13.0
2006	4,650,000	1,065,000	22.9	2006	5,501,615	698,705	12.7
2005	4,700,000	1,010,000	21.5	2005	5,182,650	647,831	12.5
DUCTILE IRON (Tons)				**STAINLESS STEEL (Tons)**			
2011	3,070,000	638,900	20.8	2011	2,082,021	425,447	20.4
2010	2,850,000	571,000	20.0	2010	1,661,971	358,985	21.6
2009	3,262,000	667,000	20.4	2009	1,620,125	340,225	21.0
2008	3,994,000	839,000	21.0	2008	1,876,668	401,320	21.4
2007	4,440,000	1,005,000	22.6	2007	2,275,823	455,164	20.0
2006	4,500,000	1,015,000	22.6	2006	2,524,434	499,838	19.8
2005	4,400,000	1,136,000	25.8	2005	2,361,300	448,647	19.0
TOTAL IRON (Tons)				**TOTAL STEEL (Tons)**			
2011	5,820,000	1,051,900	18.1	2011	91,865,449	12,468,000	13.6
2010	5,550,000	982,000	17.7	2010	83,443,836	10,602,000	12.7
2009	6,619,000	1,261,000	19.1	2009	62,165,938	8,043,253	12.9
2008	8,152,000	1,632,000	20.0	2008	101,964,789	12,842,000	12.6
2007	8,880,000	1,920,000	21.6	2007	110,169,806	13,631,755	12.4
2006	9,150,000	2,080,000	22.7	2006	109,501,703	15,528,000	14.2
2005	9,100,000	2,146,000	23.6	2005	104,970,522	14,477,000	13.8
LEAD (Metric Tons)				**ZINC (Tons)**			
2011	1,530,000	1,169,600	76.4	2011	923,000	213,700	23.2
2010	1,430,000	1,100,800	77.0	2010	919,000	212,289	23.1
2009	1,430,000	1,040,600	72.8	2009	891,000	201,900	22.7
2008	1,470,000	1,109,400	75.5	2008	1,000,000	230,000	23.0
2007	1,590,000	1,162,800	73.1	2007	1,110,000	244,200	22.0
2006	1,510,000	1,132,500	75.0	2006	1,130,000	248,600	22.0
2005	1,510,000	1,126,400	74.6	2005	939,000	206,580	22.0

NOTE: For most materials listed, automotive consumption includes materials used for cars, trucks, buses and replacement parts.
SOURCE: Ward's Automotive Group from various sources.

Material Usage, Vehicles Retired From Use and Vehicle Recycling

AVERAGE MATERIALS CONTENT OF NORTH AMERICAN LIGHT VEHICLES

Material	2010 Pounds	2010 Percent	2005 Pounds	2005 Percent	2000 Pounds	2000 Percent	1995 Pounds	1995 Percent
Regular Steel	1,542	38.2	1,634	40.7	1,655	42.4	1,630	44.1
High and Medium Strength Steel	559	13.8	491	12.2	408	10.5	324	8.8
Stainless Steel	73	1.8	71	1.8	62	1.6	51	1.4
Other Steels	33	0.8	35	0.9	26	0.7	46	1.2
Iron Castings	237	5.9	328	8.2	432	11.1	466	12.6
Aluminum	344	8.5	316	7.9	268	6.9	231	6.3
Magnesium Castings	13	0.3	10	0.2	8	0.2	4	0.1
Copper and Brass	65	1.6	59	1.5	52	1.3	50	1.4
Lead	40	1.0	37	0.9	36	0.9	33	0.9
Zinc Castings	9	0.2	10	0.2	13	0.3	19	0.5
Powder Metal	41	1.0	42	1.0	36	0.9	29	0.8
Other Metals	6	0.1	4	0.1	4	0.1	4	0.1
Plastics and Plastic Composites	378	9.4	332	8.3	286	7.3	240	6.5
Rubber	200	5.0	173	4.3	166	4.3	149	4.0
Coatings	34	0.8	27	0.7	25	0.6	23	0.6
Textiles	54	1.3	48	1.2	44	1.1	42	1.1
Fluids and Lubricants	226	5.6	210	5.2	207	5.3	192	5.2
Glass	94	2.3	104	2.6	103	2.6	97	2.6
Other Materials	92	2.3	86	2.1	71	1.9	64	1.7
Total	**4,040**	**100.0**	**4,017**	**100.0**	**3,902**	**100.0**	**3,694**	**100.0**

SOURCE: American Chemistry Council. Data reflects Light Vehicles built in North America.

VEHICLES RETIRED FROM USE
(in Thousands)

Year	Cars	Trucks & Buses	Total
2011	7,395	4,603	11,998
2010	6,360	4,269	10,629
2009	10,462	4,917	15,379
2008	6,882	7,134	14,016
2007	7,008	5,699	12,707
2006	6,750	5,258	12,008
2005	6,478	3,511	9,989
2004	5,524	6,379	11,903
2003	6,864	5,226	12,090
2002	7,310	5,986	13,296
2001	7,650	6,472	14,122
2000	8,085	6,214	14,299
1999	7,216	4,447	11,663
1998	6,819	4,846	11,665
1997	8,244	4,265	12,509
1996	7,527	3,284	10,811
1995	7,414	2,918	10,332
1994	7,824	4,545	12,369
1993	7,366	1,048	8,414
1992	11,194	1,587	12,781
1991	8,565	2,284	10,849
1989	8,981	2,189	11,170
1987	8,103	2,364	10,467
1985	7,729	2,100	9,829
1983	6,243	1,491	7,734
1981	7,542	1,519	9,061
1979	9,312	1,916	11,228
1977	8,234	1,668	9,902
1975	5,669	908	6,577
1973	7,987	1,208	9,195

NOTE: Data as of July 1 each calendar year except 2009, which is Oct. 1. Beginning in 2010, data as of Dec. 31. Car and truck splits are estimated. Figures represent vehicles which are not re-registered.
SOURCE: The Polk Company. Permission for further use must be obtained from The Polk Company.

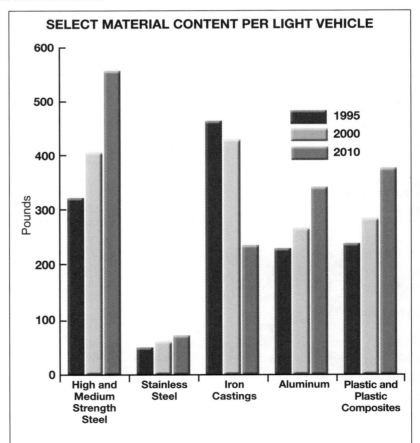

SELECT MATERIAL CONTENT PER LIGHT VEHICLE

Licensed Drivers by Age Group, Gender and State

LICENSED DRIVERS BY STATE, 2010

State	Male (000)	Female (000)	Total (000)
Alabama	1,858	1,948	3,806
Alaska	274	242	516
Arizona	2,236	2,208	4,444
Arkansas	1,022	1,056	2,078
California	12,078	11,676	23,754
Colorado	1,937	1,842	3,779
Connecticut	1,457	1,478	2,935
Delaware	339	356	695
Dist. of Columbia	189	196	385
Florida	6,796	7,154	13,950
Georgia	3,114	3,394	6,508
Hawaii	476	433	909
Idaho	538	532	1,070
Illinois	4,123	4,251	8,374
Indiana	2,785	2,766	5,551
Iowa	1,066	1,101	2,167
Kansas	1,007	1,026	2,033
Kentucky	1,457	1,493	2,950
Louisiana	1,515	1,619	3,134
Maine	505	514	1,019
Maryland	1,923	1,996	3,919
Massachusetts	2,255	2,337	4,592
Michigan	3,464	3,619	7,083
Minnesota	1,650	1,631	3,281
Mississippi	918	1,011	1,929
Missouri	2,086	2,160	4,246
Montana	377	366	743
Nebraska	677	674	1,351
Nevada	871	820	1,691
New Hampshire	520	517	1,037
New Jersey	2,924	3,029	5,953
New Mexico	701	705	1,406
New York	5,816	5,470	11,286
North Carolina	3,186	3,351	6,537
North Dakota	245	238	483
Ohio	3,851	4,112	7,963
Oklahoma	1,073	1,275	2,348
Oregon	1,381	1,388	2,769
Pennsylvania	4,340	4,398	8,738
Rhode Island	367	381	748
South Carolina	1,739	1,598	3,337
South Dakota	302	300	602
Tennessee	2,177	2,242	4,419
Texas	7,520	7,638	15,158
Utah	836	824	1,660
Vermont	255	258	513
Virginia	2,619	2,783	5,402
Washington	2,645	2,461	5,106
West Virginia	599	607	1,206
Wisconsin	2,070	2,063	4,133
Wyoming	216	203	419
Total	**104,375**	**105,740**	**210,115**

SOURCE: U.S. Department of Transportation, Federal Highway Administration.

U.S. DRIVERS BY AGE GROUP AND GENDER, 2010

Age (in Years)	Male (000)	Female (000)	Total (000)
Under 16	199	198	397
16	608	605	1,213
17	1,025	1,004	2,029
18	1,408	1,323	2,731
19	1,641	1,546	3,187
20	1,744	1,682	3,426
21	1,756	1,717	3,473
22	1,757	1,725	3,482
23	1,767	1,748	3,515
24	1,792	1,779	3,571
25-29	9,179	9,253	18,432
30-34	8,934	8,915	17,849
35-39	9,079	9,082	18,161
40-44	9,613	9,565	19,178
45-49	10,381	10,433	20,814
50-54	10,241	10,388	20,629
55-59	9,126	9,313	18,439
60-64	7,847	8,011	15,858
65-69	5,652	5,816	11,468
70-74	4,029	4,202	8,231
75-79	2,966	3,192	6,158
80-84	2,090	2,373	4,463
85 and over	1,541	1,870	3,411
Total	**104,375**	**105,740**	**210,115**

SOURCE: U.S. Department of Transportation, Federal Highway Administration.

U.S. DRIVERS BY GENDER

Year	Male (000)	Percent Male	Female (000)	Percent Female	Total (000)
2010	104,375	49.68	105,740	50.32	210,115
2009	104,262	49.74	105,357	50.26	209,619
2008	103,622	49.74	104,704	50.26	208,326
2007	102,465	49.80	103,277	50.20	205,742
2006	101,116	49.86	101,694	50.14	202,810
2005	100,252	49.99	100,297	50.01	200,549
2004	99,571	50.06	99,318	49.94	198,889
2003	98,228	50.07	97,937	49.93	196,165
2002	97,461	50.16	96,834	49.84	194,295
2001	95,792	50.08	95,483	49.92	191,275
2000	95,796	50.30	94,829	49.70	190,625
1999	94,166	50.31	93,004	49.69	187,170
1998	93,105	50.33	91,875	49.67	184,980
1997	91,905	50.30	90,804	49.70	182,709
1996	90,519	50.42	89,021	49.58	179,540
1995	89,214	50.51	87,414	49.49	176,628
1994	89,194	50.85	86,209	49.15	175,403
1993	87,993	50.82	85,156	49.18	173,149
1992	88,387	51.05	84,738	48.95	173,125
1991	86,665	51.28	82,330	48.72	168,995
1990	85,792	51.37	81,223	48.63	167,015
1989	85,378	51.57	80,177	48.43	165,555
1988	85,230	51.91	78,967	48.09	164,197
1987	84,084	51.91	77,891	48.09	161,975
1986	82,494	52.02	76,100	47.98	158,594
1985	81,592	52.01	75,276	47.99	156,868
1984	80,977	52.10	74,447	47.90	155,424
1983	80,894	52.40	73,495	47.60	154,389
1982	78,553	52.29	71,681	47.71	150,234
1981	77,888	52.96	69,187	47.04	147,075

SOURCE: U.S. Department of Transportation, Federal Highway Administration.

Demographics of New Vehicle Buyers and Initial Vehicle Quality

DEMOGRAPHICS OF NEW VEHICLE BUYERS AND INITIAL VEHICLE QUALITY, 2012 MODEL YEAR

Characteristic	New Passenger Car Buyers				New Light Trucks Buyers				New CUV Buyers			
	Domestic[1]	European[2]	Asian[2]	Total	Domestic[1]	European[2]	Asian[2]	Total	Domestic[1]	European[2]	Asian[2]	Total
Gender												
Male	61.0%	63.4%	54.8%	58.0%	79.6%	63.6%	69.2%	75.3%	52.6%	57.7%	50.5%	52.2%
Female	39.0	36.6	45.2	42.0	20.4	36.4	30.8	24.7	47.4	42.3	49.5	47.8
Total	100.0	100.0	100.0	100.0	100.0	100.0	100.0	100.0	100.0	100.0	100.0	100.0
Age of Principal Purchaser (In Years)												
Under 25	3.7%	2.7%	5.1%	4.3%	1.8%	1.1%	1.1%	1.5%	1.7%	1.3%	1.3%	1.5%
25-29	3.4	5.0	5.9	5.0	3.7	2.6	3.8	3.7	3.6	3.3	4.0	3.7
30-34	3.8	6.0	5.7	5.2	5.5	5.7	7.9	6.4	5.5	6.2	5.1	5.4
35-39	4.4	6.4	5.0	5.1	6.4	10.7	10.8	8.2	5.5	8.7	5.3	5.8
40-44	6.7	9.1	7.3	7.4	8.2	18.5	11.6	9.8	7.4	11.6	7.6	8.0
45-49	9.6	10.9	9.3	9.6	9.6	15.8	10.0	9.9	8.3	12.8	8.9	9.1
50-54	11.9	12.8	11.7	11.9	13.4	13.3	11.2	12.6	10.0	13.0	12.3	11.4
55-59	12.3	13.7	12.7	12.9	13.1	9.5	11.0	12.2	12.6	12.7	13.9	13.2
60-64	12.5	13.2	12.3	12.6	14.8	8.8	12.3	13.7	15.5	13.4	14.9	15.0
65 and over	31.7	20.2	25.0	26.0	23.5	14.0	20.3	22.0	29.9	17.0	26.7	26.9
Total	100.0	100.0	100.0	100.0	100.0	100.0	100.0	100.0	100.0	100.0	100.0	100.0
Highest Education Level												
8th Grade or Less	0.6%	0.2%	0.3%	0.4%	0.5%	0.2%	0.7%	0.6%	0.3%	0.2%	0.1%	0.2%
Some High School	2.1	0.6	1.2	1.3	2.0	0.2	1.3	1.7	1.3	0.2	0.8	0.9
High School Graduate	19.8	6.2	14.0	14.3	21.1	5.3	12.4	17.4	18.3	4.8	11.7	13.7
Technical/Trade School	10.6	5.1	7.2	7.8	11.5	2.1	7.4	9.7	9.0	3.6	6.5	7.2
Some College	26.1	18.2	24.3	23.8	25.2	14.7	21.4	23.5	25.3	14.9	21.1	22.1
College Graduate	20.3	28.6	24.8	24.2	20.0	36.1	25.8	22.6	23.0	31.9	26.0	25.4
Post Graduate	5.1	8.0	6.1	6.1	5.4	7.6	5.9	5.6	5.6	7.5	6.8	6.4
Advanced Degree	15.4	33.1	22.1	22.1	14.3	33.8	25.1	18.9	17.2	36.9	27.0	24.1
Total	100.0	100.0	100.0	100.0	100.0	100.0	100.0	100.0	100.0	100.0	100.0	100.0
Census Region												
Northeast	18.5%	23.5%	22.2%	21.4%	19.2%	21.6%	19.5%	19.4%	18.5%	26.4%	25.7%	22.7%
Midwest	36.8	13.2	17.0	21.9	33.2	11.4	16.5	26.4	40.0	14.1	19.9	27.7
South	30.7	33.4	39.1	35.8	31.4	36.6	41.5	35.3	29.8	33.4	34.2	32.3
West	14.0	29.9	21.7	20.9	16.2	30.4	22.5	18.9	11.7	26.1	20.2	17.3
Total	100.0	100.0	100.0	100.0	100.0	100.0	100.0	100.0	100.0	100.0	100.0	100.0
Median Household Income	$73,468	$131,450	$78,977	$83,198	$93,854	$320,740	$99,815	$97,595	$87,297	$173,334	$94,919	$96,795
Initial Quality (Problems per 100 Passenger Cars)												
Study Results	110	109	93	101	99	117	94	97	116	112	97	107

NOTE: Study conducted among personal use buyers of '12 model year vehicles.
(1) Domestic figures include captive import buyers.
(2) Import figures include buyers of North American assembled vehicles.
SOURCE: J.D. Power and Associates, 2012 Initial Quality Study.

Car Operating Costs

CAR OPERATING COSTS

| Model Year | Variable Cost in Cents Per Mile | | | | Cost Per 10,000 Miles | | | |
	Gas & Oil	Maintenance	Tires	Total	Variable Cost	Fixed Cost	Total Cost	Total Cost Per Mile
2012	14.17	4.47	1.00	19.64	$1,964	$5,746	$7,710	77.10
2011	12.34	4.44	0.96	17.74	1,774	5,857	7,631	76.31
2010	11.36	4.54	0.83	16.73	1,673	5,719	7,392	73.92
2009	10.09	4.56	0.77	15.42	1,542	5,526	7,068	70.68
2008	11.67	4.57	0.72	16.96	1,696	5,399	7,095	70.95
2007	8.90	4.90	0.70	14.50	1,450	4,765	6,215	62.15
2006	9.50	4.90	0.70	15.10	1,510	4,686	6,196	61.96
2005	8.20	5.30	0.60	14.10	1,410	5,412	6,822	68.22
2004	6.50	5.40	0.70	12.60	1,260	5,633	6,893	68.93
2003	7.20	4.10	1.80	13.10	1,310	4,884	6,194	61.94
2002	5.90	4.10	1.80	11.80	1,180	4,874	6,054	60.54
2001	7.90	3.90	1.80	13.60	1,360	4,621	5,981	59.81
2000	6.90	3.60	1.70	12.20	1,220	4,724	5,944	59.44
1999	5.60	3.30	1.70	10.60	1,060	4,660	5,720	57.20
1998	6.20	3.10	1.40	10.70	1,070	4,528	5,598	55.98
1997	6.60	2.80	1.40	10.80	1,080	4,348	5,428	54.28
1996	5.60	2.80	1.20	9.60	960	4,193	5,153	51.53
1995	5.80	2.60	1.20	9.60	960	4,005	4,965	49.65
1994	5.60	2.50	1.00	9.10	910	3,836	4,746	47.46
1993	5.90	2.40	0.90	9.20	920	3,722	4,642	46.42
1992	5.90	2.20	0.90	9.00	900	3,784	4,684	46.84
1990	5.40	2.10	0.90	8.40	840	3,256	4,096	40.96
1985	5.57	1.20	0.65	7.42	742	2,061	2,803	28.03
1980	5.86	1.12	0.64	7.62	762	2,033	2,795	27.95

ANNUAL FIXED COST OF OPERATING A CAR

| Model Year | Insurance | | | License, Registration & Taxes | Depreciation | Finance Charge | Total | Average Fixed Cost Per Day |
	Fire & Theft[2]	Collision[3]	Property Damage & Liability[4]					
2012[1]	NA	$1,001	NA	$610	$3,544	$846	$6,001	$16.44
2011[1]	NA	968	NA	595	3,728	823	6,114	16.75
2010[1]	NA	1,031	NA	585	3,554	806	5,976	16.37
2009[1]	NA	976	NA	567	3,461	779	5,783	15.84
2008[1]	NA	943	NA	554	3,321	758	5,576	15.28
2007[1]	NA	985	NA	538	3,392	733	5,648	15.47
2006[1]	NA	926	NA	535	3,392	716	5,569	15.26
2005[1]	NA	1,288	NA	389	3,879	739	6,295	17.25
2004[1]	NA	1,603	NA	415	3,782	741	6,541	17.92
2003	203	401	498	205	3,738	744	5,789	15.86
2002	173	357	484	201	3,721	828	5,764	15.79
2001	167	345	479	208	3,548	866	5,613	15.38
2000	163	326	481	223	3,492	849	5,534	15.16
1999	162	324	484	226	3,436	828	5,460	14.96
1998	134	287	479	226	3,364	813	5,303	14.53
1997	120	326	401	216	3,272	768	5,103	13.98
1996	144	275	426	215	3,170	718	4,948	13.56
1995	121	252	410	203	3,073	686	4,745	13.00
1994	123	246	400	194	2,940	648	4,551	12.47
1993	116	243	385	178	2,830	670	4,422	12.12
1992	128	286	373	174	2,717	796	4,474	12.26
1990	110	245	318	165	2,357	680	3,875	10.62
1985	75	177	213	110	1,262	534	2,371	6.50
1980	70	172	248	82	1,038	423	2,033	5.57

NOTE: Methodology changed beginning in 2004; data is not comparable to prior years. Beginning in 1985 ownership costs are based on a six year/60,000 mile retention cycle rather than four year/60,000 miles.
NA - Not available.
(1) Individual component costs of insurance are no longer available, therefore insurance costs for 2004 forward reflect the total amount of a full coverage policy.
(2) $100 deductible 1981-1992; $250 deductible 1993-2003, $100 deductible 2004-2012.
(3) $250 deductible 1981-1992; $500 deductible 1993-2012.
(4) Coverage: 1980 to 2012-$100,000/$300,000
SOURCE: American Automobile Association.

Light Truck Operating Costs

LIGHT TRUCK OPERATING COSTS

	Variable Cost in Cents Per Mile				Cost Per 10,000 Miles			
Model Year	Gas & Oil	Maintenance	Tires	Total	Variable Cost	Fixed Cost	Total Cost	Total Cost Per Mile
2012	18.65	4.88	1.27	24.80	$2,480	$7,365	$9,845	98.45
2011	17.04	4.80	1.14	22.98	2,298	7,517	9,815	98.15
2010	16.38	4.95	0.98	22.31	2,231	7,463	9,694	96.94
2009	14.39	4.94	0.95	20.28	2,028	6,942	8,970	89.70
2008	17.05	5.47	0.93	23.45	2,345	6,750	9,095	90.95
2007	12.60	5.50	0.90	19.00	1,900	6,247	8,147	81.47
2006	13.70	5.60	0.80	20.10	2,010	5,890	7,900	79.00
2005	10.80	5.30	0.90	17.00	1,700	6,074	7,774	77.74
2004	8.40	4.30	1.00	13.70	1,370	5,903	7,273	72.73
2003	7.90	4.10	1.50	13.50	1,350	5,527	6,877	68.77
2002	5.80	4.10	1.70	11.60	1,160	4,332	5,492	54.92

ANNUAL FIXED COST OF OPERATING A LIGHT TRUCK

	Insurance							
Model Year	Fire & Theft[2]	Collision[3]	Property Damage & Liability[4]	License, Registration & Taxes	Depreciation	Finance Charge	Total	Average Fixed Cost Per Day
2012[1]	NA	$934	NA	$794	$4,784	$1,128	$7,640	$20.93
2011[1]	NA	912	NA	757	5,052	1,071	7,792	21.35
2010[1]	NA	964	NA	735	5,003	1,036	7,738	21.20
2009[1]	NA	948	NA	727	4,519	1,023	7,217	19.77
2008[1]	NA	888	NA	715	4,327	1,000	6,930	18.99
2007[1]	NA	950	NA	695	4,531	971	7,147	19.58
2006[1]	NA	918	NA	683	4,254	935	6,790	18.60
2005[1]	NA	1,398	NA	435	4,300	891	7,024	19.24
2004[1]	NA	1,491	NA	454	4,043	865	6,853	18.78
2003	159	402	389	289	4,286	867	6,392	17.51
2002	204	451	389	261	3,220	662	5,187	14.21

NOTE: Methodology changed beginning in 2004; data is not comparable to prior years.
NA - Not available
(1) Individual component costs of insurance are no longer available, therefore insurance costs for 2004 forward reflect the total amount of a full coverage policy.
(2) $250 deductible 2002-2003, $100 deductible 2004-2012.
(3) $500 deductible 2002-2012.
(4) Coverage: 2002 to 2012-$100,000/$300,000
SOURCE: American Automobile Association.

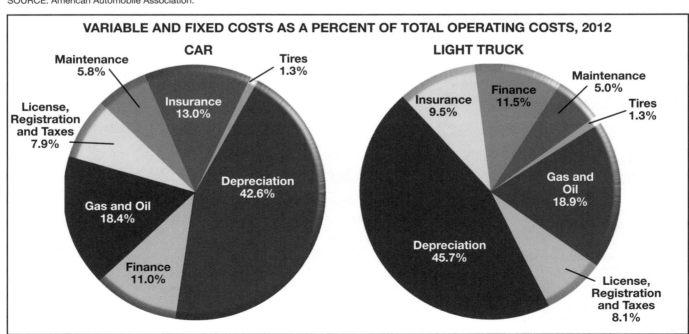

VARIABLE AND FIXED COSTS AS A PERCENT OF TOTAL OPERATING COSTS, 2012

CAR

- Maintenance 5.8%
- Tires 1.3%
- Insurance 13.0%
- License, Registration and Taxes 7.9%
- Depreciation 42.6%
- Gas and Oil 18.4%
- Finance 11.0%

LIGHT TRUCK

- Finance 11.5%
- Maintenance 5.0%
- Tires 1.3%
- Insurance 9.5%
- Gas and Oil 18.9%
- Depreciation 45.7%
- License, Registration and Taxes 8.1%

Automobile Financing

NEW AND USED CAR FINANCING WITH FINANCE COMPANIES

Year	% Average Interest Rate	Average Maturity (Months)	Average Amount Financed	Average Monthly Payment	Year	% Average Interest Rate	Average Maturity (Months)	Average Amount Financed	Average Monthly Payment
NEW CARS					**USED CARS**				
2011	4.7	62.3	$26,673	$483.33	2011	7.7	64.5	$18,723	$355.40
2010	4.3	63.0	27,959	496.56	2010	8.2	62.6	18,124	356.82
2009	3.8	62.0	28,272	502.95	2009	9.4	59.2	16,225	343.57
2008	5.5	63.4	26,178	476.73	2008	8.7	59.8	16,664	344.41
2007	4.9	62.0	28,287	517.35	2007	9.2	60.7	17,095	353.29
2006	5.0	63.0	26,620	481.30	2006	9.6	59.4	16,671	353.70
2005	6.0	60.0	24,133	466.56	2005	8.8	58.6	16,228	341.68
2004	4.9	60.7	24,888	463.76	2004	8.8	57.9	15,136	321.77
2003	3.4	61.4	26,295	467.19	2003	9.7	57.7	14,613	317.90
2002	4.3	56.8	24,747	482.31	2002	10.7	57.6	14,532	323.70
2001	5.7	55.1	22,822	471.73	2001	12.2	57.5	14,416	332.33
2000	6.6	54.9	20,923	442.58	2000	13.6	57.0	14,058	336.16
1999	6.7	52.7	19,880	436.49	1999	12.6	55.9	13,642	324.15
1998	6.3	52.1	19,083	419.60	1998	12.6	53.5	12,691	311.51
1997	7.1	54.1	18,077	391.45	1997	13.3	51.0	12,281	316.54
1996	9.8	51.6	16,987	404.75	1996	13.5	51.4	12,182	313.39
1995	11.2	54.1	16,210	382.98	1995	14.5	52.2	11,590	300.66
1994	9.8	54.0	15,375	353.25	1994	13.5	50.2	10,709	280.37
1993	9.5	54.5	14,332	324.79	1993	12.8	48.8	9,875	260.63
1992	9.8	54.0	13,607	313.01	1992	13.7	47.9	9,211	250.70
1991	12.4	55.1	12,494	298.14	1991	15.6	47.2	8,884	253.11
1990	12.5	54.6	12,071	291.31	1990	16.0	46.1	8,289	249.35
1989	12.6	54.2	12,001	291.50	1989	16.2	46.6	7,954	231.08
1988	12.6	56.2	11,663	275.95	1988	15.1	46.7	7,824	222.68
1987	10.7	53.5	11,203	264.22	1987	14.6	45.2	7,420	214.39
1986	9.4	50.0	10,665	258.74	1986	16.0	42.6	6,555	202.52
1985	12.0	51.1	9,883	248.44	1985	17.6	41.2	6,091	198.03
1984	14.6	48.3	9,337	256.90	1984	17.9	39.7	5,691	190.92
1983	12.7	45.9	8,787	242.24	1983	18.8	38.0	5,033	176.77
1982	15.9	46.0	8,178	238.16	1982	20.8	37.0	4,746	174.84
1981	16.0	45.3	7,339	216.41	1981	20.0	35.8	4,339	162.02
1980	14.8	45.0	6,322	183.91	1980	19.1	34.8	3,810	143.44

SOURCE: Board of Governors of The Federal Reserve.

Expenditures for Transportation

AVERAGE EXPENDITURE PER NEW CAR

Year	Average Expenditure Per New Car[1]			Estimated Average New Car Price for a 1967 "Comparable Car"		Annual Median Family Earnings[4]	Average New Car Expenditure[5]	Weeks of Median Family Earnings to Equal Cost of "Comparable Car"	
	Domestic*	Import	Average	With Added Safety & Emissions Equipment[2]	Without Added Safety & Emissions Equipment[3]			With Added Safety & Emissions Equipment[6]	Without Added Safety & Emissions Equipment[7]
2011	$23,359	$29,621	$25,233	$14,136	$8,835	$79,606	16.5	9.2	5.8
2010	23,020	27,681	24,520	13,722	8,807	75,743	16.8	9.4	6.0
2009	22,153	25,500	23,280	13,539	8,815	75,291	16.1	9.4	6.1
2008	22,205	25,903	23,442	13,378	8,793	78,591	15.5	8.9	5.8
2007	22,284	27,465	23,892	13,364	8,797	75,254	16.5	9.2	6.1
2006	22,166	27,062	23,634	13,389	8,800	71,196	17.3	9.8	6.4
2005	21,593	26,621	23,017	13,094	8,799	66,977	17.9	10.2	6.8
2004	20,536	25,941	22,076	12,882	8,784	63,485	18.1	10.6	7.2
2003	19,971	26,081	21,646	12,923	8,838	60,135	18.7	11.2	7.6
2001	20,042	25,787	21,474	13,160	9,116	56,628	19.2	12.3	8.4
1999	19,032	27,542	20,710	13,164	9,157	50,784	20.9	13.6	9.4
1997	17,600	27,509	19,236	13,240	9,297	45,326	22.4	15.2	10.7
1995	16,864	23,202	17,959	12,989	9,115	40,572	23.0	16.5	11.7
1993	15,976	20,261	16,871	12,153	8,631	36,764	23.9	16.7	12.2
1991	15,192	16,327	15,475	11,321	8,224	34,775	23.1	16.7	12.3
1989	13,936	15,510	14,371	10,282	7,825	32,448	23.0	16.5	12.5
1987	12,922	14,470	13,386	9,775	7,518	29,744	23.4	17.1	13.1
1985	11,589	12,853	11,838	9,014	6,958	27,144	22.7	17.3	13.3
1983	10,516	10,868	10,606	8,415	6,544	24,580	22.4	17.8	13.8
1981	8,912	8,896	8,910	7,726	6,115	22,388	20.7	17.9	14.2
1979	6,889	6,704	6,847	6,198	5,337	19,661	18.1	16.4	14.1
1967	3,313	2,276	3,216	3,196	3,185	7,933	21.1	20.9	20.9

NOTE: *Includes transplants.

(1) U.S. Departments of Commerce, Bureau of Economic Analysis (BEA) , "Average Transaction Price Per New Car." Includes purchases by business, government, and consumers.

(2) 1967 "Average Transaction Price" plus the value of added safety and emissions equipment as determined by the U.S. Bureau of Labor Statistics (BLS), all inflated to current dollars using the BLS, "New Car Consumer Price Index-All Urban Consumers." For example, 1969 is equal to the 1968 value plus the BLS stated value of added safety and emissions equipment for the 1969 model year multiplied by 1968-1969 monthly changes in the New Car Consumer Price Index. The cost to improve fuel economy, which prior to 1980 was included with "Other Quality Adjustments", has since been included by the BLS with the cost of emissions improvements.

(3) 1967 "Average Transaction Price" inflated to current dollars.

(4) BLS, "Median Family Earnings."

(5) "Average Expenditure," as reported by the BEA, divided by "Annual Median Family Earnings", multiplied by 52 weeks. This index is not a good reflection of car prices because it includes upgrading-the purchase of more expensive types of vehicles with more options-and downgrading.

(6) "Estimated Average New Car Price of Comparable Cars With New Safety and Emissions Equipment Added", divided by "Annual Median Family Earnings," multiplied by 52 weeks. This index is a good reflection of price as seen by car purchasers who would not otherwise buy safety/emissions equipment. (7) "Estimated Average New Car Price of Comparable Cars Without New Safety and Emissions Equipment" divided by "Annual Median Family Earnings," multiplied by 52 weeks. This index is a good reflection of price as seen by purchasers who place full value on new safety/emissions equipment.

INDICES OF CONSUMER COSTS

Year	Consumer Price Index - All Urban Consumers (1982-84 = 100)							
	All Items	Housing	Medical Care	Public Transportation	Gasoline	New Cars	New Trucks	Used Cars & Trucks
2011	224.9	219.1	400.3	269.4	301.7	142.2	146.5	149.0
2010	218.1	216.3	388.4	251.4	238.6	138.1	142.7	143.1
2009	214.5	217.1	375.6	236.3	201.6	136.7	138.8	128.0
2008	215.3	216.3	364.1	250.5	277.5	135.4	137.1	134.0
2007	207.3	209.6	351.1	230.0	237.9	135.9	140.7	135.7
2006	201.6	203.2	336.2	226.6	219.9	136.4	142.9	140.0
2005	195.3	195.7	323.2	217.3	194.7	135.2	145.3	139.4
2004	188.9	189.5	310.1	209.1	159.7	133.9	145.0	133.3
2003	184.0	184.8	297.1	209.3	135.1	134.7	146.1	142.9
2002	179.9	180.3	285.6	207.4	116.0	137.3	147.8	152.0
2001	177.1	176.4	272.8	210.6	124.0	138.9	150.7	158.7
2000	172.2	169.6	260.8	209.6	128.6	139.6	151.7	155.8
1999	166.6	163.9	250.6	197.7	100.1	139.6	153.1	152.0
1998	163.0	160.4	242.1	190.3	91.6	140.7	152.1	150.6
1997	160.5	156.8	234.6	186.7	105.8	141.7	151.4	151.1

SOURCE: U.S. Department of Labor, Bureau of Labor Statistics.

Personal Consumption Expenditures for Transportation

PERSONAL CONSUMPTION EXPENDITURES FOR TRANSPORTATION

	2011	2010	2009	2008	2007	2006	2005	2004
User-Operated Transportation								
New Autos	81,468	69,773	72,374	85,672	95,922	99,982	97,448	91,909
New Light Trucks	123,207	108,692	93,574	99,193	137,230	133,065	151,447	160,522
Net Purchases of Used Motor Vehicles	121,264	112,437	104,171	106,137	116,713	113,524	112,707	107,115
Tires, Tubes, Accessories and Parts	52,631	49,223	46,429	52,237	52,644	50,561	48,046	45,188
Motor Vehicle Maintenance and Repair, Storage, Rental and Leasing	155,598	153,027	151,196	159,213	162,630	157,148	155,128	148,336
Gasoline, Oil and Lubricants	402,708	331,391	279,113	384,516	342,973	314,665	283,798	231,555
Parking Fees and Tolls	17,585	17,107	16,734	15,585	14,702	14,778	14,771	13,722
Insurance Premiums, Less Claims Paid	62,858	60,092	59,701	61,801	61,767	56,974	57,614	53,515
Total User-Operated Transportation	**1,017,319**	**901,742**	**823,292**	**964,354**	**984,581**	**940,697**	**920,959**	**851,862**
Purchased Public Transportation								
Transit Systems	16,994	16,483	16,033	15,493	14,558	14,624	13,415	12,769
Taxicabs	4,923	4,669	4,469	4,341	4,383	4,448	4,086	3,776
Railway Excluding Commutation	1,105	1,033	919	996	906	810	733	719
Bus	1,184	1,149	1,091	1,302	1,206	1,303	1,306	1,353
Airline	55,776	50,465	45,058	51,603	51,596	49,368	47,654	46,163
Other	10,407	10,053	9,861	10,760	10,511	10,036	9,589	9,151
Total Purchased Public Transportation	**90,389**	**83,852**	**77,431**	**84,495**	**83,160**	**80,589**	**76,783**	**73,931**
Total Transportation Expenditures	**1,107,708**	**985,594**	**900,723**	**1,048,849**	**1,067,741**	**1,021,286**	**997,742**	**925,793**
Total Personal Consumption Expenditures	**10,725,959**	**10,245,518**	**9,866,119**	**10,035,524**	**9,806,312**	**9,322,662**	**8,819,002**	**8,285,080**
Transportation spending share of Total PCE	**10.3%**	**9.6%**	**9.1%**	**10.5%**	**10.9%**	**11.0%**	**11.3%**	**11.2%**

NOTE: Data in millions of dollars.
SOURCE: U.S. Department of Commerce, Bureau of Economic Analysis.

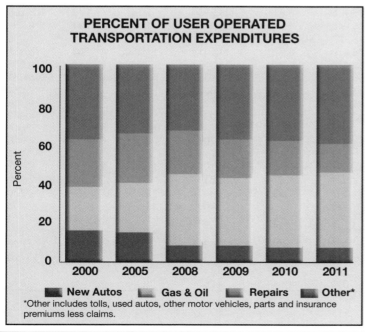

PERCENT OF USER OPERATED TRANSPORTATION EXPENDITURES

Legend: New Autos, Gas & Oil, Repairs, Other*

*Other includes tolls, used autos, other motor vehicles, parts and insurance premiums less claims.

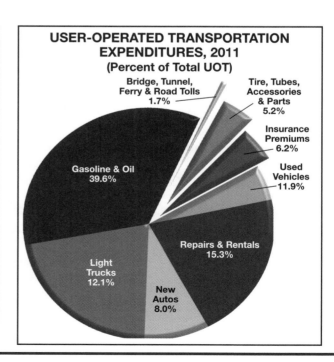

USER-OPERATED TRANSPORTATION EXPENDITURES, 2011 (Percent of Total UOT)

- Gasoline & Oil 39.6%
- Bridge, Tunnel, Ferry & Road Tolls 1.7%
- Tire, Tubes, Accessories & Parts 5.2%
- Insurance Premiums 6.2%
- Used Vehicles 11.9%
- Repairs & Rentals 15.3%
- Light Trucks 12.1%
- New Autos 8.0%

Vehicle Miles of Travel and Fuel Consumption

VEHICLE MILES OF TRAVEL AND FUEL CONSUMPTION

	Cars	Light Trucks	Light Vehicle Total	Medium Duty Trucks	Heavy Duty Trucks	Buses	Motorcycles	Total Vehicles
Vehicle Miles of Travel (in Millions)								
2010	—	—	2,647,665	110,676	175,912	13,790	18,463	2,966,506
2009	—	—	2,633,248	120,207	168,100	14,387	20,822	2,956,764
2008	1,615,850	1,108,603	2,724,453	83,951	143,507	7,114	14,484	2,973,509
2007	1,670,994	1,111,277	2,782,271	81,954	145,008	6,976	13,612	3,029,821
2006	1,682,671	1,089,013	2,771,684	80,331	142,706	6,994	12,401	3,014,116
2005	1,708,421	1,041,051	2,749,472	79,174	144,028	6,980	10,454	2,990,108
2004	1,699,890	1,027,164	2,727,054	78,441	142,370	6,801	10,122	2,964,788
2003	1,672,079	984,094	2,656,173	77,757	140,160	6,783	9,577	2,890,450
2002	1,658,474	966,034	2,624,508	75,866	138,737	6,845	9,552	2,855,508
2000	1,600,287	923,059	2,523,346	70,500	135,020	7,590	10,469	2,746,925
1990	1,417,823	574,571	1,992,394	51,901	94,341	5,726	(1)	2,144,362
1980	1,121,810	290,935	1,412,745	39,813	68,678	6,059	(1)	1,527,295
Average Annual Miles Traveled Per Vehicle								
2010	—	—	11,489	13,469	68,907	16,298	2,248	11,853
2009	—	—	11,231	14,386	64,231	17,087	2,626	11,631
2008	11,788	10,951	11,432	12,362	64,764	8,436	1,868	11,619
2007	12,293	10,952	11,720	12,040	65,290	8,360	1,907	11,910
2006	12,427	11,857	12,197	13,038	70,986	8,509	1,855	12,408
2005	12,510	10,920	11,856	12,274	69,020	8,649	1,679	12,082
2004	12,460	11,184	11,946	12,732	70,819	8,552	1,755	12,200
2003	12,325	11,287	11,919	13,295	73,445	8,734	1,783	12,208
2002	12,202	11,364	11,879	13,426	60,939	8,998	1,909	12,171
2000	11,976	11,672	11,863	11,897	64,399	10,173	2,409	12,164
1990	10,277	11,902	10,693	11,567	55,206	9,133	(1)	11,107
1980	8,813	10,437	9,112	9,103	48,472	11,458	(1)	9,458
Fuel Consumed (Millions of Gallons)								
2010	—	—	122,373	15,071	29,885	1,924	426	169,679
2009	—	—	121,368	16,253	28,050	1,987	482	168,140
2008	71,947	61,199	133,146	9,889	26,814	1,110	256	171,215
2007	74,355	61,816	136,171	10,036	28,515	1,144	242	176,108
2006	74,983	60,662	135,645	9,843	28,075	1,147	221	174,931
2005	77,418	58,869	136,287	9,501	27,689	1,120	189	174,786
2004	75,402	63,417	138,819	8,959	24,191	1,360	202	173,531
2003	75,455	60,758	136,213	8,880	23,815	969	192	170,069
2002	75,471	55,220	130,691	10,321	26,480	1,000	191	168,683
2000	73,065	52,939	126,004	9,563	25,666	1,112	209	162,554
1990	69,759	35,611	105,370	8,357	16,133	895	(1)	130,755
1980	70,186	23,796	93,982	6,923	13,037	1,018	(1)	114,960
Average Annual Fuel Consumption Per Vehicle (Gallons)								
2010	—	—	531	1,834	11,706	2,274	52	678
2009	—	—	518	1,945	10,718	2,360	61	661
2008	522	605	557	1,456	12,101	1,316	33	667
2007	547	609	574	1,474	12,839	1,371	34	692
2006	554	660	597	1,598	13,965	1,396	33	720
2005	567	617	588	1,486	13,269	1,388	30	706
2004	553	690	608	1,454	12,033	1,710	35	714
2003	556	697	611	1,518	12,479	1,248	36	718
2002	555	650	592	1,826	11,631	1,314	38	719
2000	547	669	592	1,614	12,241	1,490	48	720
1990	506	738	569	1,862	9,441	1,428	(1)	677
1980	551	854	610	1,583	9,201	1,926	(1)	712

NOTE: Car and light truck combined into light vehicle beginning in 2009.
NA - Not available. (1) Cars include motorcycles through 1994.
SOURCE: U.S. Department of Transportation, Federal Highway Administration.

Annual Vehicle Miles of Travel

VEHICLE MILES OF TRAVEL, 2010

	Rural Interstate	Total Rural	Urban Interstate	Total Urban	Total
Alabama	5,745	30,566	7,552	33,597	64,163
Alaska	859	2,205	663	2,594	4,799
Arizona	7,005	17,286	5,935	42,777	60,063
Arkansas	4,328	18,792	4,093	14,713	33,505
California	17,565	58,060	68,207	264,789	322,849
Colorado	4,149	14,720	7,489	32,220	46,940
Connecticut	711	3,902	9,633	27,393	31,295
Delaware	—	2,779	1,191	6,169	8,948
Dist. of Columbia	—	—	477	3,591	3,591
Florida	9,459	35,403	25,371	160,352	195,755
Georgia	10,007	36,770	19,088	74,953	111,723
Hawaii	109	2,424	1,746	7,571	9,995
Idaho	2,204	9,232	1,271	6,570	15,802
Illinois	9,066	26,827	23,053	78,961	105,788
Indiana	7,143	28,362	9,363	47,398	75,760
Iowa	4,858	19,019	2,592	12,370	31,389
Kansas	3,192	14,568	3,641	15,331	29,899
Kentucky	6,875	27,753	6,178	20,254	48,007
Louisiana	5,404	19,052	7,569	26,386	45,438
Maine	2,249	10,486	838	4,064	14,550
Maryland	3,555	14,287	13,485	41,839	56,126
Massachusetts	1,373	4,139	15,092	50,223	54,362
Michigan	5,792	31,923	15,435	65,645	97,568
Minnesota	4,108	24,586	8,260	32,045	56,631
Mississippi	3,835	23,444	3,382	16,397	39,841
Missouri	6,329	30,731	11,642	40,133	70,864
Montana	2,393	8,401	355	2,789	11,190
Nebraska	2,624	11,110	1,376	8,328	19,438
Nevada	1,870	4,839	3,481	16,280	21,119
New Hampshire	1,297	5,742	1,597	7,324	13,066
New Jersey	1,583	6,423	13,513	66,604	73,027
New Mexico	4,406	14,330	2,643	10,995	25,325
New York	6,135	32,926	20,317	98,326	131,252
North Carolina	5,996	40,007	14,907	62,378	102,385
North Dakota	1,527	5,959	422	2,303	8,262
Ohio	9,137	36,159	22,652	75,677	111,836
Oklahoma	5,143	21,773	4,885	25,973	47,746
Oregon	4,243	14,931	4,511	18,843	33,774
Pennsylvania	10,372	35,734	13,154	64,595	100,329
Rhode Island	407	884	1,717	7,396	8,280
South Carolina	7,596	23,682	6,144	25,442	49,124
South Dakota	2,032	6,360	627	2,506	8,866
Tennessee	8,656	28,412	11,641	42,027	70,439
Texas	15,480	69,024	39,732	164,992	234,016
Utah	3,166	8,002	6,105	18,583	26,585
Vermont	1,265	5,396	379	1,852	7,248
Virginia	9,342	29,866	14,913	52,304	82,170
Washington	4,606	17,177	10,884	40,014	57,191
West Virginia	2,787	11,059	2,753	8,144	19,203
Wisconsin	5,194	31,739	5,267	27,681	59,420
Wyoming	2,470	6,899	472	2,669	9,568
U.S. Total	**245,647**	**984,148**	**477,693**	**1,982,358**	**2,966,506**

NOTE: Data in millions. Includes travel by motorcycle.
SOURCE: U.S. Department of Transportation, Federal Highway Administration.

TOTAL VEHICLE MILES TRAVELED

Year	Rural	Urban	Total	% Change
2010	984	1,982	2,966	0.3
2009	982	1,975	2,957	-0.5
2008	990	1,983	2,973	-1.9
2007	1,035	1,995	3,030	0.5
2006	1,037	1,977	3,014	0.8
2005	1,038	1,952	2,990	0.9
2004	1,070	1,892	2,962	2.5
2003	1,085	1,806	2,891	1.2
2002	1,128	1,728	2,856	2.7
2001	1,105	1,676	2,781	1.1
2000	1,085	1,665	2,750	2.2
1999	1,063	1,628	2,691	2.5
1998	1,033	1,592	2,625	3.7
1997	985	1,547	2,532	2.0
1996	960	1,522	2,482	2.5
1995	933	1,489	2,422	2.7
1994	909	1,449	2,358	2.7
1993	887	1,410	2,297	2.2
1992	884	1,363	2,247	3.4
1991	884	1,289	2,173	1.2
1990	870	1,277	2,147	1.9
1989	849	1,258	2,107	4.0
1988	818	1,208	2,026	5.5
1987	780	1,141	1,921	4.7
1986	748	1,087	1,835	3.4
1985	730	1,044	1,774	3.1
1984	718	1,002	1,720	4.1
1983	701	952	1,653	3.6
1982	689	906	1,595	2.7
1981	686	867	1,553	1.7
1980	672	855	1,527	-0.2
1979	676	854	1,530	-0.9
1978	682	862	1,544	5.2
1977	651	816	1,467	4.6
1976	625	777	1,402	5.6
1975	602	726	1,328	3.8
1974	585	695	1,280	-2.5
1973	606	707	1,313	4.2
1972	590	670	1,260	6.9
1971	573	606	1,179	6.3
1970	539	570	1,109	4.5
1969	524	537	1,061	4.4
1968	506	510	1,016	5.4
1967	481	483	964	4.1
1966	476	450	926	4.3
1965	464	424	888	5.0
1964	441	405	846	5.1
1963	420	385	805	5.0
1962	399	368	767	3.9
1961	398	340	738	2.6
1960	387	332	719	2.6
1959	377	324	701	5.4
1958	358	307	665	2.8
1957	350	297	647	2.5
1956	344	287	631	4.1
1955	331	275	606	7.8
1954	314	248	562	3.3
1953	308	236	544	6.0
1952	289	224	513	4.5
1951	268	223	491	7.2

NOTE: Data in billions.
SOURCE: U.S. Department of Transportation, Federal Highway Administration.

Selected Travel Data by State

TRAVEL DATA BY STATE, 2010

State	Resident Population in Thousands	Population Per Vehicle	Annual Miles Traveled Per Vehicle	Annual Miles Traveled Per Licensed Driver	Public Road and Street Mileage Rural	Public Road and Street Mileage Urban	Public Road and Street Mileage Total	State Gasoline Tax Rate
Alabama	4,780	1.03	13,787	16,859	76,384	25,190	101,575	18.0
Alaska	710	1.00	6,755	9,314	13,718	2,585	16,303	8.0
Arizona	6,392	1.48	13,903	13,517	41,242	23,066	64,308	18.0
Arkansas	2,916	1.41	16,159	16,125	87,112	12,956	100,068	21.5
California	37,254	1.20	10,410	13,592	82,046	90,092	172,139	18.0
Colorado	5,029	1.20	11,229	12,420	68,923	19,430	88,353	22.0
Connecticut	3,574	1.16	10,154	10,664	6,216	15,175	21,391	25.0
Delaware	898	1.12	11,199	12,874	3,346	2,991	6,337	23.0
District of Columbia	602	2.84	16,966	9,329	--	1,503	1,503	23.5
Florida	18,801	1.31	13,620	14,033	40,189	81,513	121,702	16.0
Georgia	9,688	1.26	14,506	17,167	83,093	39,824	122,917	7.5
Hawaii	1,360	1.50	11,051	10,991	2,050	2,345	4,395	17.0
Idaho	1,568	1.18	11,926	14,775	42,949	5,822	48,771	25.0
Illinois	12,831	1.27	10,496	12,633	98,199	41,320	139,519	19.0
Indiana	6,484	1.14	13,296	13,649	70,111	26,877	96,988	18.0
Iowa	3,046	0.92	9,475	14,487	102,992	11,391	114,383	21.0
Kansas	2,853	1.17	12,273	14,706	127,675	12,978	140,653	24.0
Kentucky	4,339	1.21	13,376	16,273	66,628	12,556	79,184	25.6
Louisiana	4,533	1.11	11,120	14,500	44,992	16,335	61,327	20.0
Maine	1,328	1.26	13,807	14,268	19,859	3,005	22,864	29.5
Maryland	5,774	1.27	12,316	14,324	14,089	17,437	31,526	23.5
Massachusetts	6,548	1.23	10,192	11,837	7,983	28,265	36,248	21.0
Michigan	9,884	1.06	10,507	13,775	85,985	35,983	121,969	19.0
Minnesota	5,304	1.09	11,681	17,258	117,532	20,632	138,164	27.5
Mississippi	2,967	1.47	19,763	20,659	64,050	11,031	75,080	18.4
Missouri	5,989	1.16	13,751	16,689	106,767	23,592	130,360	17.0
Montana	989	1.07	12,086	15,048	71,619	3,174	74,793	27.8
Nebraska	1,826	1.01	10,784	14,382	87,225	6,428	93,653	27.1
Nevada	2,701	1.98	15,510	12,487	27,028	8,033	35,061	24.0
New Hampshire	1,316	1.09	10,861	12,599	11,150	4,935	16,085	19.6
New Jersey	8,792	1.33	11,018	12,268	7,373	31,868	39,242	10.5
New Mexico	2,059	1.28	15,706	18,013	60,469	7,909	68,378	18.9
New York	19,378	1.89	12,799	11,630	66,146	48,427	114,574	24.4
North Carolina	9,535	1.66	17,828	15,663	70,086	35,567	105,653	32.2
North Dakota	673	0.91	11,231	17,102	84,923	1,919	86,842	23.0
Ohio	11,537	1.18	11,411	14,044	78,185	45,007	123,192	28.0
Oklahoma	3,751	1.12	14,221	20,329	96,784	16,089	112,873	17.0
Oregon	3,831	1.26	11,073	12,194	46,252	12,899	59,151	24.0
Pennsylvania	12,702	1.27	10,042	11,483	73,506	46,180	119,685	31.2
Rhode Island	1,053	1.35	10,582	11,071	1,223	5,267	6,490	32.0
South Carolina	4,625	1.26	13,419	14,720	49,651	16,372	66,024	16.0
South Dakota	814	0.88	9,579	14,721	79,486	2,961	82,447	22.0
Tennessee	6,346	1.24	13,774	15,943	69,971	24,236	94,207	20.0
Texas	25,146	1.46	13,611	15,439	213,313	97,936	311,249	20.0
Utah	2,764	1.04	10,014	16,017	33,885	11,239	45,124	24.5
Vermont	626	1.10	12,791	14,115	12,970	1,466	14,437	20.0
Virginia	8,001	1.30	13,364	15,210	50,526	23,852	74,378	17.5
Washington	6,725	1.44	12,213	11,200	60,312	23,510	83,822	37.5
West Virginia	1,853	1.29	13,377	15,923	33,258	5,367	38,625	32.2
Wisconsin	5,687	1.14	11,961	14,376	92,512	22,451	114,963	30.9
Wyoming	564	0.85	14,426	22,810	25,392	2,713	28,105	14.0
Total	**308,746**	**1.28**	**12,255**	**14,118**	**2,977,376**	**1,089,701**	**4,067,077**	**21.8**

SOURCE: U.S. Department of Commerce, Bureau of the Census, and U.S. Department of Transportation.

State Highway Agency Capital Outlay and Maintenance

STATE HIGHWAY AGENCY CAPITAL OUTLAY AND MAINTENANCE

	Capital Outlay		Maintenance		Total		'10 vs. '09 Percent Change
	2010	2009	2010	2009	2010	2009	
Alabama	1,117,114	1,182,119	141,484	158,245	1,258,598	1,340,364	-6.1
Alaska	401,372	578,918	32,827	72,610	434,199	651,528	-33.4
Arizona	1,234,542	1,273,127	82,930	117,821	1,317,472	1,390,948	-5.3
Arkansas	613,195	561,904	243,486	240,028	856,681	801,932	6.8
California	6,338,983	6,198,986	1,093,485	963,106	7,432,468	7,162,092	3.8
Colorado	709,148	925,307	242,397	101,393	951,545	1,026,700	-7.3
Connecticut	817,795	659,277	71,355	71,838	889,150	731,115	21.6
Delaware	452,803	334,746	7,047	54,261	459,850	389,007	18.2
District of Columbia	378,477	285,947	66,242	55,108	444,719	341,055	30.4
Florida	4,773,259	4,589,386	610,308	685,611	5,383,567	5,274,997	2.1
Georgia	1,716,667	2,198,897	126,925	156,094	1,843,592	2,354,991	-21.7
Hawaii	249,537	276,618	38,351	36,969	287,888	313,587	-8.2
Idaho	583,968	537,617	87,233	82,842	671,201	620,459	8.2
Illinois	3,000,966	3,000,966	426,167	429,340	3,427,133	3,430,306	-0.1
Indiana	1,646,704	1,823,311	533,445	65,495	2,180,149	1,888,806	15.4
Iowa	763,931	680,583	98,548	87,774	862,479	768,357	12.2
Kansas	846,310	904,092	126,307	133,294	972,617	1,037,386	-6.2
Kentucky	1,557,099	1,735,079	385,831	354,691	1,942,930	2,089,770	-7.0
Louisiana	1,773,985	2,973,935	278,057	226,341	2,052,042	3,200,276	-35.9
Maine	351,451	299,913	129,556	121,667	481,007	421,580	14.1
Maryland	1,068,354	1,474,659	112,311	116,675	1,180,665	1,591,334	-25.8
Massachusetts	1,345,806	1,046,031	147,473	114,500	1,493,279	1,160,531	28.7
Michigan	2,416,196	2,260,625	207,072	192,948	2,623,268	2,453,573	6.9
Minnesota	973,934	848,952	356,697	344,285	1,330,631	1,193,237	11.5
Mississippi	935,289	867,005	93,170	101,583	1,028,459	968,588	6.2
Missouri	1,531,532	1,595,920	388,416	390,532	1,919,948	1,986,452	-3.3
Montana	513,614	435,888	77,260	64,764	590,874	500,652	18.0
Nebraska	682,848	606,510	231,260	273,790	914,108	880,300	3.8
Nevada	565,371	738,746	59,577	89,267	624,948	828,013	-24.5
New Hampshire	332,387	230,115	2,667	120,100	335,054	350,215	-4.3
New Jersey	2,499,863	1,594,245	242,810	185,605	2,742,673	1,779,850	54.1
New Mexico	490,571	528,548	75,048	147,028	565,619	675,576	-16.3
New York	3,392,295	3,229,953	737,358	698,057	4,129,653	3,928,010	5.1
North Carolina	2,111,677	1,989,813	600,619	609,270	2,712,296	2,599,083	4.4
North Dakota	396,647	314,349	13,693	17,355	410,340	331,704	23.7
Ohio	1,980,049	2,068,001	141,014	341,647	2,121,063	2,409,648	-12.0
Oklahoma	1,401,130	1,040,529	122,324	129,856	1,523,454	1,170,385	30.2
Oregon	981,108	820,255	146,929	161,803	1,128,037	982,058	14.9
Pennsylvania	4,569,696	3,638,187	453,158	1,026,411	5,022,854	4,664,598	7.7
Rhode Island	264,408	153,323	111,065	80,049	375,473	233,372	60.9
South Carolina	861,879	645,602	396,750	387,342	1,258,629	1,032,944	21.8
South Dakota	398,474	349,865	35,231	49,593	433,705	399,458	8.6
Tennessee	1,228,642	1,035,883	239,184	305,894	1,467,826	1,341,777	9.4
Texas	4,899,668	5,364,789	1,228,654	1,133,383	6,128,322	6,498,172	-5.7
Utah	1,250,471	911,965	208,522	202,917	1,458,993	1,114,882	30.9
Vermont	251,590	191,853	65,363	71,851	316,953	263,704	20.2
Virginia	1,024,147	1,091,029	803,996	1,052,926	1,828,143	2,143,955	-14.7
Washington	2,139,134	1,981,924	550,789	509,519	2,689,923	2,491,443	8.0
West Virginia	793,051	841,764	208,533	216,260	1,001,584	1,058,024	-5.3
Wisconsin	1,531,341	1,369,599	59,343	64,735	1,590,684	1,434,334	10.9
Wyoming	413,103	429,025	33,441	39,446	446,544	468,471	-4.7
Total	**72,571,581**	**70,715,680**	**12,971,708**	**13,453,919**	**85,543,289**	**84,169,599**	**1.6**

NOTE: Data in thousands of dollars.
SOURCE: U.S. Department of Transportation, Federal Highway Administration.

Vehicle and Equipment Manufacturing Employment by State

VEHICLE AND EQUIPMENT MANUFACTURING EMPLOYMENT BY STATE, 2009

State	Vehicle Manufacturing	Vehicle Body & Trailer	Engine & Engine Parts	Electrical Components	Transmission, Brake & Suspension Parts	Other Vehicle Parts Manufacturing
Alabama	10,699	3,466	1,410	1,780	2,750	7,161
Alaska	—	10	—	180	—	—
Arizona	50	609	300	180	289	1,391
Arkansas	650	884	852	2,110	1,890	1,977
California	6,502	6,115	2,039	10	2,021	9,363
Colorado	10	671	50	1,164	84	360
Connecticut	—	10	140	60	770	630
Delaware	330	10	10	—	—	100
District of Columbia	—	—	—	510	—	—
Florida	650	2,693	317	581	300	1,947
Georgia	1,413	2,089	413	—	2,117	2,909
Hawaii	—	10	—	180	10	10
Idaho	10	551	10	4,949	20	20
Illinois	4,139	2,098	1,425	3,814	2,365	6,890
Indiana	12,055	22,138	3,913	780	18,952	11,242
Iowa	50	5,448	610	1,053	530	1,582
Kansas	1,520	2,219	50	1,772	10	522
Kentucky	12,056	1,192	2,514	10	7,914	10,743
Louisiana	1,520	630	140	60	230	280
Maine	—	181	10	10	150	50
Maryland	50	123	50	760	240	327
Massachusetts	50	318	162	5,154	80	335
Michigan	25,696	2,129	8,153	253	18,583	28,463
Minnesota	1,520	1,990	300	1,780	1,032	465
Mississippi	3,260	340	146	816	629	1,468
Missouri	5,266	1,375	1,410	10	2,237	4,403
Montana	50	169	10	380	10	60
Nebraska	10	1,533	300	10	500	2,029
Nevada	150	44	149	760	20	60
New Hampshire	10	149	10	89	190	310
New Jersey	59	310	260	60	80	268
New Mexico	10	77	10	2,255	10	60
New York	650	883	1,410	1,780	2,318	3,148
North Carolina	3,260	3,140	1,369	380	5,375	6,406
North Dakota	330	344	10	6,807	180	97
Ohio	14,860	4,111	6,511	265	14,368	15,666
Oklahoma	1,520	2,145	199	437	990	630
Oregon	1,520	2,569	111	2,775	120	632
Pennsylvania	650	5,755	140	60	3,330	2,161
Rhode Island	—	55	10	1,180	—	190
South Carolina	6,506	817	3,034	—	3,847	3,718
South Dakota	330	915	140	3,810	110	905
Tennessee	6,506	1,840	3,034	1,525	6,780	12,522
Texas	5,371	5,768	1,133	10	1,024	6,829
Utah	10	888	24	—	170	3,141
Vermont	10	50	10	692	—	140
Virginia	1,520	1,451	1,410	216	1,820	1,496
Washington	180	789	137	180	56	1,259
West Virginia	150	165	1,410	728	110	310
Wisconsin	3,260	4,673	3,035	10	858	3,874
Wyoming	—	27	50	5	10	50
Total	**134,418**	**95,966**	**48,340**	**52,390**	**105,479**	**158,599**

NOTE: In some cases, an average was taken based on the Bureau of the Census employment range.
Omission of data for individual states is due to either the absences of such business from the state or the necessity of withholding the data to avoid disclosure of individual firms data.
SOURCE: U.S. Department of Commerce, Bureau of the Census.

Vehicle and Equipment Manufacturing Employment by State

VEHICLE AND EQUIPMENT MANUFACTURING EMPLOYMENT BY STATE, 2009 — continued

State	Vehicle Metal Stamping	Tire Manufacturing	Storage Batteries	Total Vehicle & Equipment Manufacturing	Total State Manufacturing Employment	Vehicle and Equipment % of Total State Manufacturing Employment
Alabama	3,285	4,956	—	35,507	246,259	14.4
Alaska	—	10	—	200	11,927	1.7
Arizona	—	127	10	2,956	145,520	2.0
Arkansas	10	1,520	160	10,053	163,825	6.1
California	1,093	742	846	28,731	1,246,464	2.3
Colorado	60	124	50	2,573	121,919	2.1
Connecticut	649	50	160	2,469	166,398	1.5
Delaware	—	10	160	620	30,410	2.0
District of Columbia	—	—	—	510	1,800	28.3
Florida	442	346	328	7,604	294,519	2.6
Georgia	679	2,753	680	13,053	351,203	3.7
Hawaii	—	10	—	220	12,854	1.7
Idaho	10	10	—	5,580	55,345	10.1
Illinois	3,628	3,771	429	28,559	566,887	5.0
Indiana	6,266	2,128	565	78,039	442,399	17.6
Iowa	736	1,520	535	12,064	203,998	5.9
Kansas	60	1,520	680	8,353	167,416	5.0
Kentucky	3,551	176	340	38,496	214,746	17.9
Louisiana	—	102	—	2,962	134,803	2.2
Maine	—	50	—	451	53,059	0.8
Maryland	380	50	160	2,140	111,657	1.9
Massachusetts	214	45	50	6,408	239,914	2.7
Michigan	21,881	204	160	105,522	470,900	22.4
Minnesota	216	132	—	7,435	307,822	2.4
Mississippi	357	1,520	50	8,586	149,363	5.7
Missouri	380	458	1,944	17,483	259,237	6.7
Montana	10	50	—	739	17,226	4.3
Nebraska	180	104	—	4,666	93,831	5.0
Nevada	—	50	10	1,243	42,775	2.9
New Hampshire	60	50	—	868	71,259	1.2
New Jersey	73	50	50	1,210	252,418	0.5
New Mexico	10	10	—	2,442	28,623	8.5
New York	750	1,520	160	12,619	462,496	2.7
North Carolina	278	5,867	340	26,415	439,637	6.0
North Dakota	—	50	—	7,818	24,350	32.1
Ohio	14,352	3,268	1,157	74,558	638,489	11.7
Oklahoma	10	3,250	50	9,231	134,603	6.9
Oregon	10	270	340	8,347	152,428	5.5
Pennsylvania	347	1,436	6,760	20,639	574,683	3.6
Rhode Island	10	—	10	1,455	44,008	3.3
South Carolina	1,360	4,456	—	23,738	223,092	10.6
South Dakota	10	10	—	6,230	40,477	15.4
Tennessee	2,886	6,501	680	42,274	311,239	13.6
Texas	1,195	656	160	22,146	784,367	2.8
Utah	60	50	—	4,343	110,538	3.9
Vermont	60	10	340	1,312	32,504	4.0
Virginia	180	3,250	10	11,353	252,213	4.5
Washington	75	68	50	2,794	234,232	1.2
West Virginia	103	50	—	3,026	55,357	5.5
Wisconsin	1,028	45	722	17,505	431,014	4.1
Wyoming	—	10	—	152	10,453	1.5
Total	**66,944**	**53,415**	**18,146**	**733,697**	**11,632,956**	**6.3**

NOTE: In some cases, an average was taken based on the Bureau of the Census employment range.
Omission of data for individual states is due to either the absences of such business from the state or the necessity of withholding the data to avoid disclosure of individual firms data.
SOURCE: U.S. Department of Commerce, Bureau of the Census.

U.S. Vehicle and Related Industries Employment

U.S. EMPLOYMENT IN VEHICLE AND RELATED INDUSTRIES, 2009

Industry	Companies	Employees	Payrolls $ (000)
Motor Vehicle and Equipment Manufacturing			
Light vehicle manufacturing	265	111,683	7,278,895
Heavy truck manufacturing	90	22,735	1,076,038
Motor vehicle body & trailers	2,007	95,966	3,618,595
Motor vehicle engine and engine parts	890	48,340	2,476,776
Motor vehicle electrical & electrical equipment	754	52,390	2,560,589
Motor vehicle suspension, brake and powertrains	952	105,479	5,335,798
Motor vehicle seating and Interior trim	409	40,921	1,592,801
Other motor vehicle parts manufacturing	1,496	117,678	4,495,115
Motor vehicle metal stamping	769	66,944	3,226,109
Tires and Inner Tubes	580	53,415	2,594,538
Storage Batteries	112	18,146	835,521
Subtotal	**8,324**	**733,697**	**35,090,775**
Motor Freight Transportation and Related Services			
Trucking and courier services[1]	123,685	1,875,606	71,520,074
Road transportation support activities	9,978	74,975	2,189,378
Arrangement of transportation of freight & cargo	20,583	228,886	10,729,453
Misc. services incidental to transportation	1,519	24,981	1,196,135
Subtotal	**155,765**	**2,204,448**	**85,635,040**
Petroleum Refining and Wholesale Distribution			
Petroleum Refining	303	63,960	6,158,865
Asphalt paving mixtures and blocks	1,364	13,568	777,427
Lubricating oils and greases	300	9,717	599,428
Petroleum bulk stations and terminals	4,500	70,000	4,070,732
Petroleum and petroleum products wholesalers, except bulk stations and terminals	2,740	32,082	2,203,032
Subtotal	**9,207**	**189,327**	**13,809,484**
Passenger Transportation			
Local and suburban transportation	2,589	70,684	2,500,393
Taxi & Limousine service	7,243	64,655	1,465,107
Intercity and rural bus transportation	422	13,379	349,292
Bus charter service	1,327	29,173	727,555
School and Employee bus transportation	4,557	213,878	4,073,504
Arrangement of passenger transportation	18,030	437,011	10,118,499
Passenger car rental	7,170	NA	NA
Passenger car leasing	535	7,535	417,540
Truck, utility trailer and RV rental	5,774	48,587	2,009,003
Automobile parking	12,754	129,519	2,181,761
Recreational vehicle parks and campsites	7,202	37,766	1,116,269
Subtotal	**67,603**	**1,052,187**	**24,958,923**
Automotive Sales and Servicing			
Retail automotive dealers-New	22,936	940,917	40,203,039
Retail automotive dealers-Used	24,012	110,928	3,591,294
Auto parts, accessories and tire stores	57,013	466,747	12,730,974
Gasoline service stations[2]	112,144	855,915	15,072,179
Recreational vehicle dealers	2,791	31,122	1,135,047
Wholesale trade in motor vehicles	24,882	362,348	16,599,797
Automotive repair and maintenance	157,102	805,631	23,784,789
Motor Vehicle Towing	8,263	52,293	1,551,868
Subtotal	**409,143**	**3,625,901**	**114,668,987**
Total of Motor Vehicle and Related Industries	**650,042**	**7,805,560**	**274,163,209**
U.S. Total	**7,433,465**	**114,509,626**	**4,855,545,239**
Motor Vehicle Percent of U.S. Total	**8.7%**	**6.8%**	**5.6%**

NA is not available.
(1) Except by air or by the U.S. Postal Service. (2) Includes truck stops and stations with and without convenience stores.
SOURCE: U.S. Department of Commerce, Bureau of the Census.

New Car Dealerships

FRANCHISED NEW CAR DEALERSHIPS BY STATE, 2011

State	Dealer-ships[1]	Sales (Millions $)	Paid Employees	Payrolls (Millions $)	State	Dealer-ships[1]	Sales (Millions $)	Paid Employees	Payrolls (Millions $)
Alabama	297	8,924	14,048	632	Nebraska	181	4,655	6,946	307
Alaska	32	1,249	2,055	101	Nevada	99	4,044	6,827	376
Arizona	235	12,753	20,503	1,020	New Hampshire	140	4,097	5,828	308
Arkansas	218	5,360	7,842	350	New Jersey	463	21,929	26,771	1,611
California	1,307	63,510	95,187	5,071	New Mexico	114	3,101	5,746	255
Colorado	260	10,605	14,560	753	New York	886	36,743	42,586	2,352
Connecticut	263	8,488	12,401	699	North Carolina	587	17,733	27,800	1,262
Delaware	53	2,337	4,072	199	North Dakota	87	2,666	3,897	171
Florida	842	42,092	61,270	3,015	Ohio	756	24,104	38,775	1,689
Georgia	510	19,090	28,555	1,394	Oklahoma	277	18,211	16,054	744
Hawaii	66	1,664	3,113	167	Oregon	236	5,981	10,930	494
Idaho	109	2,452	4,621	201	Pennsylvania	943	26,322	44,158	2,010
Illinois	769	25,894	39,682	1,951	Rhode Island	50	1,831	2,690	134
Indiana	429	11,843	19,653	835	South Carolina	258	7,499	13,223	588
Iowa	319	7,184	11,710	510	South Dakota	99	2,425	3,857	172
Kansas	231	5,380	9,011	408	Tennessee	349	12,430	20,559	970
Kentucky	260	6,626	11,328	498	Texas	1,178	52,090	76,674	4,047
Louisiana	292	8,530	14,081	660	Utah	141	5,270	8,153	374
Maine	128	2,806	4,541	202	Vermont	86	1,560	2,621	120
Maryland	301	12,489	20,541	1,042	Virginia	489	16,879	28,857	1,412
Massachusetts	411	14,774	19,880	1,137	Washington	334	10,398	18,685	921
Michigan	643	12,783	28,285	1,417	West Virginia	143	3,677	6,136	240
Minnesota	364	7,869	15,660	697	Wisconsin	514	10,905	20,753	814
Mississippi	196	4,389	7,176	307	Wyoming	65	1,293	2,242	102
Missouri	414	12,147	19,301	902	**Total**	**17,539**	**609,353**	**933,503**	**45,790**
Montana	115	2,272	3,659	149					

(1) The number of establishments are NADA estimates as of Jan. 1, 2012.
SOURCE: Industry Analysis Div., National Automobile Dealers Assn.

DEALER SERVICE AND PARTS SALES

Year	$ Billions	% Change
2011	80.57	3.8
2010	77.63	1.9
2009	76.21	-6.9
2008	81.84	-1.8
2007	83.35	3.6
2006	80.45	-5.5
2005	85.16	-0.4
2004	85.48	0.2
2003	85.35	2.7
2002	83.11	3.8
2001	80.10	8.5
2000	73.83	9.1

SOURCE: Industry Analysis Div., National Automobile Dealers Assn.

DEALER SERVICE AND PARTS SALES BY TYPE
(Billions of Dollars)

Service Labor Sales	2011	% Chg. '11 vs. '10	2010	Parts Sales	2011	% Chg. '11 vs. '10	2010
Customer Mechanical	$16.16	3.7	$15.59	Customer Mechanical	13.45	4.5	12.87
Customer Body	3.81	-1.0	3.85	Customer Body	2.97	-1.0	3.00
Warranty	6.17	-1.9	6.29	Wholesale	12.15	5.6	11.51
Sublet	2.54	8.5	2.34	Counter	2.50	0.4	2.49
Internal	5.60	9.8	5.10	Warranty	7.50	0.7	7.45
Other	1.40	2.2	1.37	Internal	3.92	8.9	3.60
				Other	2.40	11.1	2.16
Total Service Labor	**35.67**	**3.2**	**34.55**	**Total Parts**	**44.90**	**4.2**	**43.08**

SOURCE: Industry Analysis Div., National Automobile Dealers Assn.

SHARE OF TOTAL DEALERSHIP SALES DOLLARS BY DEPARTMENT, 2011

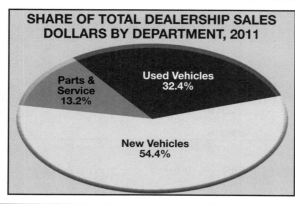

Parts & Service 13.2%
Used Vehicles 32.4%
New Vehicles 54.4%

PROFILE OF FRANCHISED DEALER SERVICE AND PARTS OPERATIONS, 2011

	Average Dealership	All Dealers
Total service and parts sales	$4,593,905	$80.57 Billion
Total gross profit as percent of service and parts sales	46.1%	—
Total net profit as percent of service and parts sales	7.1%	—
Total number of repair orders written	14,140	248 Million
Total service and parts sales per customer repair order	$241	—
Total service and parts sales per warranty repair order	$250	—
Number of technicians	15	252,400
Number of service bays (excluding body)	19	333,260
Total parts inventory	$294,214	$5.16
Average customer mechanical labor rate	$95	—

SOURCE: Industry Analysis Div., National Automobile Dealers Assn.

Personal Income of Vehicle and Equipment Manufacturing Employees by State

PERSONAL INCOME OF VEHICLE AND EQUIPMENT MANUFACTURING EMPLOYEES

State	Vehicle and Equipment Manufacturing Employees		All Manufacturing Employees		2010 Vehicle & Equipment Percent of Total Manufacturing	2009 Vehicle & Equipment Percent of Total Manufacturing
	Personal Income (in Millions of Dollars)					
	2010	2009	2010	2009		
Alabama	1,512	1,942	14,381	15,357	10.5%	12.6%
Alaska	—	—	689	695	—	—
Arizona	—	—	12,884	12,714	—	—
Arkansas	—	—	8,334	8,316	—	—
California	768	2,258	119,002	119,103	0.6%	1.9%
Colorado	68	114	9,761	10,282	0.7%	1.1%
Connecticut	—	—	15,899	16,334	—	—
Delaware	—	—	2,219	2,325	—	—
District of Columbia	—	—	144	155	—	—
Florida	194	640	22,884	22,934	0.8%	2.8%
Georgia	588	778	22,682	23,517	2.6%	3.3%
Hawaii	—	—	746	789	—	—
Idaho	—	—	3,537	3,525	—	—
Illinois	1,980	2,014	43,276	44,909	4.6%	4.5%
Indiana	4,505	6,334	31,539	32,569	14.3%	19.4%
Iowa	—	—	13,312	12,705	—	—
Kansas	—	519	11,214	11,746	—	—
Kentucky	622	2,737	12,173	13,830	5.1%	19.8%
Louisiana	—	—	11,587	11,495	—	—
Maine	16	21	3,684	3,415	0.4%	0.6%
Maryland	—	—	10,245	10,135	—	—
Massachusetts	—	—	25,115	23,313	—	—
Michigan	11,929	12,571	38,608	37,701	30.9%	33.3%
Minnesota	297	305	22,580	21,398	1.3%	1.4%
Mississippi	—	—	7,540	7,757	—	—
Missouri	1,200	1,576	17,443	17,344	6.9%	9.1%
Montana	—	—	1,031	1,060	—	—
Nebraska	—	—	5,365	5,274	—	—
Nevada	—	—	2,619	2,781	—	—
New Hampshire	22	27	5,244	5,212	0.4%	0.5%
New Jersey	130	161	27,213	26,416	0.5%	0.6%
New Mexico	—	—	2,181	2,096	—	—
New York	916	1,182	38,061	37,825	2.4%	3.1%
North Carolina	1,079	1,453	30,813	30,075	3.5%	4.8%
North Dakota	—	—	1,445	1,355	—	—
Ohio	5,712	6,179	47,311	44,935	12.1%	13.8%
Oklahoma	311	367	8,957	10,884	3.5%	3.4%
Oregon	284	285	12,261	12,152	2.3%	2.3%
Pennsylvania	350	—	39,725	40,833	0.9%	—
Rhode Island	—	9	2,573	2,792	—	0.3%
South Carolina	1,008	—	13,842	14,117	—	—
South Dakota	—	—	1,991	1,970	—	—
Tennessee	1,629	2,842	19,955	20,793	8.2%	13.7%
Texas	1,571	2,233	70,756	74,433	2.2%	3.0%
Utah	—	—	7,523	7,531	—	—
Vermont	—	—	2,144	2,143	—	—
Virginia	—	—	14,698	16,026	—	—
Washington	—	—	19,946	22,463	—	—
West Virginia	—	—	3,396	3,355	—	—
Wisconsin	—	—	30,371	28,703	—	—
Wyoming	—	—	706	693	—	—
Total	**37,574**	**54,877**	**891,607**	**900,278**	**4.2%**	**6.1%**

NOTE: Personal Income is measured as the sum of wage and salary disbursements, other labor income, proprietors' income, rental income, personal dividend income and personal interest income.
Omission of data for individual state is due to either the absences of such business from the state or the necessity of withholding the data to avoid disclosure of individual firm's data. Total includes states not listed individually.
SOURCE: U.S. Department of Commerce, Bureau of Economic Analysis.

Automotive Employment and Compensation

LABOR COSTS IN THE AUTOMOTIVE INDUSTRY FOR SELECT COUNTRIES

Country	Hourly Compensation in US Dollars						
	2011	2010	2009	2008	2007	2006	2005
Austria	46.91	46.80	51.42	47.77	47.84	41.51	36.51
Belgium	57.19	57.10	59.66	56.38	56.45	48.27	41.96
Czech Republic	14.88	14.07	14.39	14.21	12.60	10.36	8.43
Finland	37.45	37.70	41.23	38.40	37.75	33.04	28.69
France	57.92	56.40	59.51	58.27	58.17	49.33	41.78
Germany	59.12	58.11	62.96	60.81	62.29	55.53	49.31
Italy	36.48	36.30	39.17	36.11	36.03	31.68	28.13
Japan	46.30	43.39	42.65	37.17	36.05	35.37	33.95
Netherlands	40.06	40.96	43.58	41.83	42.71	37.52	33.09
Portugal	16.42	16.75	17.79	16.98	17.52	15.46	13.83
Spain	33.03	33.42	35.96	33.35	33.20	28.54	24.82
Sweden	57.74	54.46	51.50	53.32	57.39	48.02	41.45
United Kingdom	30.00	30.85	31.20	33.58	36.99	34.87	32.85
USA	31.89	33.92	34.81	32.38	36.27	35.36	32.79

NOTE: Data is all employees.
SOURCE: VDA, European Labor Cost Survey.

U.S. VEHICLE AND EQUIPMENT MANUFACTURING EMPLOYMENT

Year	All Employees (000)	Production Workers		
		Number (000)	Percent of Total Employees	Average Hourly Earnings
2011	716.9	555.7	77.5%	$21.97
2010	678.5	524.9	77.4%	22.02
2009	664.1	510.0	76.8%	21.86
2008	875.5	695.5	79.4%	22.21
2007	994.2	804.2	80.9%	22.00
2006	1,070.0	872.7	81.6%	22.14
2005	1,096.7	892.3	81.4%	22.26
2004	1,112.8	902.9	81.1%	21.71
2003	1,125.3	906.3	80.5%	21.68
2002	1,151.2	931.0	80.9%	21.09
2001	1,212.8	986.7	81.4%	19.62
2000	1,313.6	1,073.0	81.7%	19.07
1999	1,312.6	1,075.7	82.0%	18.45
1998	1,271.5	1,050.3	82.6%	18.19
1997	1,253.9	1,062.5	84.7%	18.35
1996	1,240.3	1,052.3	84.8%	18.07
1995	1,241.5	1,048.9	84.5%	17.63
1994	1,168.5	978.4	83.7%	17.28

NOTE: The basis for industry classification has changed from the Standard Industrial Classification System (SIC) to the North American Industry Classification System (NAICS).
SOURCE: U.S. Department of Labor, Bureau of Labor Statistics.

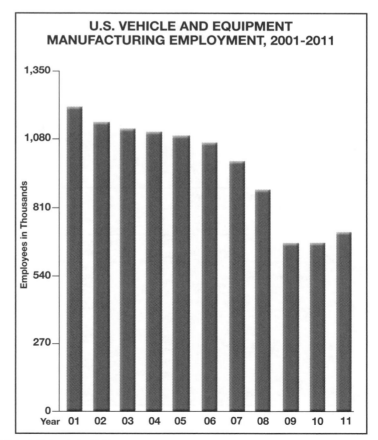

U.S. VEHICLE AND EQUIPMENT MANUFACTURING EMPLOYMENT, 2001-2011

Industrial Production and Capacity Utilization

INDUSTRIAL PRODUCTION INDEX FOR VEHICLE AND PARTS MANUFACTURERS

| | Industrial Production Index | | | |
| | Total | | Vehicle and Parts | |
Year	Index	Percent Change	Index	Percent Change
2011	91.6	4.9	83.0	9.1
2010	87.3	5.9	76.1	27.9
2009	82.4	-13.5	59.5	-25.6
2008	95.3	-4.7	80.0	-20.0
2007	100.0	3.2	100.0	-0.8
2006	96.9	2.6	100.8	-1.5
2005	94.4	4.2	102.3	0.6
2004	90.6	2.8	101.7	0.6
2003	88.1	1.6	101.1	3.6
2002	86.7	0.5	97.6	9.9
2001	86.3	-3.9	88.8	-8.8
2000	89.8	4.5	97.4	-0.7

NOTE: "Industrial Production" is an index benchmarked to 2007=100.
SOURCE: Board of Governors of the Federal Reserve System.

CAPACITY UTILIZATION FOR VEHICLE AND PARTS MANUFACTURING

Year	All Manufac-turing	Percent Change	Vehicle & Parts Mfg.	Percent Change
2011	75.4	4.9	64.6	7.3
2010	71.9	8.9	60.2	35.3
2009	66.0	-11.6	44.5	-22.1
2008	74.7	-5.6	57.1	-28.6
2007	79.1	0.8	80.0	11.7
2006	78.5	0.6	71.6	-6.9
2005	78.0	2.5	76.9	-0.1
2004	76.1	3.0	77.0	-1.8
2003	73.9	1.4	78.4	-0.4
2002	72.9	-1.1	78.7	8.1
2001	73.7	-7.9	72.8	-10.6
2000	80.0	-0.9	81.4	-3.3

NOTE: "Capacity Utilization" is a percent of capacity.
SOURCE: Board of Governors of the Federal Reserve System.

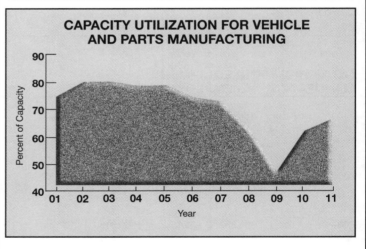

CAR AND TRUCK OUTPUT

Year	Car Output	Car Percent of GDP	Truck Output	Truck Percent of GDP	Total Vehicle Output	Percent of GDP	Gross Domestic Product (GDP)
2011	119.3	0.8	256.9	1.7	376.2	2.5	15,094.4
2010	110.1	0.8	216.1	1.5	326.2	2.2	14,526.5
2009	92.6	0.7	156.4	1.1	249.0	1.8	13,939.0
2008	137.6	1.0	185.4	1.3	323.0	2.3	14,291.5
2007	152.4	1.1	257.5	1.8	409.9	2.9	14,028.7
2006	155.4	1.2	257.2	1.9	412.7	3.1	13,377.2
2005	150.3	1.2	268.7	2.1	418.9	3.3	12,623.0
2004	129.8	1.1	264.4	2.3	394.2	3.4	11,685.9
2003	130.1	1.2	248.5	2.3	378.6	3.5	10,971.2
2002	148.0	1.4	233.7	2.2	381.7	3.6	10,469.6
2001	141.4	1.4	203.1	2.0	344.5	3.4	10,128.0
2000	151.1	1.2	213.9	2.4	365.0	3.6	9,817.0

NOTE: Data in billions of dollars.
SOURCE: U.S. Department of Commerce, Bureau of Economic Analysis.

Corporate Profits

SELECTED AUTOMAKERS' REVENUES/NET INCOME

Year	Chrysler[1] Revenues	Chrysler[1] Net Income	Ford Revenues	Ford Net Income	General Motors[2] Revenues	General Motors[2] Net Income	Honda Revenues	Honda Net Income
2011	54,981	183	136,264	8,681	150,276	7,585	108,644	6,938
2010	41,946	-652	128,954	7,149	135,592	4,668	97,470	3,286
2009	NA	NA	118,308	2,717	47,115	109,118	101,916	1,395
2008	NA	NA	146,277	-14,672	148,979	-30,860	119,801	5,989
2007	NA	NA	172,455	-2,723	178,199	-38,732	93,919	5,018
2006	200,138	4,261	160,065	-12,613	171,179	-1,978	84,345	5,082
2005	177,402	3,371	176,835	1,440	158,623	-10,417	80,429	4,521
2004	192,319	3,338	172,255	3,487	195,351	2,701	77,268	4,395
2003	171,870	564	166,040	495	185,837	2,899	—	—
2002	156,838	4,947	162,256	-9,800	186,763	1,736	—	—
2001	136,072	-589	162,412	-5,453	177,260	601	—	—
2000	152,446	7,411	170,064	3,467	184,632	4,452	—	—
1999	151,035	5,785	160,658	7,237	176,558	6,002	—	—
1998	154,615	5,656	143,350	22,071	155,445	2,956	—	—
1997	61,147	2,805	153,627	6,920	178,174	6,698	—	—
1996	61,397	3,529	146,991	4,446	164,013	4,963	—	—
1995	53,195	2,025	137,137	4,139	160,254	6,881	—	—
1994	52,235	3,713	128,439	5,308	154,951	4,901	—	—
1993	43,596	-2,551	108,521	2,529	138,676	2,466	—	—
1992	36,897	723	100,132	-7,385	132,429	-23,498	—	—
1991	29,370	-795	88,286	-2,258	123,056	-4,453	—	—
1990	30,620	68	97,650	860	124,705	-1,986	—	—
1989	35,186	359	96,146	3,835	126,932	4,224	—	—
1988	34,421	1,050	92,446	5,300	123,642	4,856	—	—
1987	28,353	1,290	79,893	4,625	114,870	3,551	—	—
1986	24,569	1,389	69,695	3,285	115,610	2,945	—	—
1984	19,717	2,373	56,323	2,907	93,145	4,517	—	—

Year	Hyundai Revenues	Hyundai Net Income	Nissan Revenues	Nissan Net Income	Toyota Revenues	Toyota Net Income	Volkswagen Revenues	Volkswagen Net Income
2011	67,070	6,987	105,866	3,852	228,427	4,909	206,318	14,594
2010	98,958	7,009	81,095	457	232,375	1,808	168,128	9,057
2009	78,334	3,463	86,720	2,402	222,566	-4,448	150,756	2,659
2008	63,408	682	108,242	4,823	262,394	17,146	160,440	6,609
2007	74,186	1,706	88,717	3,905	202,864	13,927	160,389	6,071
2006	68,468	1,355	80,584	4,428	179,083	11,681	138,463	3,631
2005	58,076	2,294	80,152	4,788	172,749	10,907	111,344	1,327
2004	50,972	1,616	70,087	4,752	163,637	10,995	120,405	969
2003	38,895	1,482	56,905	4,126	128,965	6,247	109,786	1,408
2002	40,089	1,195	46,588	2,799	107,443	4,177	82,958	2,478
2001	16,971	879	48,204	2,462	106,030	5,447	78,446	4,806
2000	14,472	530	56,649	6,486	119,656	4,540	78,314	3,791
1999	12,468	362	57,471	233	100,990	3,747	75,525	2,534
1998	7,278	-27	49,361	105	88,473	3,442	80,395	1,343
1997	—	—	—	—	99,730	3,143	63,664	765
1996	—	—	—	—	101,177	2,426	64,491	437
1995	—	—	—	—	89,715	1,458	61,168	233
1994	—	—	—	—	91,317	1,227	50,930	95
1993	—	—	—	—	95,063	1,643	44,774	-1,134
1992	—	—	—	—	80,128	1,875	53,977	93
1991	—	—	—	—	71,731	3,140	48,826	713
1990	—	—	—	—	59,962	2,878	45,429	725
1989	—	—	—	—	61,440	2,652	37,606	597
1988	—	—	—	—	—	—	—	—
1987	—	—	—	—	—	—	—	—
1986	—	—	—	—	—	—	—	—
1984	—	—	—	—	—	—	—	—

NA is not available.
NOTE: Data in millions of U.S. Dollars.
(1) Data for DaimlerChrysler for 1998-2006.
(2) Data for General Motors Corporation through July 9, 2009, and General Motors Company from 2010 forward.
SOURCE: Compiled by *WardsAuto Group* from company annual reports.

Use Tax Revenues by State

STATE USE TAX REVENUES, 2011

State	Total State Tax Revenue	State Tax on Vehicle Fuel	State License Tax on Vehicles	State License Tax on Vehicle Operators	Total Vehicle Fuel and License Taxes	Percent Vehicle of Total Taxes
Alabama	8,635,527	548,265	199,970	21,001	769,236	8.9
Alaska	5,537,679	39,617	58,285	--	97,902	1.8
Arizona	10,848,179	769,137	202,588	27,942	999,667	9.2
Arkansas	7,737,552	468,525	143,329	17,053	628,907	8.1
California	116,695,284	5,705,527	3,090,610	268,749	9,064,886	7.8
Colorado	9,467,684	622,822	420,736	28,061	1,071,619	11.3
Connecticut	13,432,252	477,772	195,286	38,664	711,722	5.3
Delaware	3,017,837	113,753	50,031	4,688	168,472	5.6
Florida	32,557,946	2,268,475	1,253,518	345,673	3,867,666	11.9
Georgia	16,003,250	932,703	296,786	30,374	1,259,863	7.9
Hawaii	4,857,729	95,310	104,923	349	200,582	4.1
Idaho	3,261,722	238,983	134,108	10,747	383,838	11.8
Illinois	29,433,475	1,314,194	1,608,090	105,406	3,027,690	10.3
Indiana	14,909,416	775,295	333,511	206,353	1,315,159	8.8
Iowa	7,236,476	447,992	500,775	10,682	959,449	13.3
Kansas	6,828,477	436,855	188,281	21,481	646,617	9.5
Kentucky	10,203,241	732,826	203,492	15,737	952,055	9.3
Louisiana	8,865,421	607,540	104,926	12,228	724,694	8.2
Maine	3,675,810	239,446	97,726	8,536	345,708	9.4
Maryland	16,002,529	752,171	444,133	26,277	1,222,581	7.6
Massachusetts	22,089,530	660,829	378,084	87,229	1,126,142	5.1
Michigan	23,540,253	975,032	891,018	61,497	1,927,547	8.2
Minnesota	18,952,919	847,897	583,498	45,161	1,476,556	7.8
Mississippi	6,714,180	428,676	129,575	37,604	595,855	8.9
Missouri	10,109,918	719,401	265,331	15,466	1,000,198	9.9
Montana	2,303,516	209,416	136,658	8,022	354,096	15.4
Nebraska	4,153,113	318,054	87,657	12,077	417,788	10.1
Nevada	6,332,128	291,238	151,688	21,474	464,400	7.3
New Hampshire	2,320,014	162,795	126,181	7,297	296,273	12.8
New Jersey	27,182,753	524,167	587,524	51,089	1,162,780	4.3
New Mexico	4,980,115	239,463	126,298	3,834	369,595	7.4
New York	67,945,152	1,609,423	1,268,900	128,684	3,007,007	4.4
North Carolina	22,405,841	1,663,047	568,268	127,852	2,359,167	10.5
North Dakota	3,822,347	170,853	92,546	4,094	267,493	7.0
Ohio	25,176,562	1,757,224	869,385	91,092	2,717,701	10.8
Oklahoma	7,766,332	447,543	637,218	15,039	1,099,800	14.2
Oregon	8,112,049	441,858	582,133	29,239	1,053,230	13.0
Pennsylvania	32,352,286	2,064,196	834,338	61,934	2,960,468	9.2
Rhode Island	2,737,952	126,294	58,741	506	185,541	6.8
South Carolina	7,687,496	527,829	133,862	42,916	704,607	9.2
South Dakota	1,379,607	127,437	52,324	3,697	183,458	13.3
Tennessee	10,858,935	845,393	262,386	45,363	1,153,142	10.6
Texas	43,188,251	3,108,416	1,618,563	170,908	4,897,887	11.3
Utah	5,475,904	369,966	186,241	13,724	569,931	10.4
Vermont	2,687,926	104,721	63,769	7,766	176,256	6.6
Virginia	17,409,072	897,405	438,904	59,064	1,395,373	8.0
Washington	17,411,033	1,205,858	472,741	70,722	1,749,321	10.0
West Virginia	5,142,771	397,749	3,547	102,876	504,172	9.8
Wisconsin	15,347,327	989,545	458,408	42,290	1,490,243	9.7
Wyoming	2,461,977	70,176	68,733	2,148	141,057	5.7
Total	**757,254,745**	**39,889,109**	**21,765,623**	**2,570,665**	**64,225,397**	**8.5**

NOTE: Data in thousands of dollars.
SOURCE: U.S. Department of Commerce, Bureau of the Census.

New Car Corporate Average Fuel Economy

NEW CAR U.S. CORPORATE AVERAGE FUEL ECONOMY PERFORMANCE BY MANUFACTURER (Miles Per Gallon)

Manufacturer	Preliminary '11 mpg	Final Sales Basis '10 mpg	'09 mpg	'08 mpg	'07 mpg	'05 mpg	'03 mpg	'01 mpg	'99 mpg	'97 mpg	'95 mpg
Domestic Fleet											
Chrysler	29.9	28.3	28.1	29.3	—	—	—	—	—	27.6	28.4
DaimlerChrysler[1][2]	—	—	—	—	28.5	28.8	29.7	27.9	27.2	—	—
Ford[1]	32.4	32.6	31.5	30.1	29.0	28.6	27.9	27.7	27.6	27.2	27.7
General Motors[1]	31.7	30.8	31.3	29.6	30.0	29.2	28.9	28.3	27.7	28.2	27.4
Honda	34.9	34.8	34.3	36.0	33.5	33.2	34.4	32.7	33.5	28.5	—
Mazda	31.7	31.4	30.9	—	—	—	—	—	—	—	—
Mitsubishi	—	—	—	—	—	27.6	—	—	—	—	—
Nissan	34.6	34.7	33.9	33.9	33.4	30.4	28.9	27.9	29.9	—	—
Subaru	—	32.3	29.0	29.0	29.5	—	—	—	—	—	—
Toyota	32.6	37.0	32.5	34.0	31.3	34.4	28.1	34.2	28.3	28.8	28.5
Import Fleet											
BMW	29.7	28.8	29.0	27.4	27.7	27.2	26.8	25.0	25.4	25.7	25.3
Chrysler	—	—	—	26.5	—	—	—	—	—	—	—
Daimler	27.0	26.9	27.1	26.9	—	—	—	—	—	—	—
DaimlerChrysler[2]	—	—	—	—	24.7	25.9	26.3	26.5	26.5	25.7	28.6
Ford	—	27.6	27.6	31.1	30.0	28.4	28.2	27.9	30.1	31.3	34.0
General Motors	32.9	34.0	30.3	31.5	32.3	30.5	28.3	26.5	25.5	32.1	36.7
Honda	42.8	40.9	39.0	33.5	39.3	33.1	31.9	29.3	29.4	32.4	32.7
Hyundai	35.7	36.3	34.1	34.2	32.4	30.3	30.4	31.3	30.8	31.4	31.2
Kia	34.6	36.6	35.2	33.6	33.4	29.5	30.4	30.5	30.9	31.0	—
Mercedes-Benz	—	—	—	—	—	—	—	—	—	25.2	24.7
Mitsubishi	33.2	32.0	30.4	30.0	28.7	30.2	—	29.4	30.0	30.0	29.9
Nissan	33.4	32.5	33.3	29.2	29.6	24.8	27.4	28.7	29.9	29.9	29.5
Subaru	30.6	28.9	29.2	28.9	28.5	27.9	27.6	27.8	27.7	28.3	28.9
Suzuki	34.1	34.6	32.7	31.6	30.3	29.6	33.0	35.1	35.5	35.2	40.8
Toyota	42.6	44.6	39.4	38.3	38.3	36.6	32.4	30.6	29.9	30.1	30.4
Volvo	28.8	27.9	—	—	—	—	—	—	26.2	25.8	26.0
Volkswagen	33.4	33.3	31.2	29.1	28.8	29.1	29.8	28.5	28.2	29.0	29.0

NOTE: Data are for model years.
(1) Domestic fleet excludes captive imports after '79.
(2) DaimlerChrysler includes Mercedes-Benz and the Chrysler Group from '99-'07.
SOURCE: U.S. Department of Transportation.

NEW CAR U.S. CORPORATE AVERAGE FUEL ECONOMY (Sales Weighted Combined City/Highway Miles Per Gallon)

Model Year	Federal Standard	Domestic Fleet	Import Fleet	Total Fleet
2011 (prelim.)	30.1	32.5	35.3	33.8
2010	27.5	33.1	35.2	33.9
2009	27.5	32.1	33.8	32.9
2008	27.5	31.2	31.8	31.5
2007	27.5	30.6	32.2	31.2
2006	27.5	30.3	29.7	30.1
2005	27.5	30.5	29.9	30.3
2004	27.5	29.9	28.7	29.5
2003	27.5	29.1	29.9	29.5
2002	27.5	29.1	28.8	29.0
2000	27.5	28.7	28.3	28.5
1998	27.5	28.6	29.2	28.8
1996	27.5	28.1	29.6	28.5
1994	27.5	27.5	29.7	28.3
1992	27.5	27.0	29.2	27.9
1990	27.5	26.9	29.9	28.0
1988	26.0	27.4	31.5	28.8
1986	26.0	26.6	31.6	28.2
1984	27.0	25.6	32.0	26.9
1982	24.0	25.0	31.1	26.6
1980	20.0	22.6	29.6	24.3
1978	18.0	18.7	27.3	19.9
1976	—	16.6	25.4	17.5

NOTE: After 1979, domestic fleet excludes captive imports.
SOURCE: U.S. Department of Transportation.

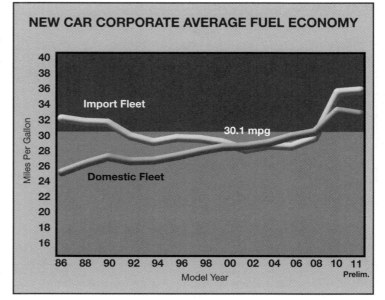

NEW CAR CORPORATE AVERAGE FUEL ECONOMY

New Light Truck Corporate Average Fuel Economy

NEW LIGHT TRUCK U.S. CORPORATE AVERAGE FUEL ECONOMY
(Sales Weighted Combined City/Highway Miles Per Gallon)

Model Year	Federal Standard	Total Fleet
2011 (prelim.)	24.2	24.5
2010	23.5	25.2
2009	23.1	24.8
2008	22.5	23.6
2007	22.2	23.1
2006	21.6	22.5
2005	21.0	22.1
2004	20.7	21.5
2003	20.7	21.8
2002	20.7	21.4
2001	20.7	20.9
2000	20.7	21.3
1999	20.7	20.9
1998	20.7	21.1
1997	20.7	20.6
1996	20.7	20.8
1995	20.6	20.5
1994	20.5	20.8
1993	20.4	21.0
1992	20.2	20.8

Light truck defined as 0-8,500 lbs.
SOURCE: U.S. Department of Transportation.

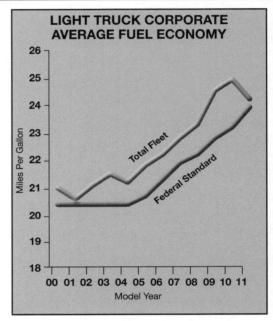

NEW LIGHT TRUCK U.S. CORPORATE AVERAGE FUEL ECONOMY PERFORMANCE BY MANUFACTURER

Manufacturer	Preliminary '11 mpg	Final Sales Basis '10 mpg	'09 mpg	'08 mpg	'07 mpg	'06 mpg	'05 mpg	'04 mpg
BMW	25.5	23.6	22.7	22.9	23.4	21.2	21.3	21.5
Chrysler	24.3	24.3	23.9	23.6	—	—	—	—
Daimler	21.5	21.4	20.8	20.8	—	—	—	—
DaimlerChrysler*	—	—	—	—	22.9	21.7	21.4	20.5
Ford	24.2	24.1	24.6	23.6	22.3	21.1	21.6	21.1
General Motors	23.1	25.4	23.6	22.8	22.4	22.8	21.8	21.4
Honda	26.2	26.8	26.1	25.5	25.1	24.7	24.9	24.6
Hyundai	28.6	30.0	25.9	25.6	25.5	25.2	24.7	24.2
Isuzu	—	—	—	—	—	—	—	23.1
Kia	28.8	25.7	25.0	24.2	24.2	22.8	21.4	20.5
Land Rover	18.5	18.7	19.1	19.3	—	—	—	—
Mazda	24.9	26.7	26.6	—	—	—	—	—
Mitsubishi	29.9	27.3	27.4	24.7	24.7	23.9	23.6	—
Nissan	24.8	24.9	25.7	23.1	22.9	21.9	21.6	21.2
Porsche	24.0	20.5	20.1	20.0	—	18.5	18.5	18.3
Subaru	30.5	29.6	28.5	27.3	27.1	—	—	—
Suzuki	25.7	26.3	25.6	23.7	23.8	24.0	22.8	22.8
Toyota	25.5	26.1	26.2	23.9	23.7	23.7	23.1	22.7
Volkswagen	27.2	25.2	24.5	20.2	19.5	20.1	20.1	19.2

NOTE: Data are for vehicles with gross vehicle weight of 8,500 lbs. or less by model years.
*DaimlerChrysler includes Mercedes-Benz and the Chrysler Group from '99-'07.
SOURCE: U.S. Department of Transportation.

Gas Guzzler Tax Receipts, Automotive Fuel Prices and New Car Quality Improvements

NEW CAR GAS GUZZLER TAX

Miles Per Gallon*	1991-12	1986-90	1985	1984	1983	1982	1981	1980
Under 12.5	$7,700	$3,850	$2,650	$2,150	$1,550	$1,200	$650	$550
12.5-13.0	6,400	3,200	2,650	1,750	1,550	950	650	550
13.0-13.5	6,400	3,200	2,200	1,750	1,250	950	550	300
13.5-14.0	5,400	2,700	2,200	1,450	1,250	750	550	300
14.0-14.5	5,400	2,700	1,800	1,450	1,000	750	450	200
14.5-15.0	4,500	2,250	1,800	1,150	1,000	600	450	200
15.0-15.5	4,500	2,250	1,500	1,150	800	600	350	0
15.5-16.0	3,700	1,850	1,500	950	800	450	350	0
16.0-16.5	3,700	1,850	1,200	950	650	450	200	0
16.5-17.0	3,000	1,500	1,200	750	650	350	200	0
17.0-17.5	3,000	1,500	1,000	750	500	350	0	0
17.5-18.0	2,600	1,300	1,000	600	500	200	0	0
18.0-18.5	2,600	1,300	800	600	350	0	0	0
18.5-19.0	2,100	1,050	800	450	350	0	0	0
19.0-19.5	2,100	1,050	600	450	0	0	0	0
19.5-20.0	1,700	850	600	0	0	0	0	0
20.0-20.5	1,700	850	500	0	0	0	0	0
20.5-21.0	1,300	650	500	0	0	0	0	0
21.0-21.5	1,300	650	0	0	0	0	0	0
21.5-22.0	1,000	500	0	0	0	0	0	0
22.0-22.5	1,000	500	0	0	0	0	0	0
22.5 & Over	0	0	0	0	0	0	0	0

NOTE: New car purchaser pays tax if car's combined city/highway fuel economy rating is lower than standard. * Combined city/highway rating.
SOURCE: Internal Revenue Service.

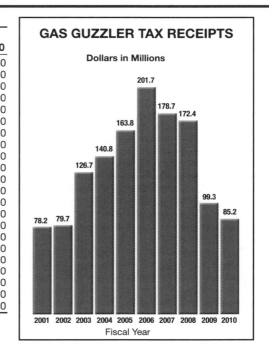

GAS GUZZLER TAX RECEIPTS

Dollars in Millions

Fiscal Year	Value
2001	78.2
2002	79.7
2003	126.7
2004	140.8
2005	163.8
2006	201.7
2007	178.7
2008	172.4
2009	99.3
2010	85.2

U.S. CITY AVERAGE RETAIL PRICES FOR AUTOMOTIVE FUEL Cents Per Gallon, Including Taxes

Year	Regular	Premium	All Types[1]	Diesel
2011	352.7	379.2	357.7	387.6
2010	278.8	304.7	283.6	301.7
2009	235.0	260.7	240.1	252.7
2008	326.6	351.9	331.7	391.5
2007	280.1	303.3	284.9	296.4
2006	258.9	280.5	263.5	281.4
2005	229.5	249.1	233.8	252.0
2004	188.0	206.8	192.3	192.1
2003	159.1	177.7	163.8	164.5
2002	135.8	155.6	144.1	142.6
2001	146.1	165.7	153.1	153.4
2000	138.2	169.3	156.3	151.1
1999	116.5	135.7	122.1	112.0
1998	105.9	125.0	111.5	104.5
1997	120.0	138.1	124.5	120.0
1996	123.1	141.3	128.8	123.6
1995	114.7	133.6	120.5	110.9
1994	111.2	130.5	117.4	112.0
1993	110.8	130.2	117.3	114.8
1992	112.7	131.6	119.0	114.5
1991	114.0	132.1	119.6	124.3
1990	116.4	134.9	121.7	134.3
1985	120.2	134.0	119.6	129.5
1980	124.5	NA	122.1	112.4

NOTE: Prices are based on city averages, cents per gallon including taxes.
NA - Not available.
(1) Includes types of motor gasoline not shown separately.
Beginning with 1991, price calculations changed from "Full Service" to "Self Service."
SOURCE: U.S. Department of Transportation.

AVERAGE RETAIL PRICE INCREASES FOR NEW CAR QUALITY IMPROVEMENTS

Model Year	Adjusted to 2011 Dollars			
	Safety	Emissions[1]	Other[2]	Total
2012	—	—	74.88	74.88
2011	4.83	—	105.96	110.79
2010	—	—	257.10	257.10
2009	—	—	192.63	192.63
2008	86.53	—	92.19	178.72
2007	59.19	—	98.71	157.90
2006	—	27.93	2.55	30.48
2005	203.11	123.47	—	326.58
2004	39.46	23.15	25.49	88.10
2003	—	—	26.44	26.44
2002	—	—	70.74	70.74
2001	25.76	69.26	122.71	217.73
2000	15.54	—	—	15.54
1999	—	78.04	415.85	493.89
1998	—	52.70	180.57	233.27
1997	9.14	20.83	156.21	186.18
1996	16.61	88.86	88.52	193.99
1995	122.60	54.74	—	177.34
1994	192.46	41.26	146.49	380.21
1993	—	—	96.35	96.35
1992	38.39	—	249.33	287.72
1991	244.07	—	—	244.07
1990	209.08	—	45.23	254.31
1989	27.62	—	190.56	218.18
1988	79.58	—	219.13	298.71
1987	—	—	58.48	58.48
1986	35.25	—	204.53	239.78
1985	—	26.90	176.08	202.98
1984	-16.72	81.46	87.53	152.27
1983	—	92.02	90.23	182.25

(1) Includes changes to improve fuel economy and emissions control.
(2) Includes improved warranties, corrosion protection and changes in standard equipment.
SOURCE: U.S. Department of Labor, Bureau of Labor Statistics.

Federal Exhaust Emission Standards for Cars and Light Trucks

FEDERAL EXHAUST EMISSION STANDARDS FOR CONVENTIONALLY FUELED CARS AND LIGHT TRUCKS (Grams Per Mile)

EPA Tier 1 Emission Standards for Passenger Cars and Light-Duty Trucks, FTP 75, (grams/mile)

Category	50,000 miles/5 years						100,000 miles/10 years[1]					
	THC	NMHC	CO	NOx diesel	NOx gasoline	PM	THC	NMHC	CO	NOx diesel	NOx gasoline	PM
LDV (Passenger cars)	0.41	0.25	3.4	1	0.4	0.08	0.8	0.31	4.2	--	0.6	0.1
LDT1 (LLDT, LVW <3,750 lbs)	—	0.25	3.4	1	0.4	0.08	0.8	0.31	4.2	1.2	0.6	0.1
LDT2 (LLDT, LVW >3,750 lbs)	—	0.32	4.4	—	0.7	0.08	0.8	0.4	5.5	1.7	0.97	0.1
LDT3 (HLDT, ALVW <5,750 lbs)	—	0.32	4.4	—	0.7	—	0.8	0.46	6.4	0.98	0.98	0.1
LDT4 (HLDT, ALVW >5,750 lbs)	—	0.39	5	—	1.1	—	0.8	0.56	7.3	1.53	1.53	0.12

1 - Useful life 120,000 miles/11 years for all HLDT standards and for THC standards for LDT

Abbreviations:
LVW - loaded vehicle weight (curb weight + 300 lbs)
ALVW - adjusted LVW (the numerical average of the curb weight and the GVWR)
LLDT - light light-duty truck (below 6,000 lbs GVWR)
HLDT - heavy light-duty truck (above 6,000 lbs GVWR)

EPA Tier 2 Emission Standards, FTP 75, (grams/mile)

Bin#	50,000 miles					120,000 miles				
	NMOG	CO	NOx	PM	HCHO	NMOG	CO	NOx*	PM	HCHO
Temporary Bins										
11[c,9]	0.195	5	0.6	—	0.022	0.28	7.3	0.9	0.12	0.032
10[a,b,d,f]	0.125 (0.160)	3.4 (4.4)	0.4	—	0.015 (0.018)	0.156 (0.230)	4.2 (6.4)	0.6	0.08	0.018
(0.027)										
9[a,b,e]	0.075 (0.140)	3.4	0.2	—	0.015	0.090 (0.180)	4.2	0.3	0.06	0.018
Permanent Bins					—					
8[b]	0.100 (0.125)	3.4	0.14	—	0.015	0.125 (0.156)	4.2	0.2	0.02	0.018
7	0.075	3.4	0.11	—	0.015	0.09	4.2	0.15	0.02	0.018
6	0.075	3.4	0.08	—	0.015	0.09	4.2	0.1	0.01	0.018
5	0.075	3.4	0.05	—	0.015	0.09	4.2	0.07	0.01	0.018
4	—	—	—	—	—	0.07	2.1	0.04	0.01	0.011
3	—	—	—	—	—	0.055	2.1	0.03	0.01	0.011
2	—	—	—	—	—	0.01	2.1	0.02	0.01	0.004
1	—	—	—	—	—	—	—	—	—	—

* - average manufacturer fleet NOx standard is 0.07 g/mi

NOTE: Tier 2 standards were phased in between 2004 and 2009. For new passenger cars and light LDT's, Tier 2 standards phased in beginning in 2004, with the standards fully phased in during 2007. For heavy LDT's and MDPV's, the Tier 2 standards were phased in beginning in 2008, with full compliance in 2009

a - Bin deleted at end of 2006 model year (2008 for HLDTs)
b - The higher temporary NMOG, CO and HCHO values applying to HLDTs expired after 2008
c - An additional temporary bin restricted to MDPVs expired after model year 2008
d - Optional temporary NMOG standard of 0.195 g/mi (50,000) and 0.280 g/mi (120,000) applies for qualifying LDT4s and MDPVs only
e - Optional temporary NMOG standard of 0.100 g/mi (50,000) and 0.130 g/mi (120,000) applies for qualifying LDT2s only
f - 50,000 mile standard optional for diesels certified to bin 10
g - Bins 9-11 expired in 2006 for light-duty vehicles and light-duty trucks and 2008 for heavy-duty light trucks and medium-duty passenger vehicles.

Traffic Deaths in Selected Countries and Countries with Safety Belt Use Laws

STATES WITH STANDARD/PRIMARY SEAT BELT ENFORCEMENT LAWS*

Alabama	Maine
Alaska	Maryland
Arkansas	Michigan
California	Minnesota
Connecticut	Mississippi
Delaware	New Jersey
District of Columbia	New Mexico
Florida	New York
Georgia	North Carolina
Hawaii	Oklahoma
Illinois	Oregon
Indiana	Rhode Island
Iowa	South Carolina
Kansas	Tennessee
Kentucky	Texas
Louisiana	Washington
	Wisconsin

*The safety belt use law may be enforced independent of another violation.
SOURCE: National Highway Traffic Safety Administration.

VEHICLE DEATHS IN SELECTED COUNTRIES

			Traffic Fatalities Per 100,000 Registered Vehicles	
	2010	2009	2010	2009
Australia	1,352	1,488	8.8	9.9
Austria	552	633	11.4	13.3
Belgium	NA	955	NA	16.0
Canada	2,100	2,207	10.0	10.2
China	65,255	67,759	83.6	110.8
Denmark	255	303	9.6	11.5
Finland	272	279	8.2	8.7
France	3,992	4,273	10.6	11.4
Germany	3,648	4,152	8.1	9.3
Hungary	740	822	21.6	23.8
Italy	4,090	4,237	9.8	10.3
Japan	5,745	5,772	7.8	7.8
Netherlands	537	644	6.0	7.2
Norway	208	212	7.3	7.6
Poland	3,907	4,572	19.2	23.6
Portugal	937	929	16.1	14.5
Spain	2,478	2,714	9.0	9.8
Sweden	266	358	5.5	7.4
Switzerland	327	349	7.3	8.0
Turkey	4,045	4,300	35.9	40.5
United Kingdom	1,905	2,337	5.4	6.6
United States	32,885	33,808	13.2	13.6

NA - Not available.
NOTE: Data varies significantly between countries both definitionally and quantitatively
SOURCE: Compiled by *Ward's* from various sources.

COUNTRIES WITH SAFETY BELT USE LAWS

Country	Effective Date	Country	Effective Date
Argentina	7/1/92	United States and Territories	
Australia	1/72	Alabama	7/18/91
Austria	7/76	Alaska	9/12/90
Belgium	6/75	Arizona	1/1/91
Brazil	6/72	Arkansas	7/15/91
Bulgaria	1976	California	1/1/86
Canadian Provinces		Colorado	7/1/87
Alberta	7/87	Connecticut	1/1/86
British Columbia	10/77	Delaware	1/1/92
Manitoba	4/84	District of Columbia	12/12/85
Newfoundland	7/82	Florida	7/1/86
New Brunswick	11/83	Georgia	9/1/88
Nova Scotia	1/85	Hawaii	2/16/85
Ontario	1/76	Idaho	7/1/86
Prince Edward Island	1/88	Illinois	7/1/85
Quebec	7/76	Indiana	7/1/87
Saskatchewan	7/77	Iowa	7/1/86
Croatia	—	Kansas	7/1/86
Cyprus	1/8/1987	Kentucky	7/13/94
Czech Republic	1/69	Louisiana	7/1/86
Denmark	1/76	Maine	12/26/95
Finland	7/75	Maryland	7/1/86
France	10/79	Massachusetts	2/1/94
Germany	1/76	Michigan	7/1/85
Greece	12/79	Minnesota	8/1/86
Hong Kong	10/83	Mississippi	3/20/90
Hungary	7/77	Missouri	9/28/85
Iceland	10/81	Montana	10/1/87
India	—	Nebraska	1/1/93
Ireland	2/79	Nevada	7/1/87
Israel	7/75	New Hampshire	—
Italy	7/03	New Jersey	3/1/85
Ivory Coast	1970	New Mexico	1/1/86
Japan	12/71	New York	12/1/84
Jordan	12/83	North Carolina	10/1/85
Luxembourg	6/75	North Dakota	7/14/94
Malaysia	4/79	Ohio	5/6/86
Netherlands	6/75	Oklahoma	2/1/87
New Zealand	6/72	Oregon	12/7/90
Norway	9/75	Pennsylvania	11/23/87
Peru	—	Puerto Rico	1/19/75
Poland	1/84	Rhode Island	6/18/91
Portugal	1/78	South Carolina	7/1/89
Singapore	7/81	South Dakota	1/1/95
Slovenia	—	Tennessee	4/21/86
South Africa	12/77	Texas	9/1/85
Spain	10/74	Utah	4/28/86
Sweden	1/75	Vermont	1/1/94
Switzerland	1/76	Virginia	1/1/88
Turkey	10/84	Washington	6/11/86
United Kingdom	1/83	West Virginia	9/1/93
USSR	1/76	Wisconsin	12/1/87
Zimbabwe	7/80	Wyoming	6/8/89

SOURCE: Compiled by *Ward's* from various sources.

INDEX

INDEX

WARDSAUTO

Contact Ward's Information Products for
more details or pricing on the products below:
Amber McLincha • 248.799.2622 • amclincha@wardsauto.com

Contact Customer Service for more
details or pricing on the products below.
Barbara Liske • 248.799.2645 • bliske@wardsauto.com

Online Subscription Services

WardsAuto.com
Call for pricing (based on number of users)

All of Ward's in one online subscription --
news, data, analysis and more.

Ward's AutoInfoBank™ on the web
Powerful web-based data reporting tool

Forecast Report Products

Ward's AutoForecasts
Call for pricing (multiple forecast products available)

Knowledgable forecasts on where the
automotive manufacturing industry is headed

Ward's Monthly Auto Data Reports

Call for details and pricing on these reports:
- Retail sales
- Production/factory sales

Magazines

Call 866-505-7173 to order or for more details:

	US & Mexico	Canada	Airmail Overseas
WardsAuto World®* 1 yr. (12 issues)	available as free digital download		
WardsAuto Dealer Business®* 1 yr. (12 issues)	$52	$72	$104

(Please do not use this form to order WardsAuto Dealer Business. Instead, please call 866-505-7173)

Newsletters

Ward's Automotive Reports®*
- ❑ One year (52 issues) with Yearbook $1,585 (airmail overseas, add $50)
- ❑ 13-week trial .... $305 (airmail overseas, add $12.50)

**Ward's Engine and
Vehicle Technology Update**®*
- ❑ One year (24 issues) .... $1,140 (airmail overseas, add $25)
- ❑ Half-year (12 issues) .... $590 (airmail overseas, add $12.50)

Reference Annuals

Ward's Automotive Yearbook®**
- ❑ 2012 Yearbook .... $590 (airmail overseas, add $30)
- ❑ 2012 Yearbook and CD-ROM set .... $925 (airmail overseas, add $30)
- ❑ 2011 Yearbook .... $580 (airmail overseas, add $30)
- ❑ 2011 Yearbook and CD-ROM set .... $910 (airmail overseas, add $30)

Ward's World Motor Vehicle Data™** (2012 Edition available Sept. 2012)
- ❑ 2012 Data Book .... $340 (airmail overseas, add $25)
- ❑ 2012 Data Book and CD-ROM set .... $395 (airmail overseas, add $25)
- ❑ 2011 Data Book .... $325 (airmail overseas, add $25)
- ❑ 2011 Data Book and CD-ROM set .... $395 (airmail overseas, add $25)

ALL ORDERS MUST INCLUDE APPLICABLE TAXES. If tax-exempt and not a govt.
agency, please provide copy of tax exempt certificate.
* Subject to sales tax in AL, CO, FL, GA, IN, KS, KY, MO, SC, TN, WA and Canada.
** Subject to sales tax in AL, AK, CA, CO, CT, FL, GA, IL, IN, KS, KY, MA, MI, MN,
MO, MS, NE, NJ, NY, OH, PA, SC, TN, TX, VA, WA, WI and Canada.

Bill to my: ❑ VISA ❑ Mastercard ❑ American Express ❑ Discover

Amount enclosed $_____ Signature _____
(Please do not use this form to order WardsAuto Dealer Business. Instead, please call 866-505-7173)

Card number_____ Exp. Date _____

Name/Title (Please print) _____

Company/Division _____

Street Address _____

City_____ State/Province _____

Zip/Postal Code_____ Country_____

Phone _____ Fax _____

E-mail Address _____

Mail Check Orders to: Penton Media, Inc. - Ward's Automotive Group • 24653 Network Place • Chicago, IL 60673-1246
Please make checks payable to: Penton Media, Inc. in U.S. funds, drawn on a U.S. bank.
Customer Service Inquiries: Contact Barbara Liske by phone: (248) 799-2645, by fax: (248) 357-9747, or email: bliske@wardsauto.com